MW00667049

IMAGES
of America

NORTH CAROLINA LIGHTHOUSES AND LIFESAVING STATIONS

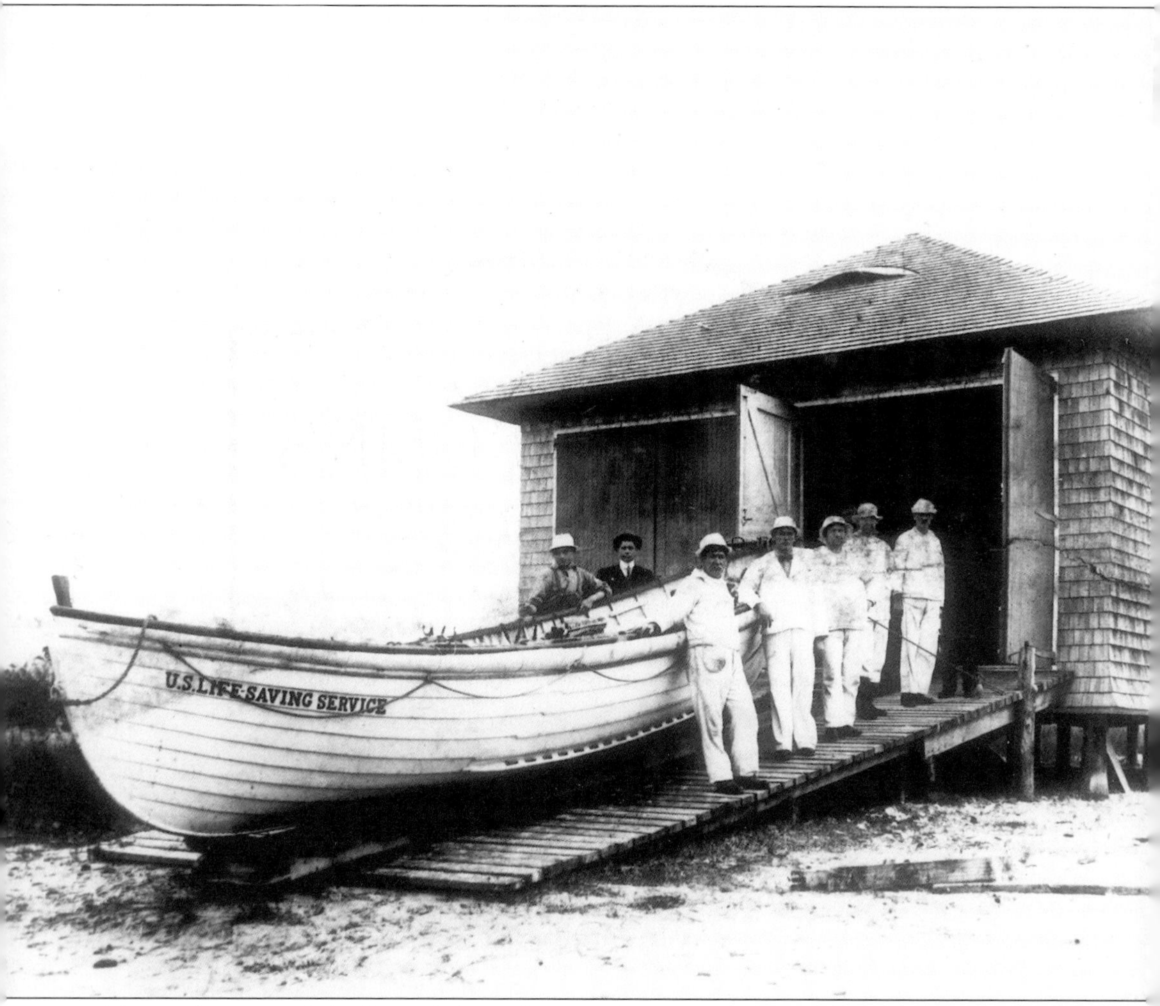

This is the crew of the Bogue Inlet Lifesaving Station near Swansboro. (Courtesy of North Carolina Archives and History.)

IMAGES
of America

NORTH CAROLINA LIGHTHOUSES AND LIFESAVING STATIONS

John Hairr

ARCADIA

ISBN 0-7385-1520-5

Published by Arcadia Publishing
Charleston SC, Chicago, Portsmouth NH, San Francisco

Printed in Great Britain

Library of Congress Catalog Card Number:

For all general information contact Arcadia Publishing at:
Telephone 843-853-2070
Fax 843-853-0044
E-mail sales@arcadiapublishing.com
For customer service and orders:
Toll-Free 1-888-313-2665

Visit us on the internet at http://www.arcadiapublishing.com

Contents

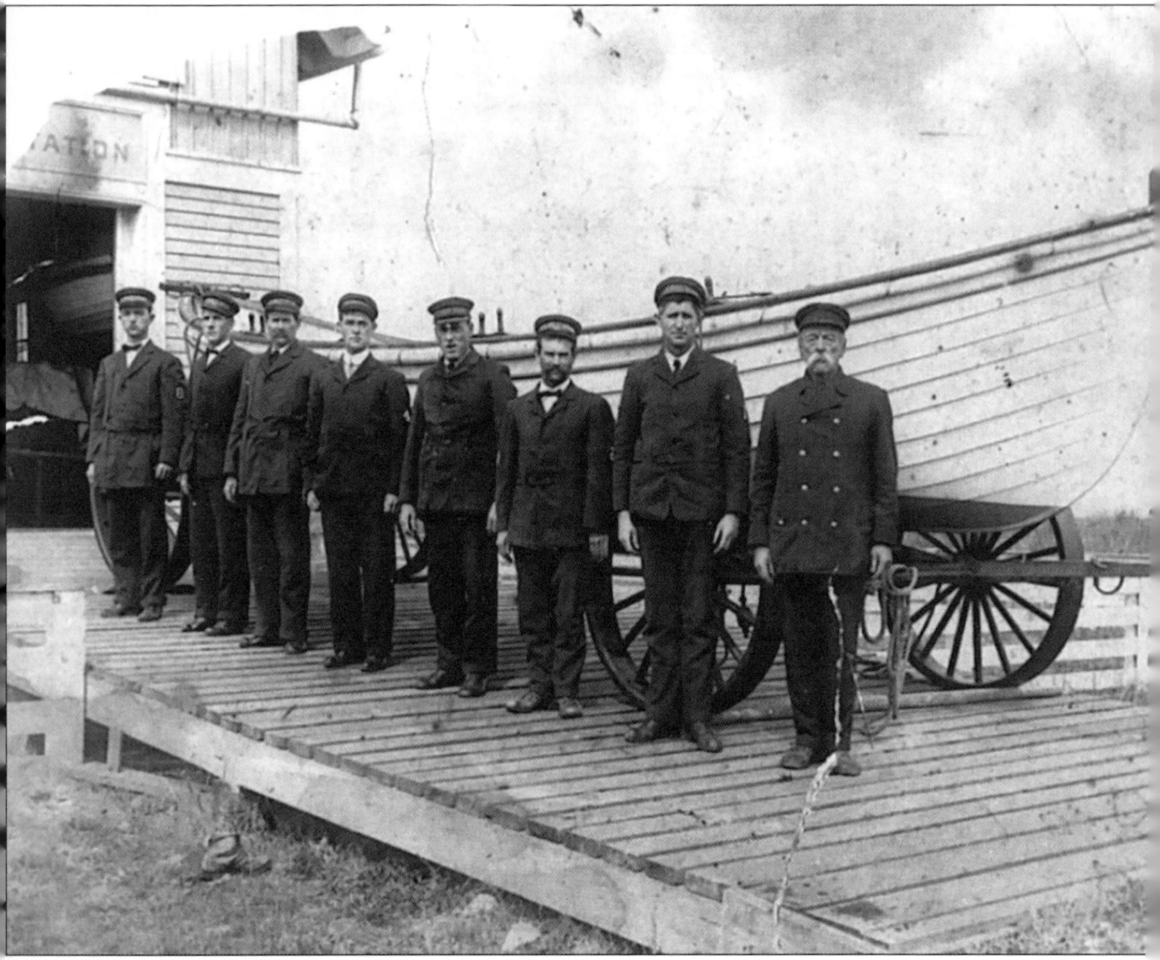

Pictured here is the crew of the Oak Island Lifesaving Station with their surfboat. Oak Island was the southernmost point along the North Carolina coast guarded by the United States Life Saving Service. The United States Coast Guard still maintains an active station at the mouth of the Cape Fear River. (Courtesy of North Carolina Archives and History.)

INTRODUCTION

Since the earliest days of European exploration, the North Carolina shores have been a hazard to mariners. With its bold capes jutting into the ocean, sandy shoals extending miles offshore, fickle weather, and treacherous currents, it is easy to understand why the shores of the Old North State came to be called "The Graveyard of the Atlantic."

With so many miles of dangerous coastline, North Carolina is blessed with world-renowned lighthouses. Tourists from all over the world visit the famous lighthouses at Currituck Beach, Bodie Island, and Cape Hatteras. Many climb to the top of these structures to gain a unique perspective of the surrounding landscape.

But these lights are more than just tourist attractions. For more than two centuries, lighthouses have guided travelers along the North Carolina coast. Some, like Old Baldy and Ocracoke, were built to safely guide ships into important harbors. Others, such as Cape Lookout and Cape Hatteras, were designed to warn mariners to steer clear of danger.

Although initiated by the state, the federal government erected and maintained North Carolina lighthouses. In 1789, the United States Congress gave the responsibility of these navigational aids to what was then called the United States Lighthouse Establishment, which was administered by the Secretary of the Treasury. After several more names, including the United States Light-House Board and the Bureau of Lighthouses, the navigational aids came under the administration of the United States Coast Guard in 1939.

Sometimes, despite the best nautical charts and lighthouses, ships still wrecked on the treacherous North Carolina coastline. Prior to 1874, stranded mariners relied on the benevolence of local inhabitants, a nearby light keeper, or perhaps a passing United States Revenue Service cutter. But in 1870, the federal government took the first steps in creating the United States Life-Saving Service, whose role was to assist shipwreck victims along the entire coastal United States.

By 1874, the first stations were constructed along the northern Outer Banks at Jones Hill, Caffeys Inlet, Kitty Hawk, Nags Head, Bodie Island, Chicamacomico and Little Kinnakeet. By 1886, the string of lifesaving stations stretched all the way down the coast to Oak Island, at the mouth of the Cape Fear River.

In 1915, the United States Life-Saving Service and the Revenue Cutter Service merged to form the United States Coast Guard. Later, in 1939, the Coast Guard took over operations of the lighthouses. From the dangerous days of World War II, when U-boats prowled the coast hunting for victims, to the 21st century with a new enemy threatening the peace, members of the United States Coast Guard have helped make the dangerous waters of North Carolina safer.

As our reliance on satellite navigation increases, many of the lighthouses along the coast are being phased out. The Coast Guard has turned several of these structures over to organizations interested in preserving an important part of our maritime tradition. To learn more about the ongoing efforts to preserve the lighthouses along the North Carolina shores, contact the Outer Banks Lighthouse Society, P.O. Box 1005, Morehead City, NC 28557.

One
The Bald Head Lighthouses

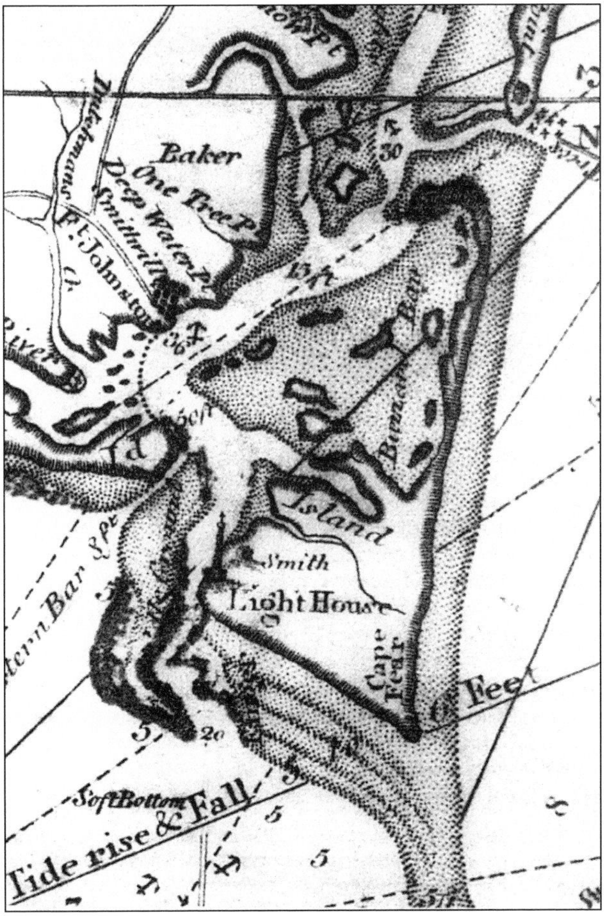

The Potts Map of Cape Fear was drawn *c.* 1800. It shows the location of the original lighthouse on Bald Head Island. (Courtesy of North Carolina Archives and History.)

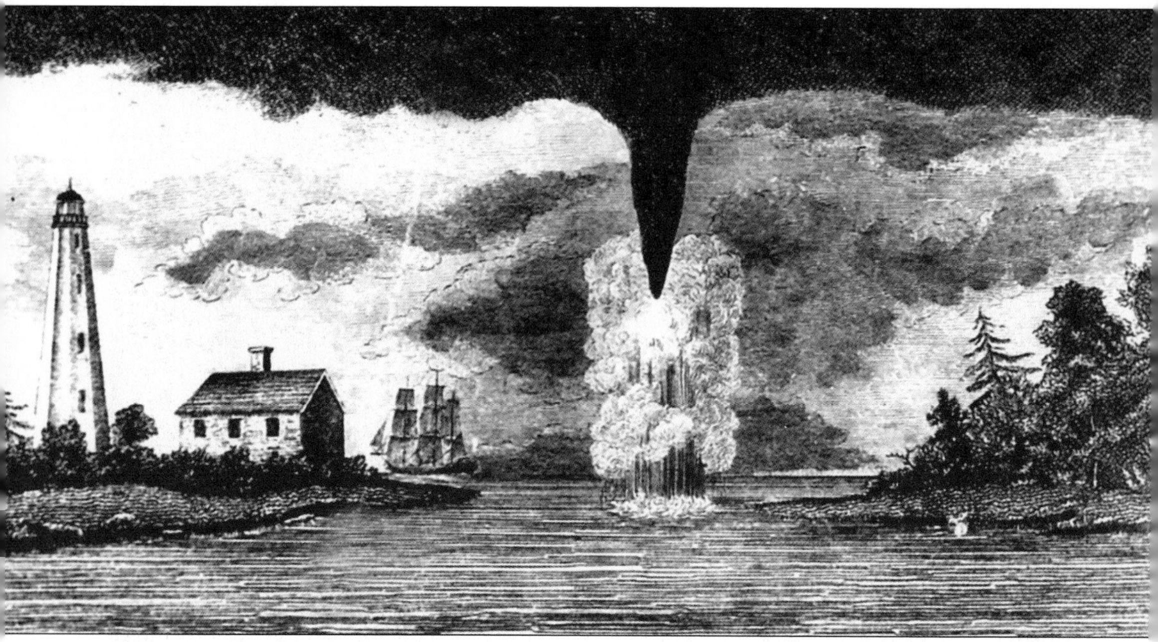

The original Bald Head Island Lighthouse was authorized by the North Carolina General Assembly in 1784. By 1790, the state ceded the 10-acre tract and lighthouse to the federal government, which completed work on the structure in 1794. It was first lighted on December 23, 1794. Unfortunately, the lighthouse was constructed too close to the edge of the water. It was only a matter of time before the encroaching sea threatened the structure. By 1813, erosion of the sandy land along the base of the tower made it necessary for treasury authorities to tear down the first Cape Fear lighthouse. This picture is the only known likeness of this historic structure. On July 24, 1806, an artist who signed his name only as "Kettle" sketched this scene of a waterspout near the mouth of the river. He noted that it was one of eleven observed in the river between one and two o'clock that day. (Courtesy of North Carolina Archives and History.)

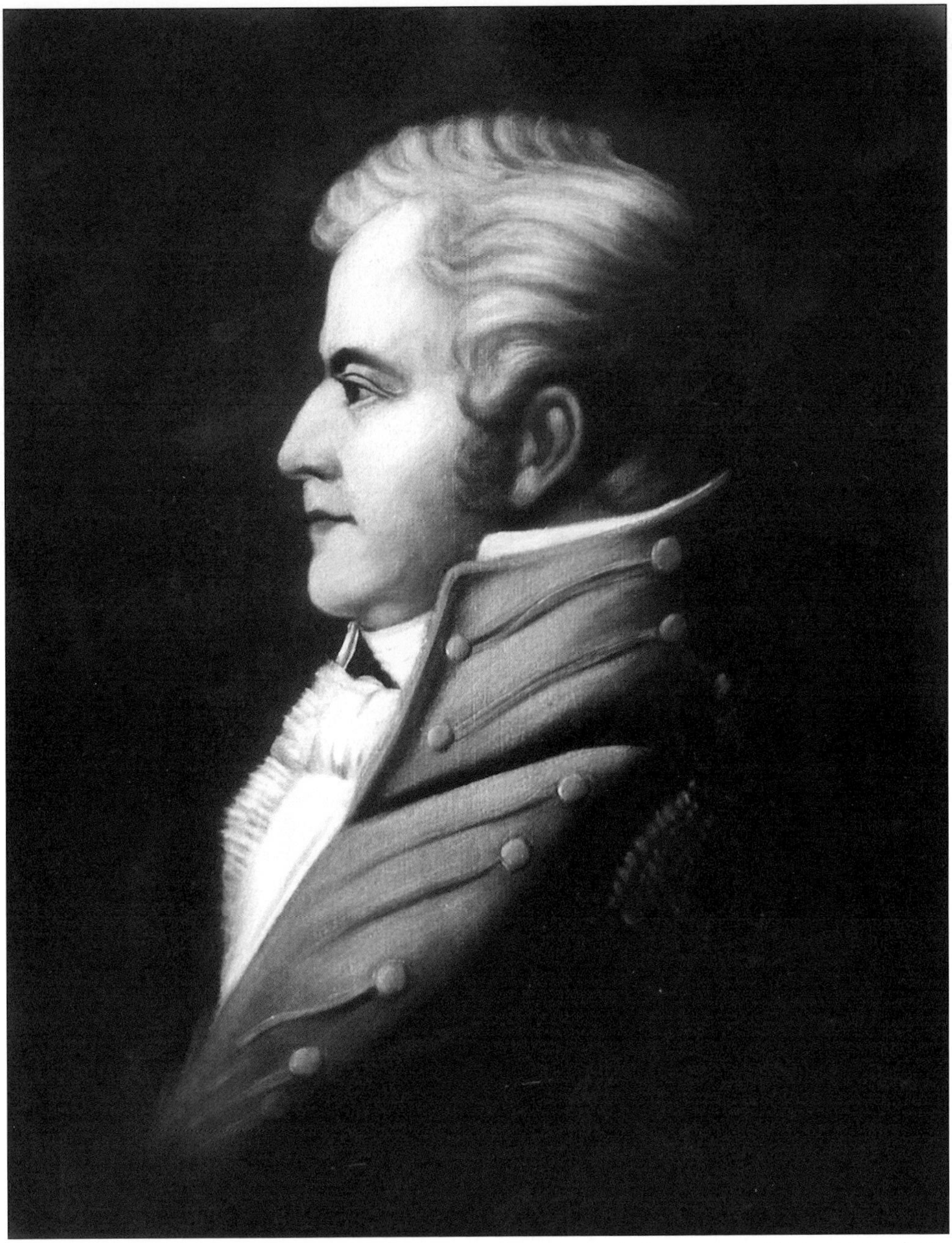

Gov. Benjamin Smith donated land for the site of the first lighthouse on Bald Head Island. He is the namesake of the town of Smithville, now known as Southport. (Courtesy of North Carolina Maritime Museum at Southport.)

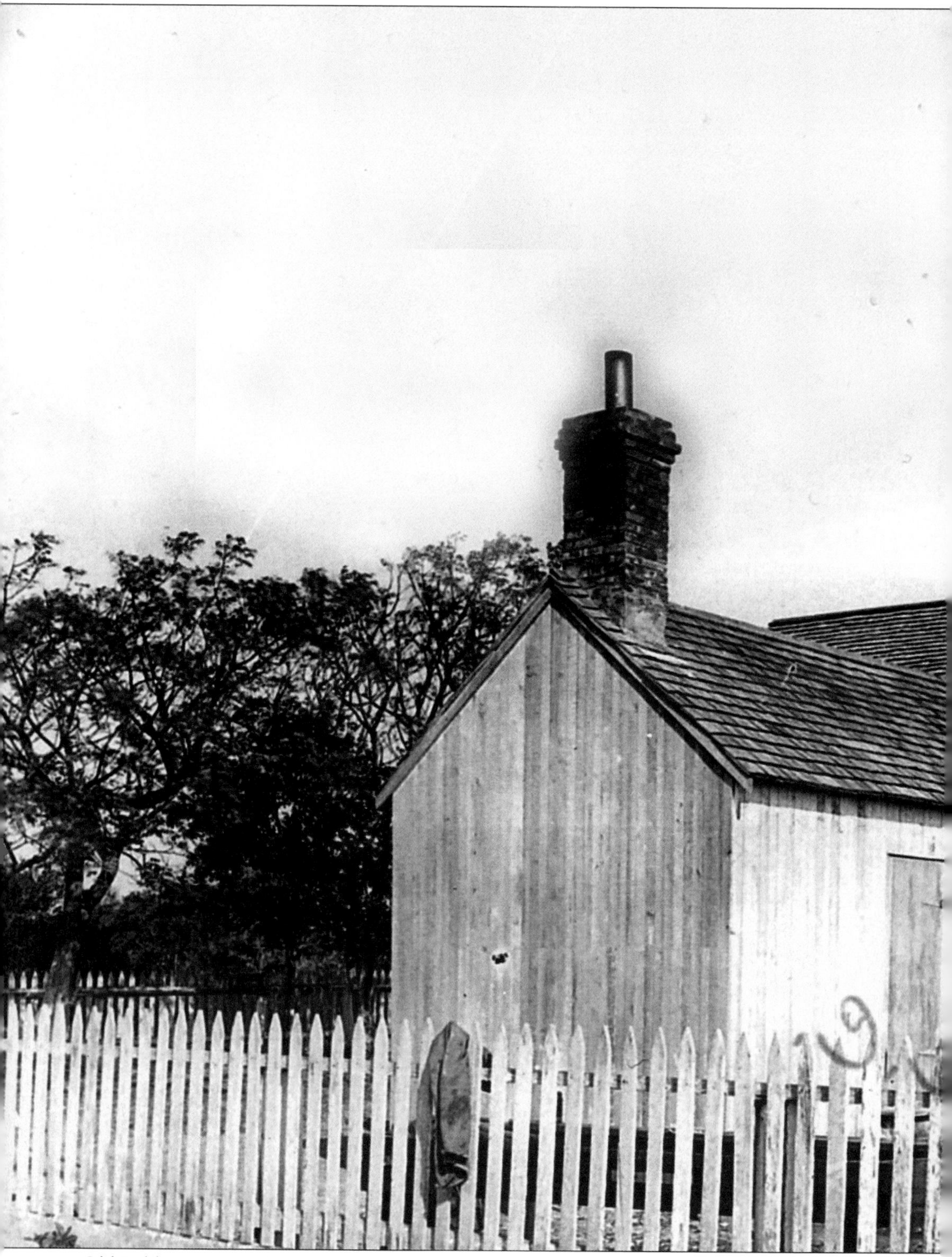

Old Baldy rises over the keeper's quarters in this 1893 photo. (Courtesy of National Archives.)

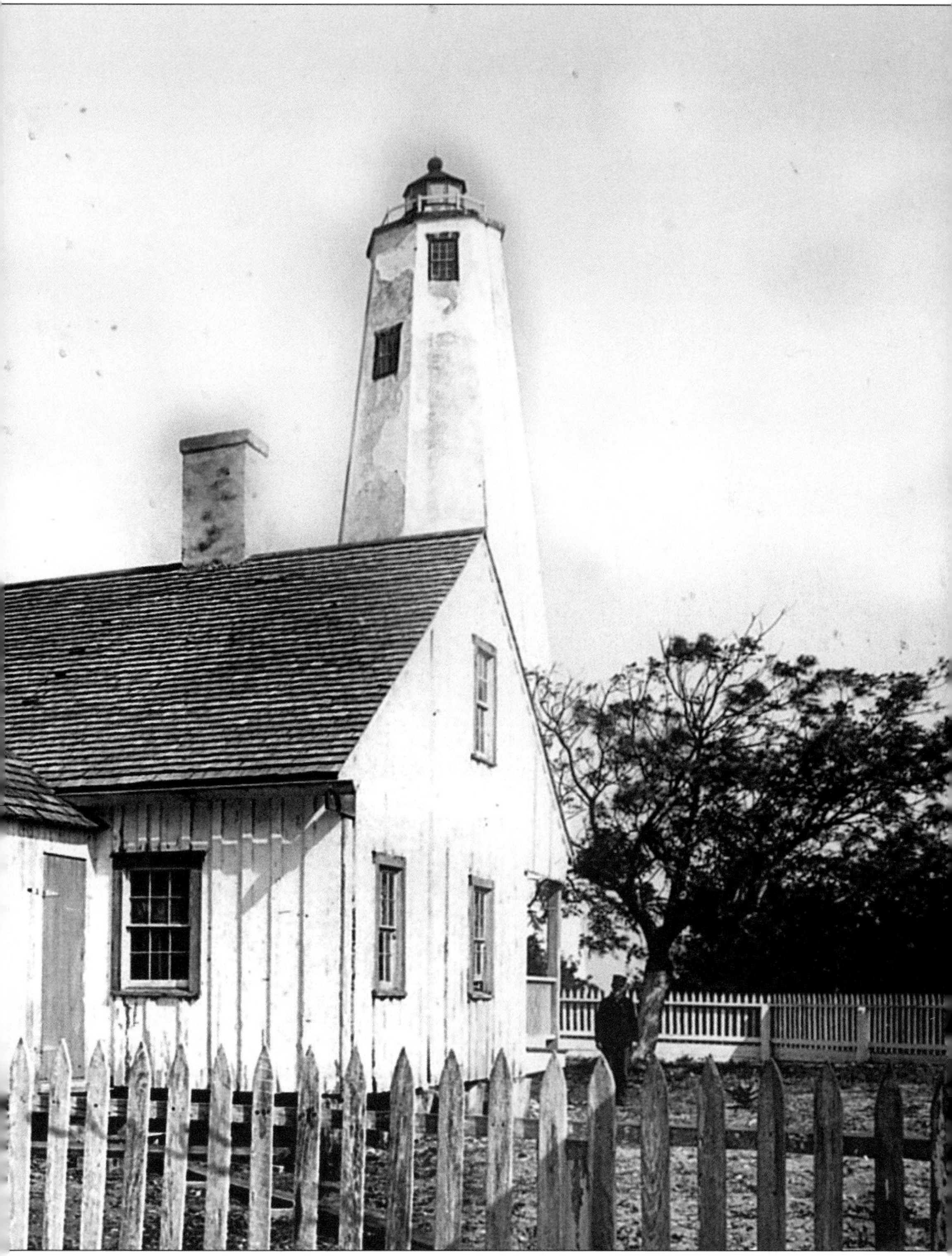

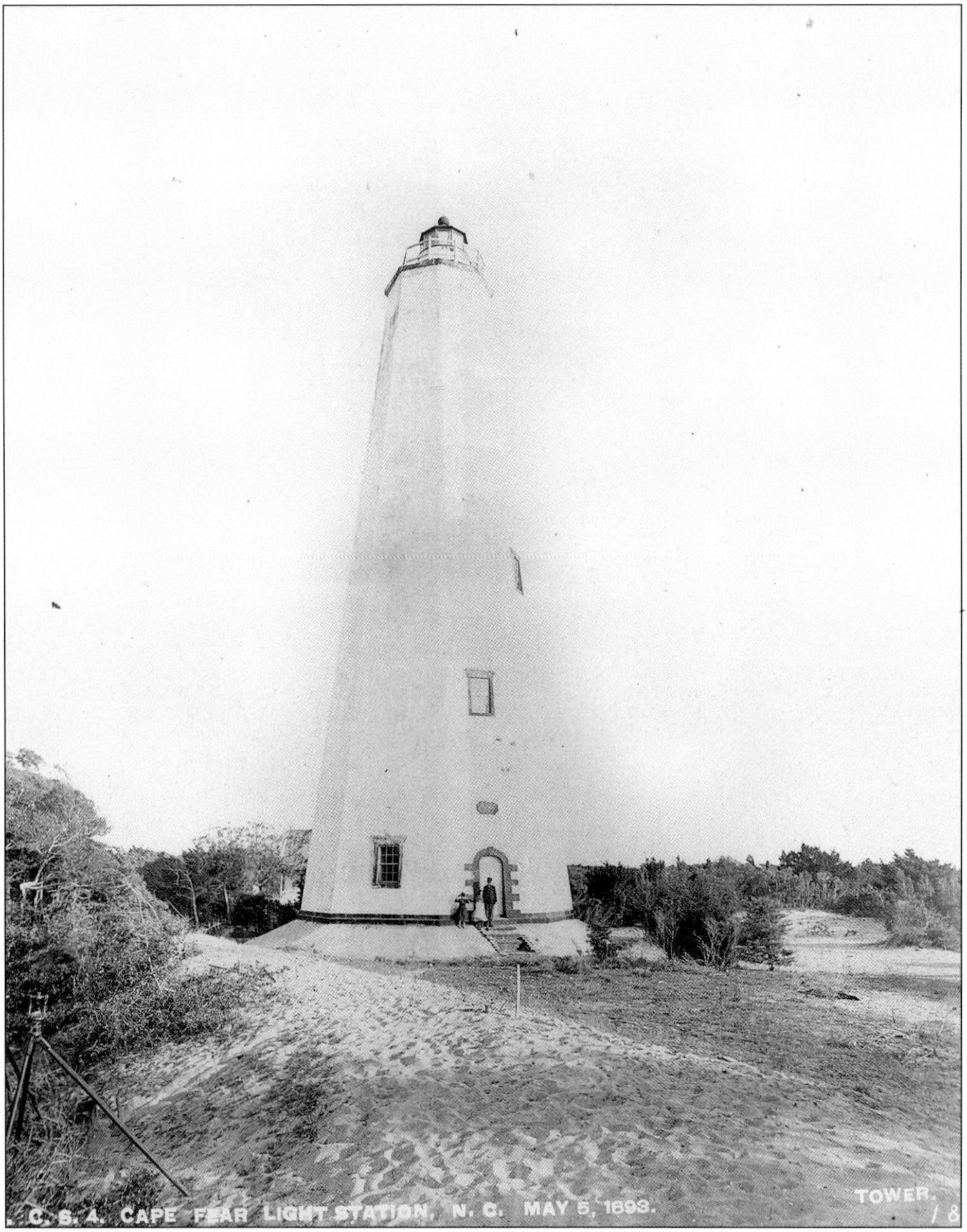

This photo, taken on May 5, 1893, shows the Old Baldy Lighthouse. The second lighthouse to guide ships into the mouth of the Cape Fear River was completed in 1817. The octagonal lighthouse was made of bricks, with walls five feet thick at the bottom, narrowing to two feet at the top. The outside of the structure was plastered and then painted. Early descriptions indicate that Old Baldy was originally painted black, distinguishing it from the nearby lighthouse on Federal Point. For most of its existence, Old Baldy has been whitewashed. With the coming of the Civil War, Confederate authorities removed the lens from this lighthouse. Fortunately, the structure was spared from destruction, unlike many other lighthouses along the Southern coast. (Courtesy of the United States Coast Guard.)

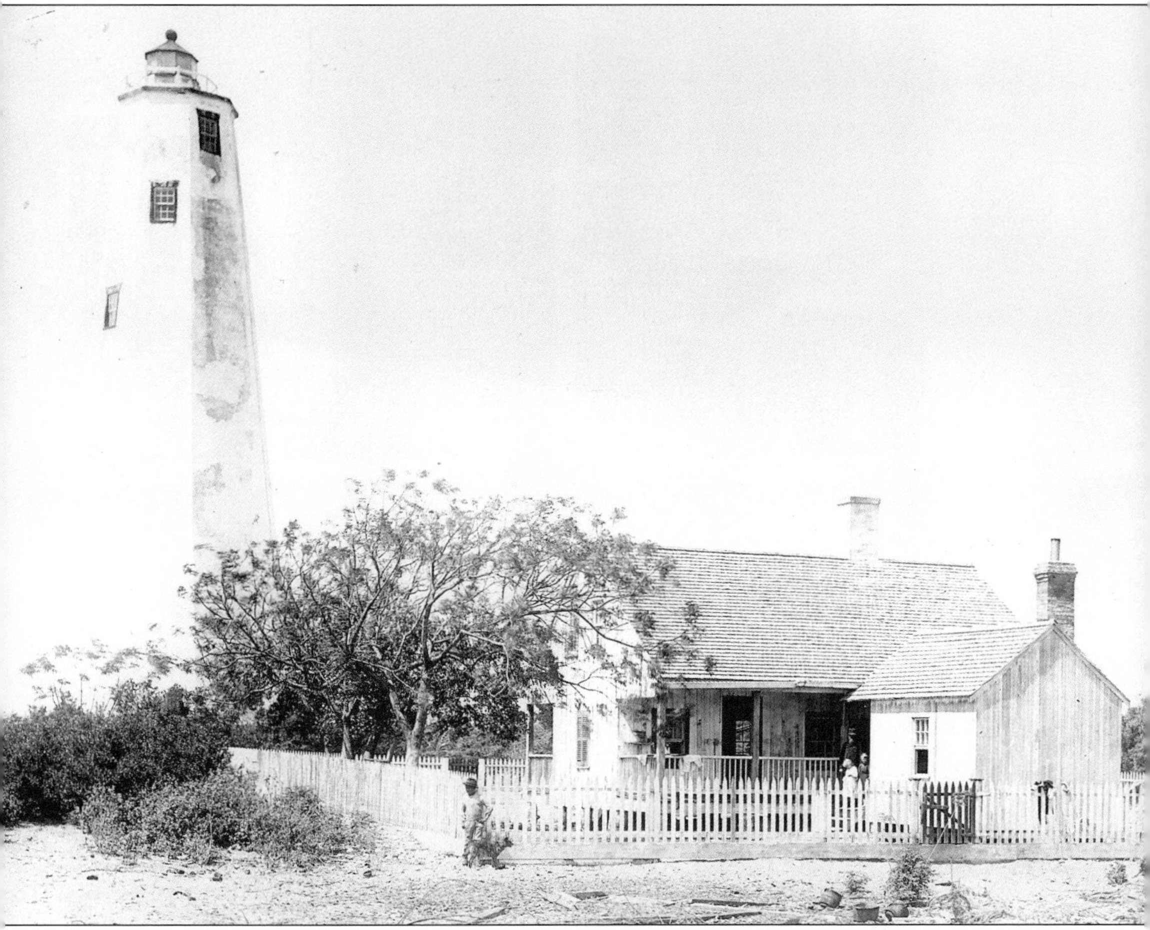

The people on the porch and the child next to the fence are believed to be the keeper of the lighthouse and his family. The photo was taken in 1893. (Courtesy of National Archives.)

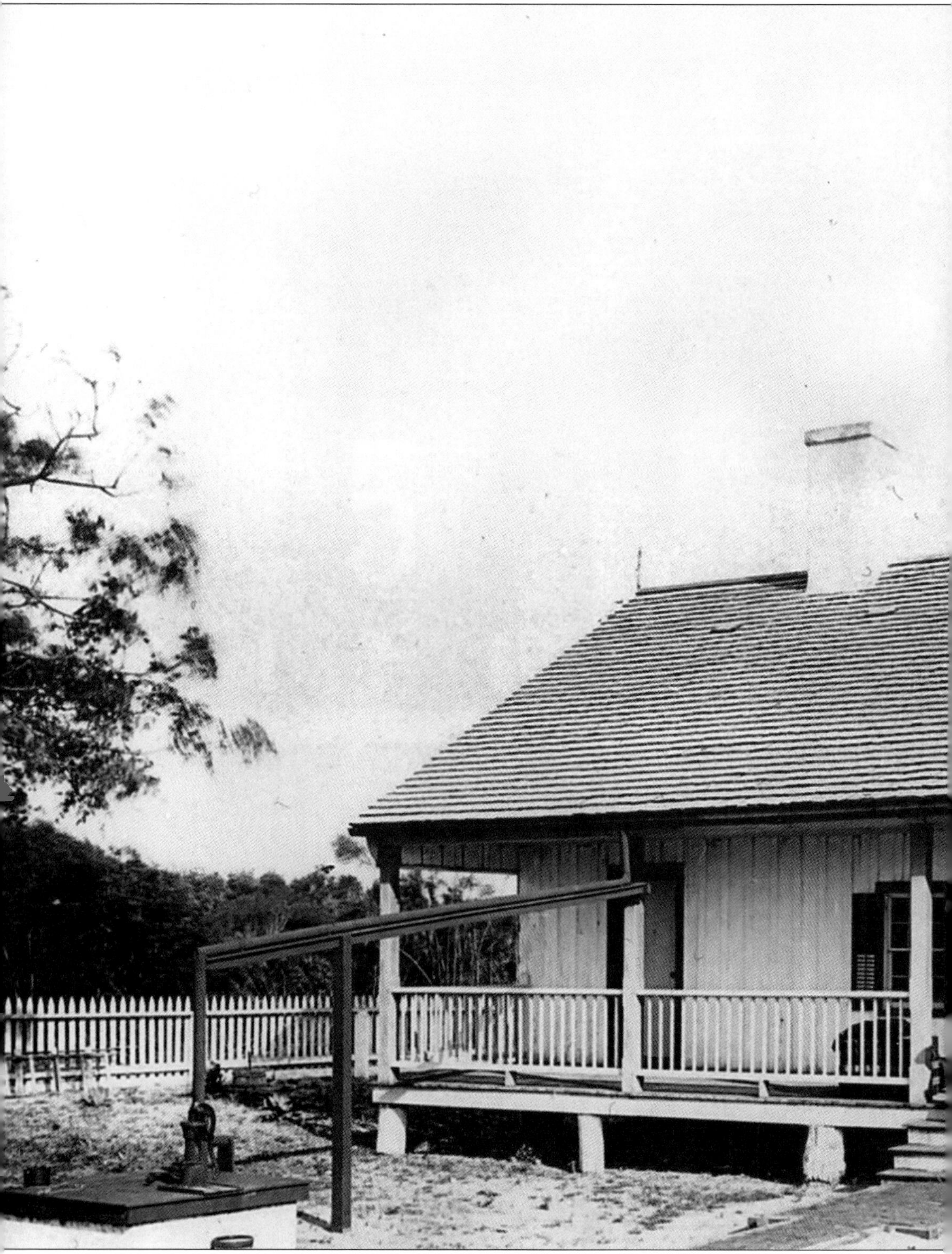

The keeper's dwelling stood adjacent to the lighthouse on Bald Head Island. (Courtesy of

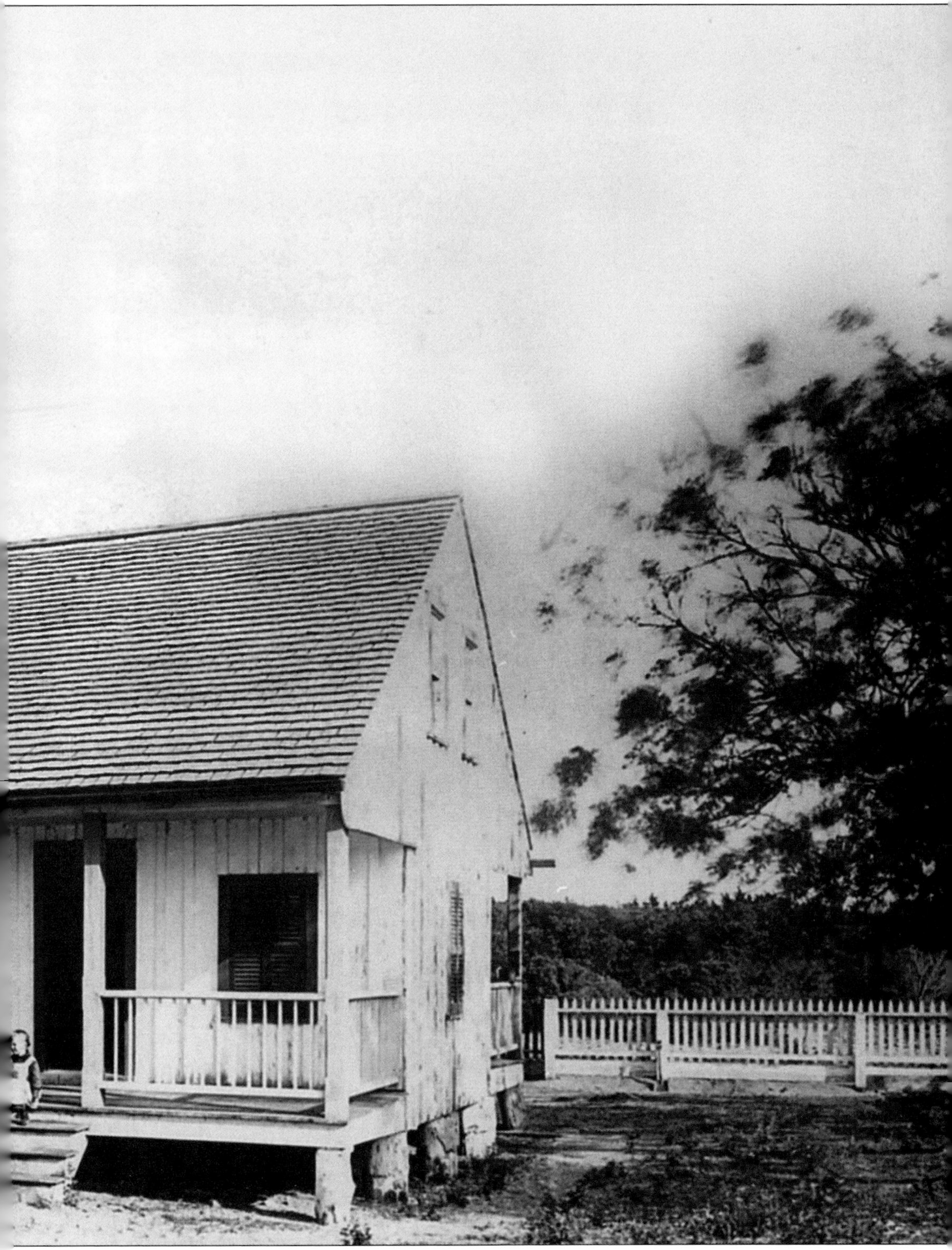

National Archives.)

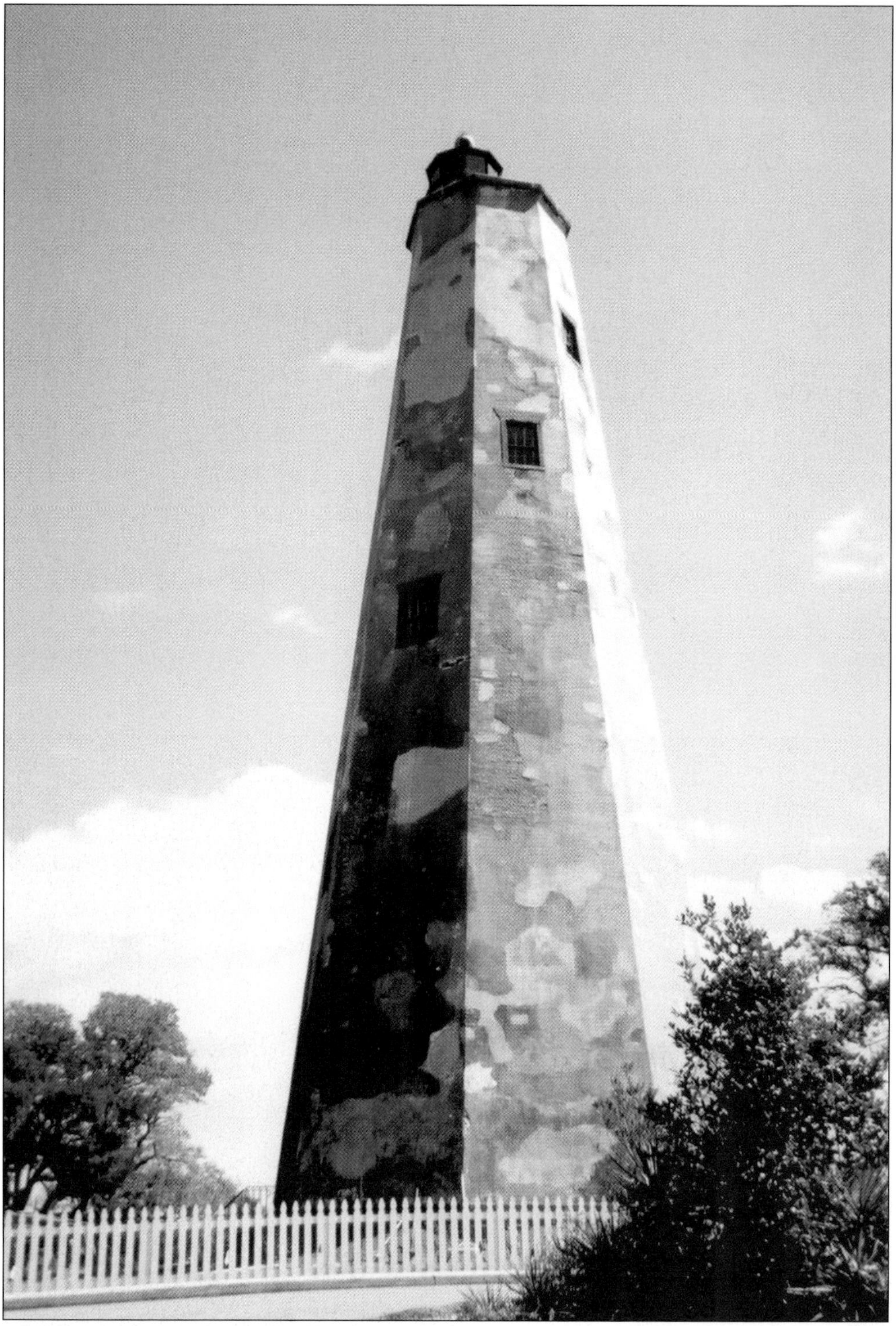

Old Baldy was deactivated in 1935, though a radio beacon remained in operation until the 1950s.

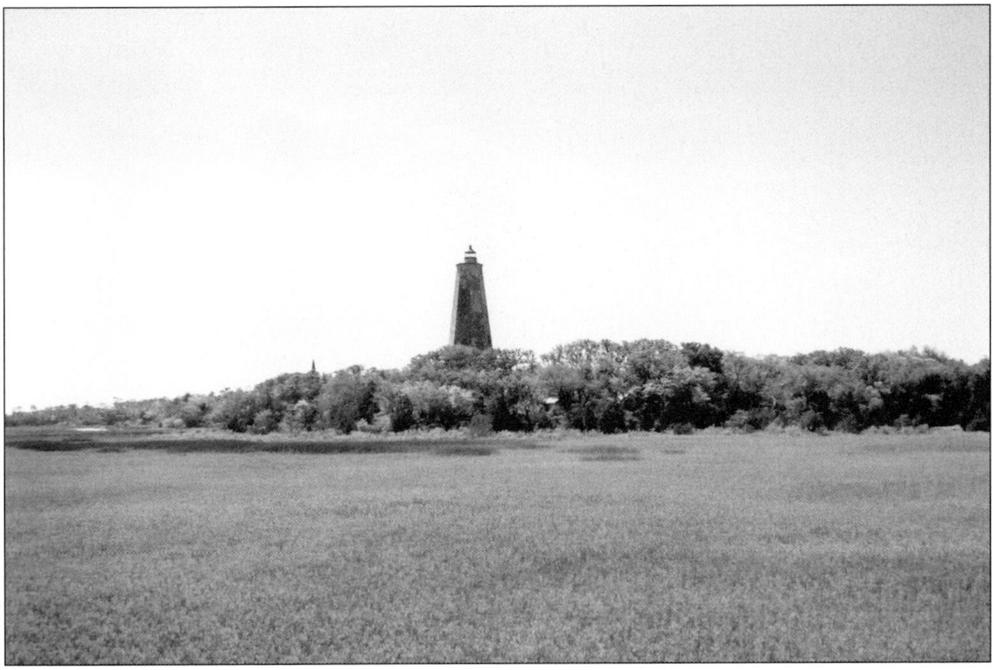

Old Baldy looms over the picturesque tidal marsh.

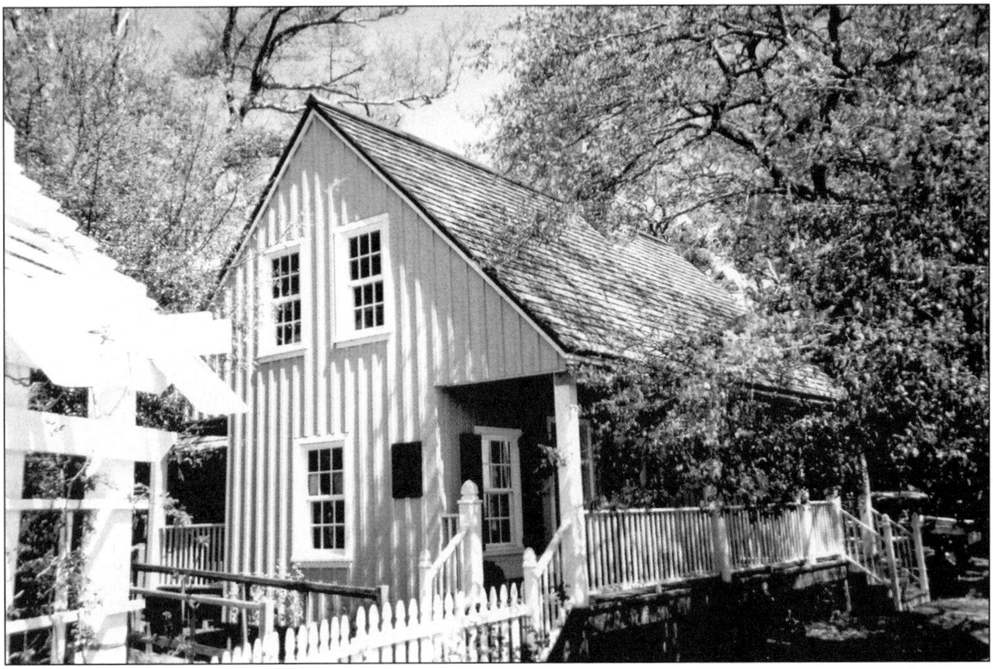

The Old Baldy Foundation Inc. operates a museum inside a reproduction of the keeper's quarters, adjacent to the lighthouse.

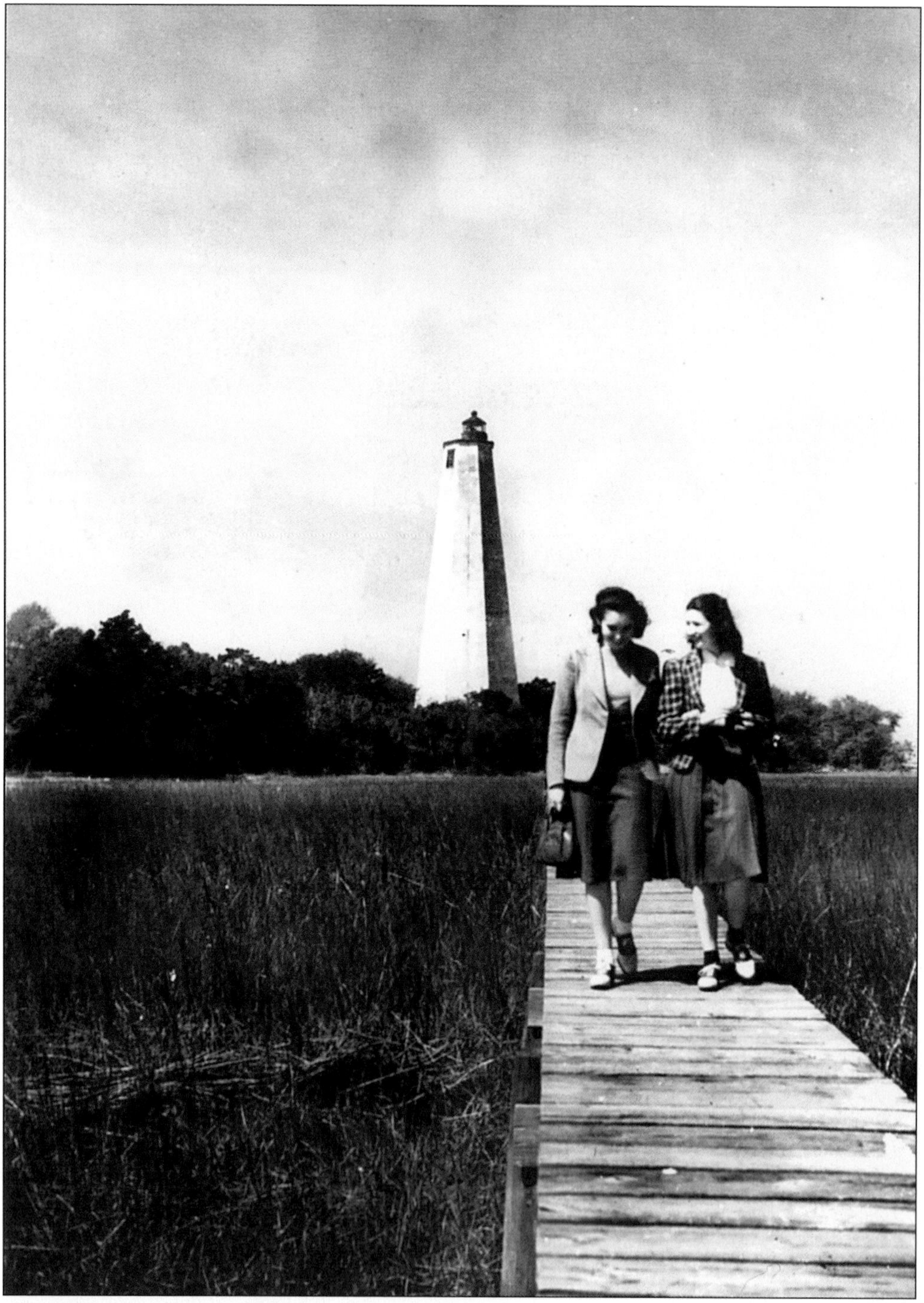

This Bald Head Island Lighthouse is pictured in 1940. (Courtesy of North Carolina Archives and History.)

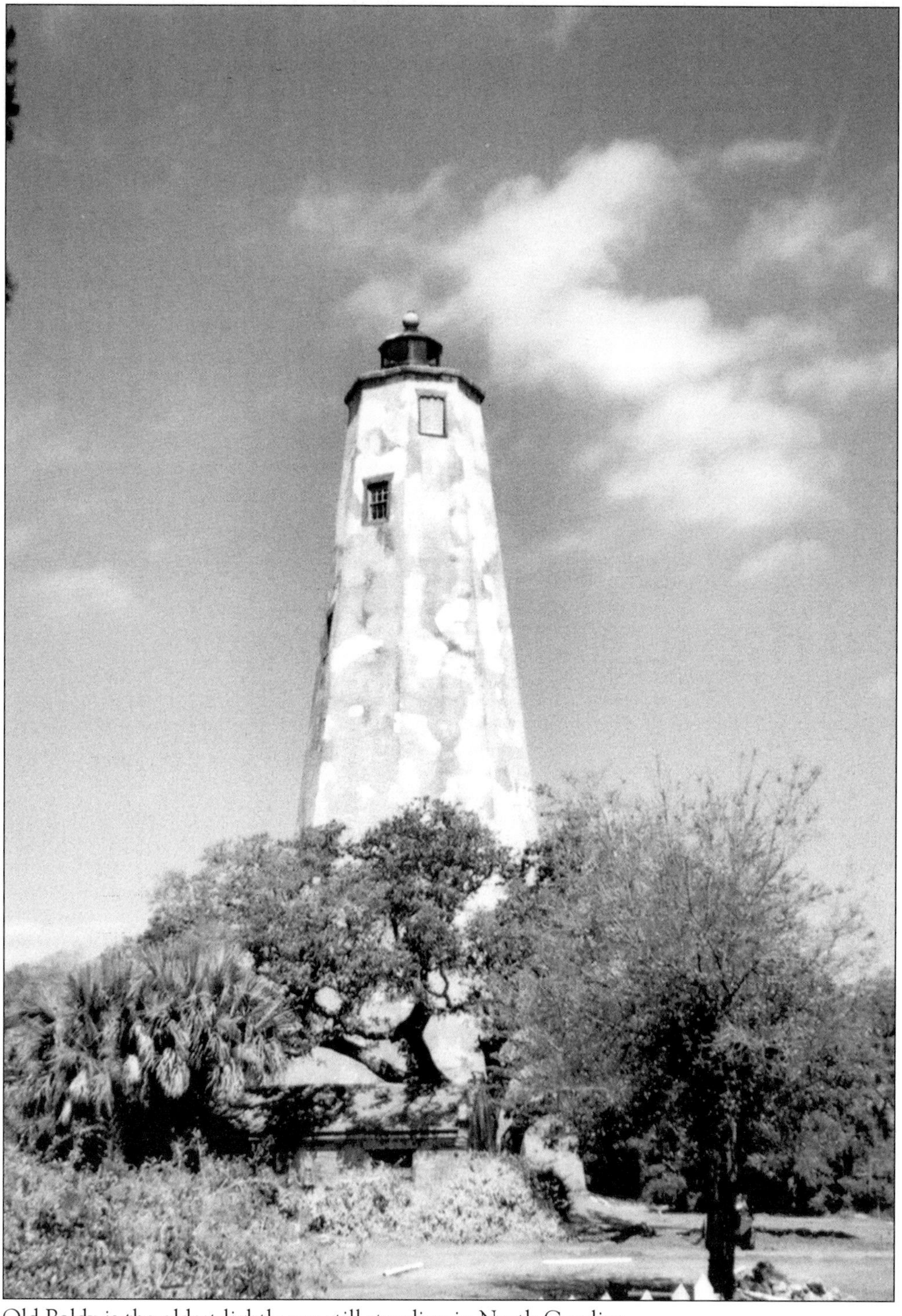

Old Baldy is the oldest lighthouse still standing in North Carolina.

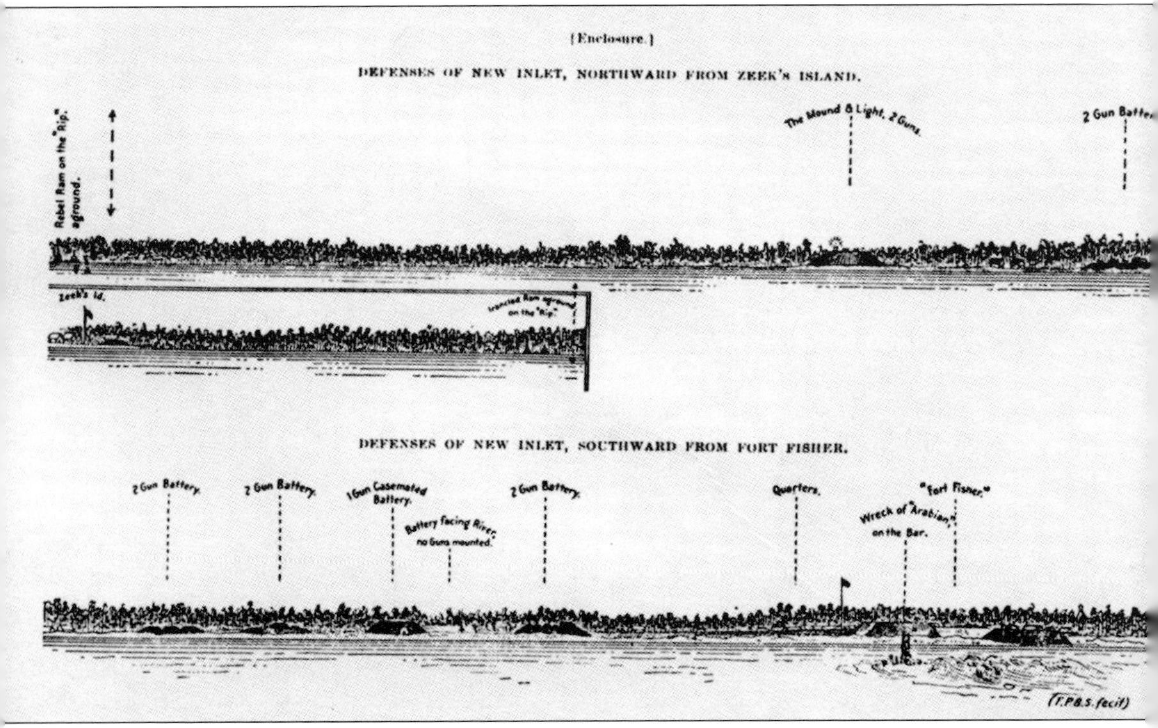

Although it is not an official aid to navigation, the light, which was erected by the Confederates atop the Mound Battery at Fort Fisher, served as a prominent landmark for blockade runners entering and leaving New Inlet during the War Between the States.

Two

FEDERAL POINT AND THE CAPE FEAR RIVER LIGHTS

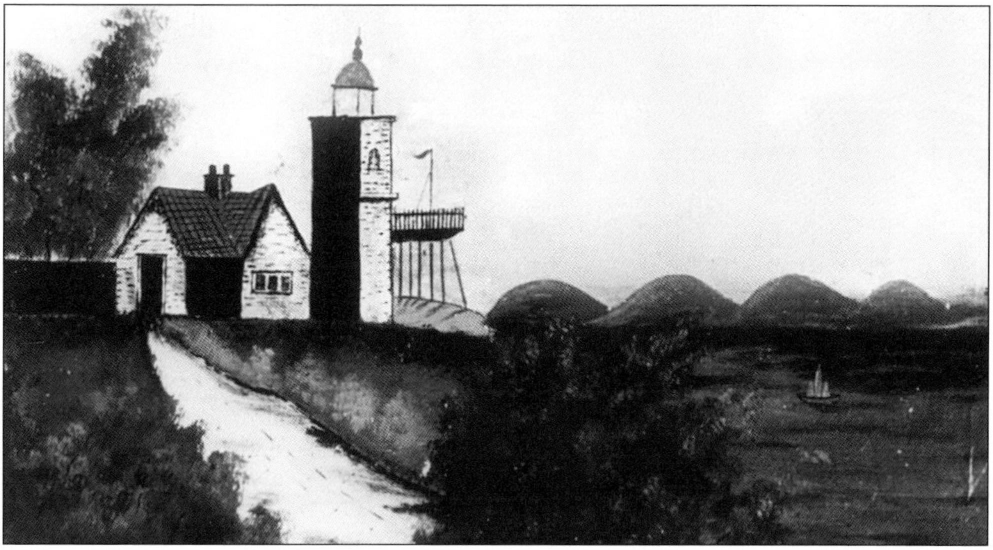

This is the second of three successive lighthouses that once stood on Federal Point, guiding mariners safely through New Inlet and into the Cape Fear River. There are no known images of the original Federal Point Lighthouse, which was built in 1817 and destroyed by fire on the night of April 13, 1836. During the Civil War, Capt. George Tate of the 40th North Carolina Regiment drew this sketch of the second Federal Point Lighthouse. The structure, which was completed in 1837, was destroyed by Confederates in 1863 during the construction of Fort Fisher. (Courtesy of North Carolina Archives and History.)

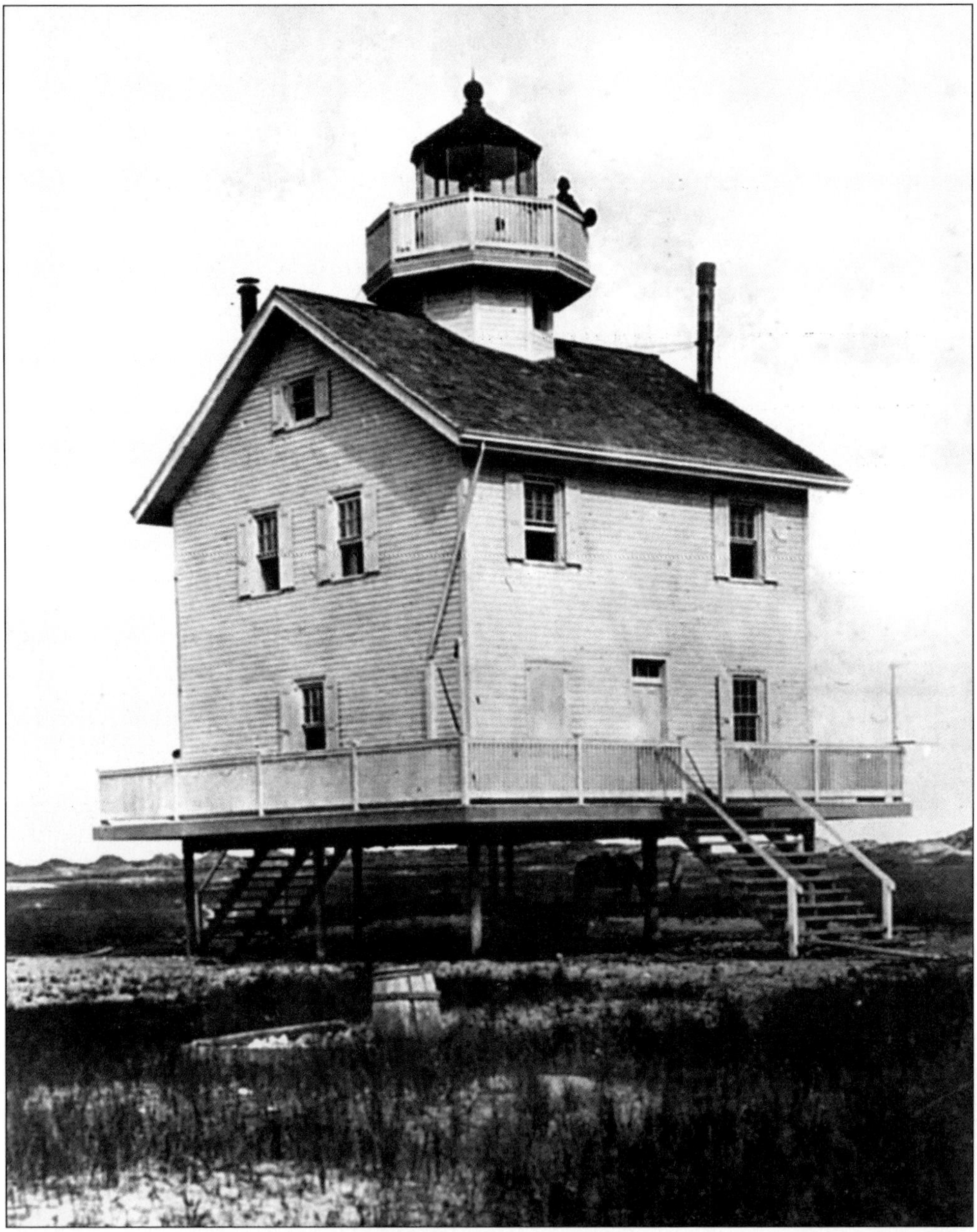

The third and final Federal Point Lighthouse was completed in the spring of 1866. It stood near where the North Carolina Aquarium at Fort Fisher stands today. The light went into operation on April 30, 1866. Due to the United States Army Corps of Engineers' project, which closed New Inlet, the Federal Point Lighthouse became unnecessary and was discontinued on December 31, 1879. According to a notice published in the *Wilmington Star*, the lighthouse on Federal Point was burned on the afternoon of August 23, 1881. The article noted, "This lighthouse has not been in use since the closing of New Inlet; but was occupied as a dwelling by Mr. Taylor, the former keeper. It was a wooden structure, situated about one mile from Fort Fisher." (Courtesy of North Carolina Archives and History.)

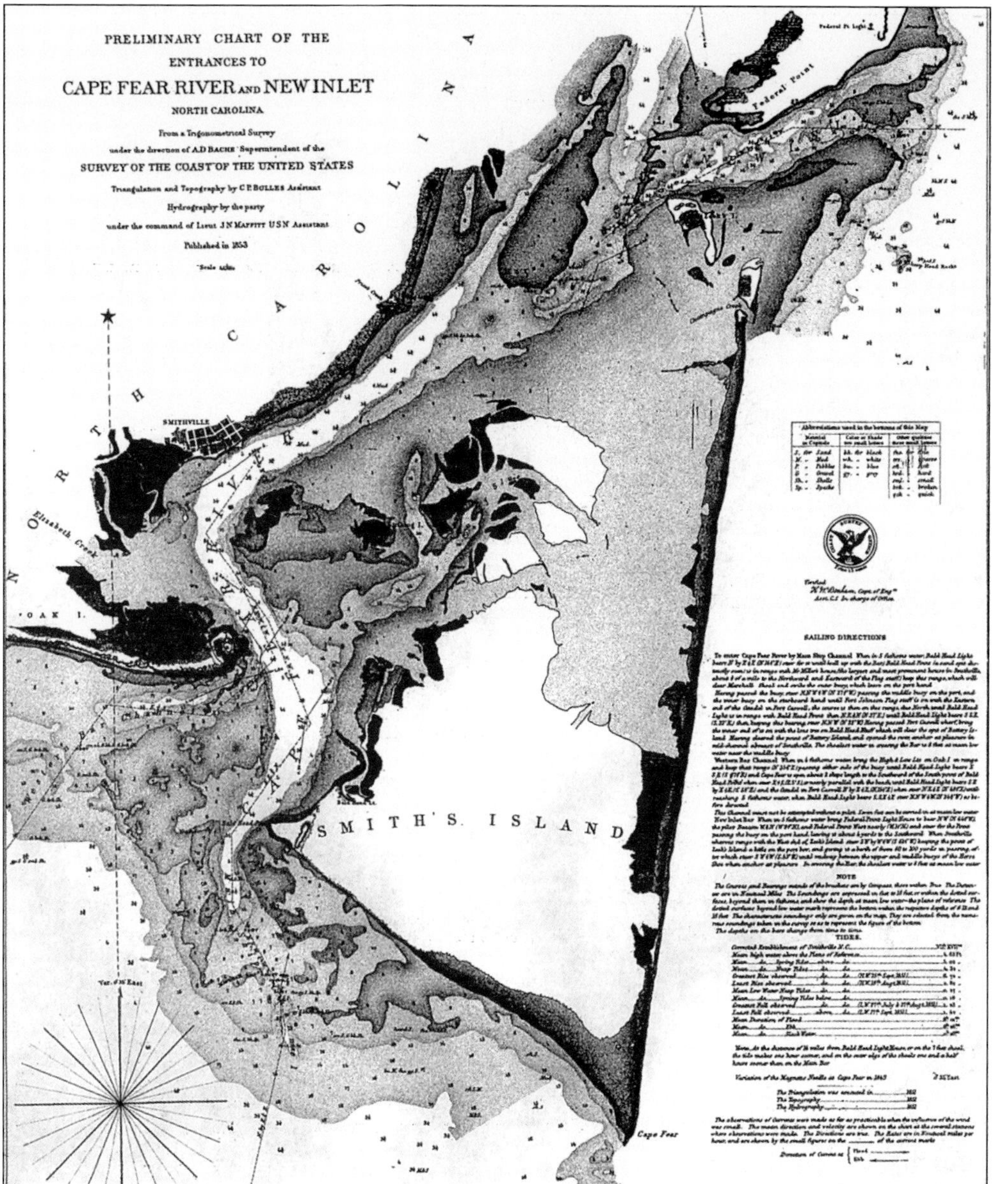

This nautical chart, showing the entrances to the Cape Fear River, was prepared in 1853. Note the locations indicated for the lighthouses at Federal Point and Smith's Island. The Federal Point Lighthouses marked the entrance to New Inlet, which was formed in 1761 when a fierce hurricane came ashore and opened an inlet across a narrow neck of land known as "The Haulover."

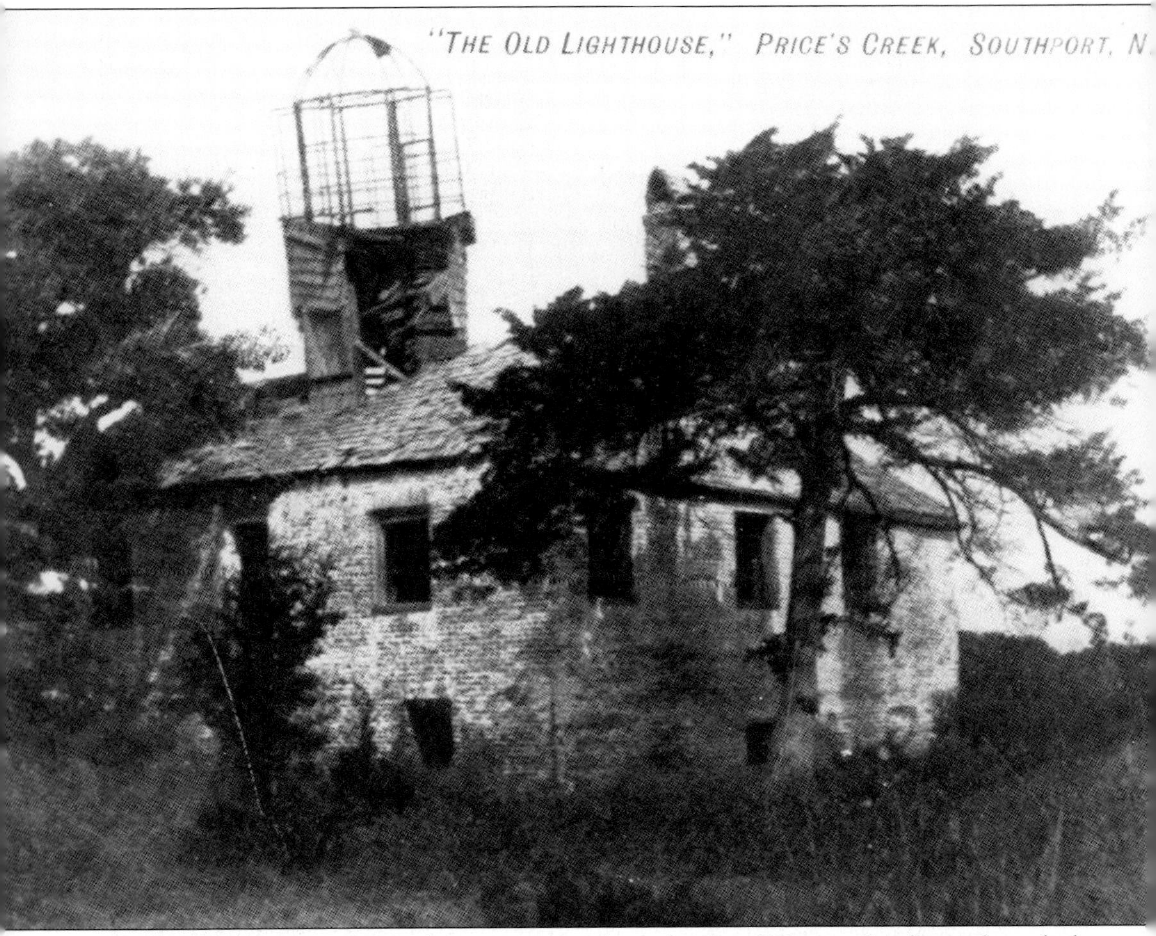

At the mouth of Price's Creek, opposite to where the Fort Fisher-to-Southport ferry docks today, stood an important pair of lighthouses. These lights were authorized by Congress in 1848, along with several other lights along Cape Fear that marked the way to Wilmington. Shown above, the main Price's Creek Lighthouse was built atop the keeper's dwelling. Although Samuel Mabson of Wilmington was appointed the first keeper of this lighthouse, he apparently never took the job. Thus, John Bell became the first keeper of the Price's Creek Lights. He officially illuminated the lighthouses for the first time on January 4, 1851. (Courtesy of North Carolina Archives and History.)

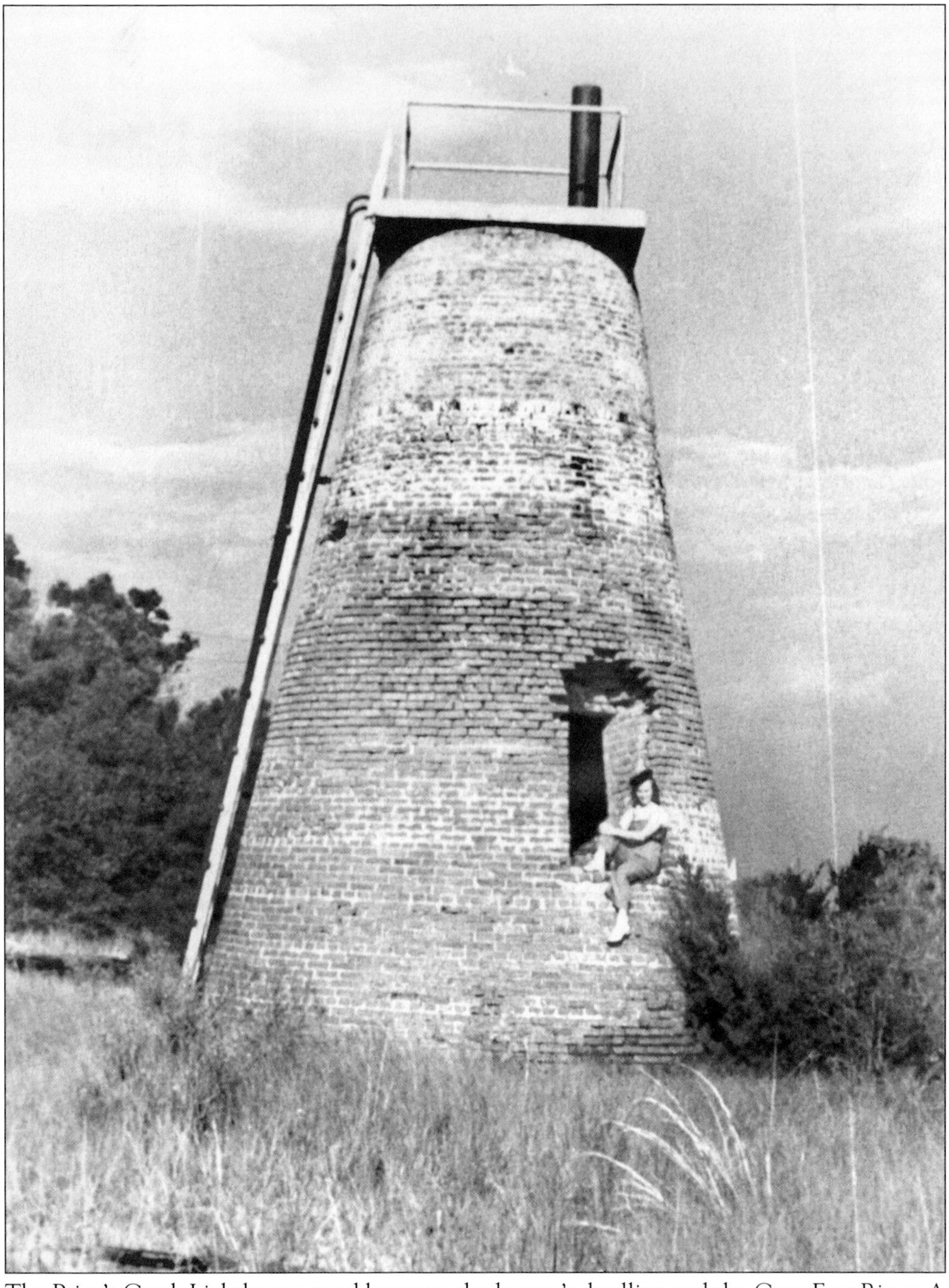

The Price's Creek Lighthouse stood between the keeper's dwelling and the Cape Fear River. A description was given in the April 27, 1850, contract: "A light house at proper distance in front of the above, to range with the channel, to be 20 feet high, to be built of hard brick. The diameter of the base to be 17 feet and that of the top 9." The tower was utilized as a signal station by Confederate forces during the Civil War. The remains of the tower are still standing and can be seen by passengers aboard the Fort Fisher-to-Southport Ferry. (Courtesy of North Carolina Archives and History.)

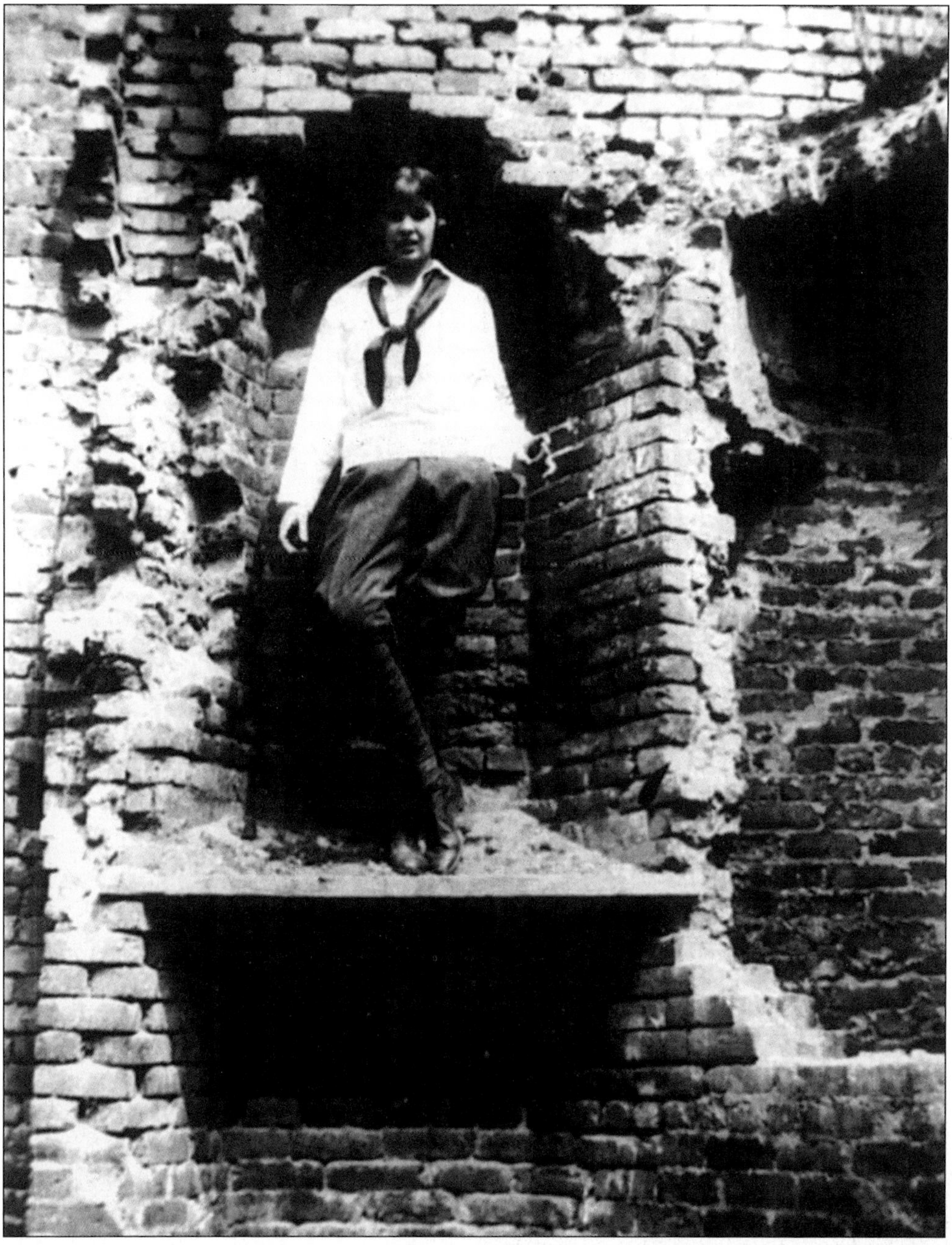

This unidentified young lady posed in the remains of the main Price's Creek Lighthouse, *c.* 1910. The light atop the keeper's quarters was thought to have been severely damaged during the Civil War, but long remained a prominent Brunswick County landmark. (Courtesy of North Carolina Archives and History.)

Three
CAPE FEAR LIGHTHOUSE

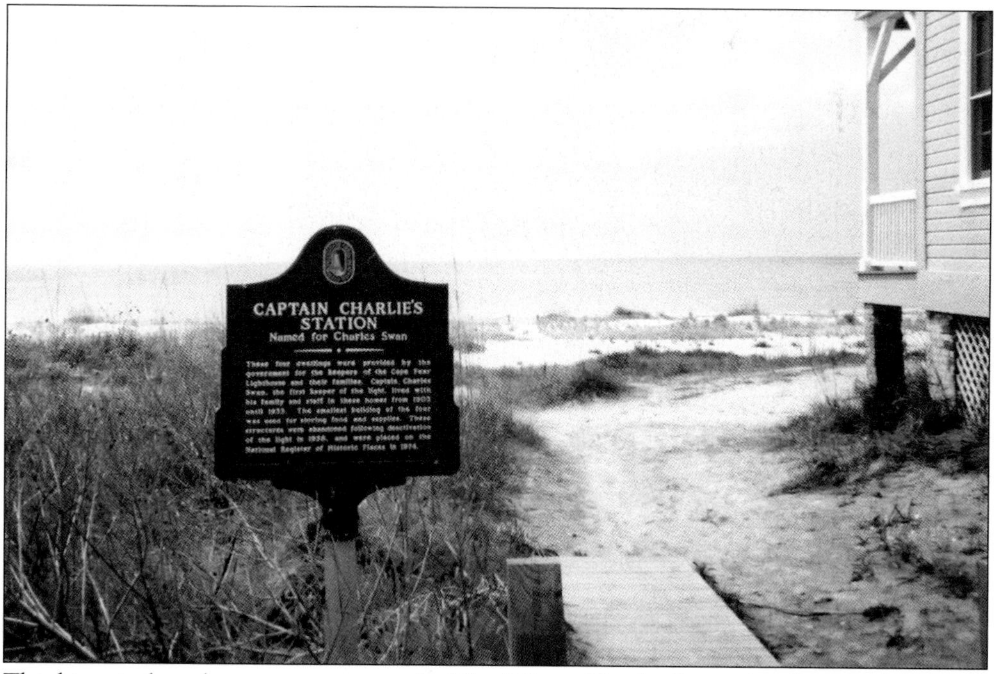

This historical marker commemorates the life of Capt. Charles Swan, first keeper of the Cape Fear Lighthouse; people affectionately referred to it as "Captain Charlie's Lighthouse."

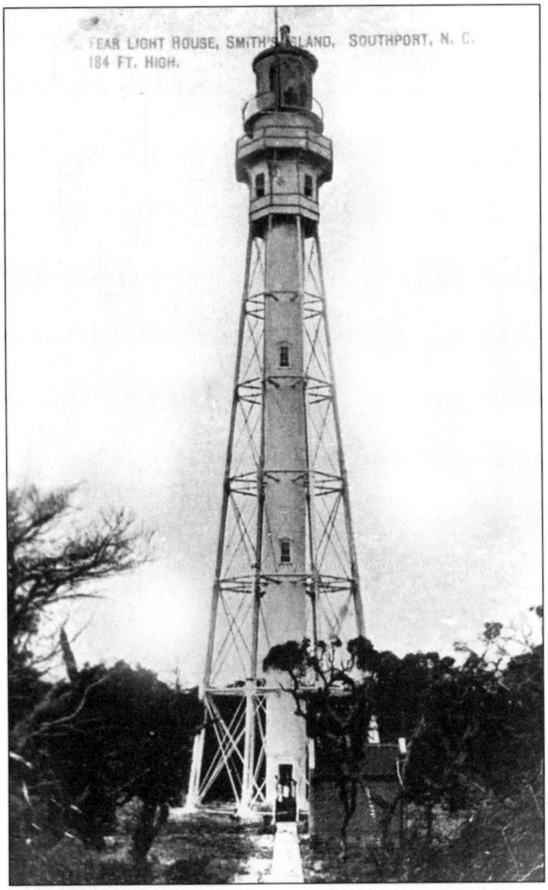

This old postcard shows the Cape Fear Lighthouse in 1909. Note the wire mesh built around the lantern room. This protected the glass from birds that often flew into the light. Captain Swan was reputedly able to distinguish what kind of bird hit the glass merely by the sound of the impact. It is also reported that the keeper's family supplemented their diet by cooking the birds that fell dead at the base of the tower. (Courtesy of North Carolina Archives and History.)

The United States Army Corps of Engineers closed New Inlet in the late 1800s with the construction of this dam, known as "The Rocks." This rendered the Federal Point Lighthouse obsolete. Because river traffic from the north was forced to go around Cape Fear and into the mouth of the river, a new lighthouse on the eastern tip of Bald Head Island was necessary.

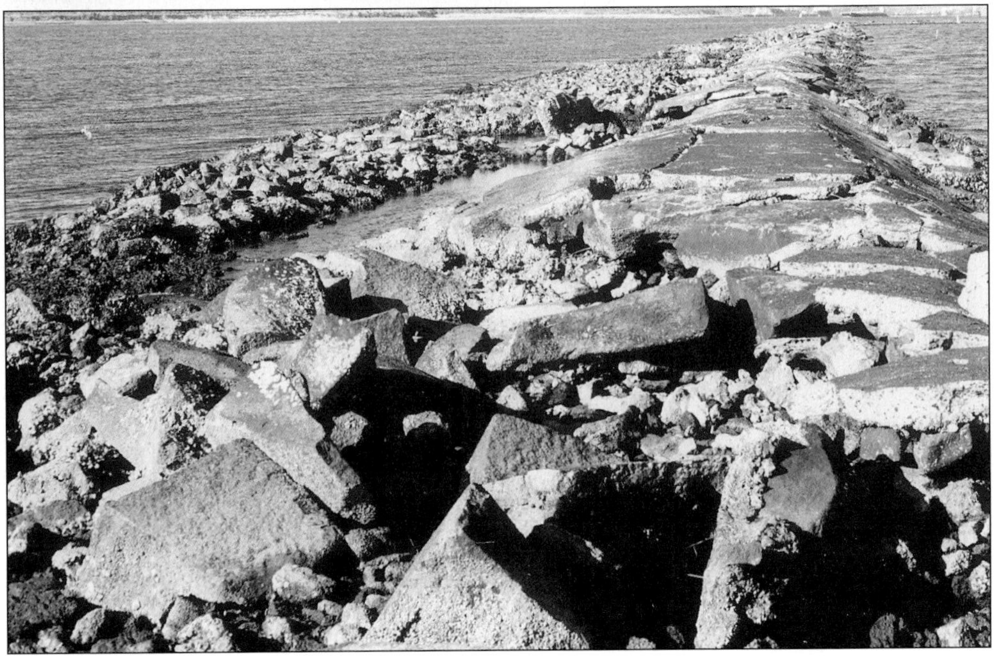

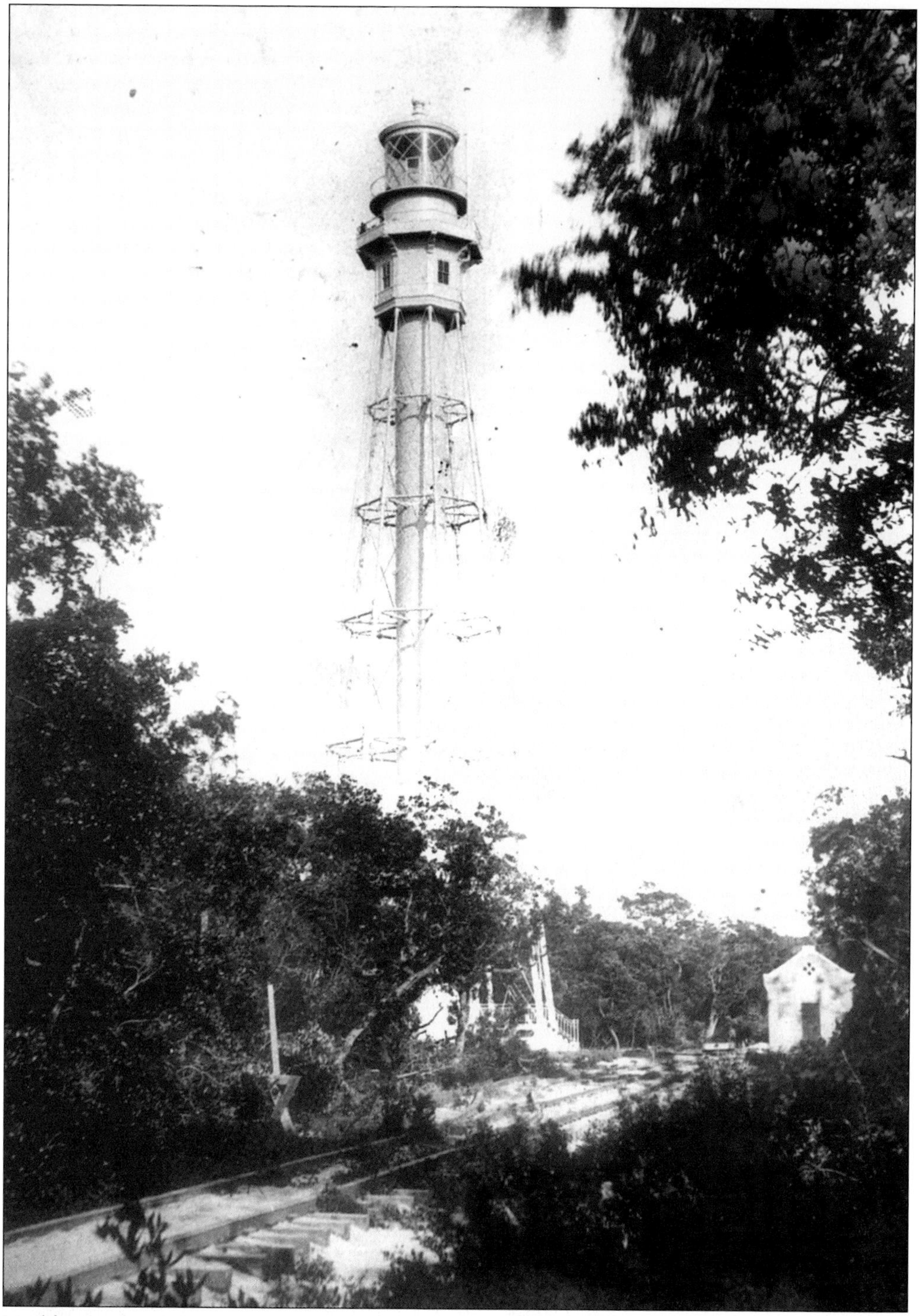

Visible in the foreground, the tram railway was built through the thick maritime forest of Bald Head Island so that the materials for the Cape Fear Lighthouse could be hauled from the Cape Fear River landing. The route of this old road is still used today. (Courtesy of National Archives.)

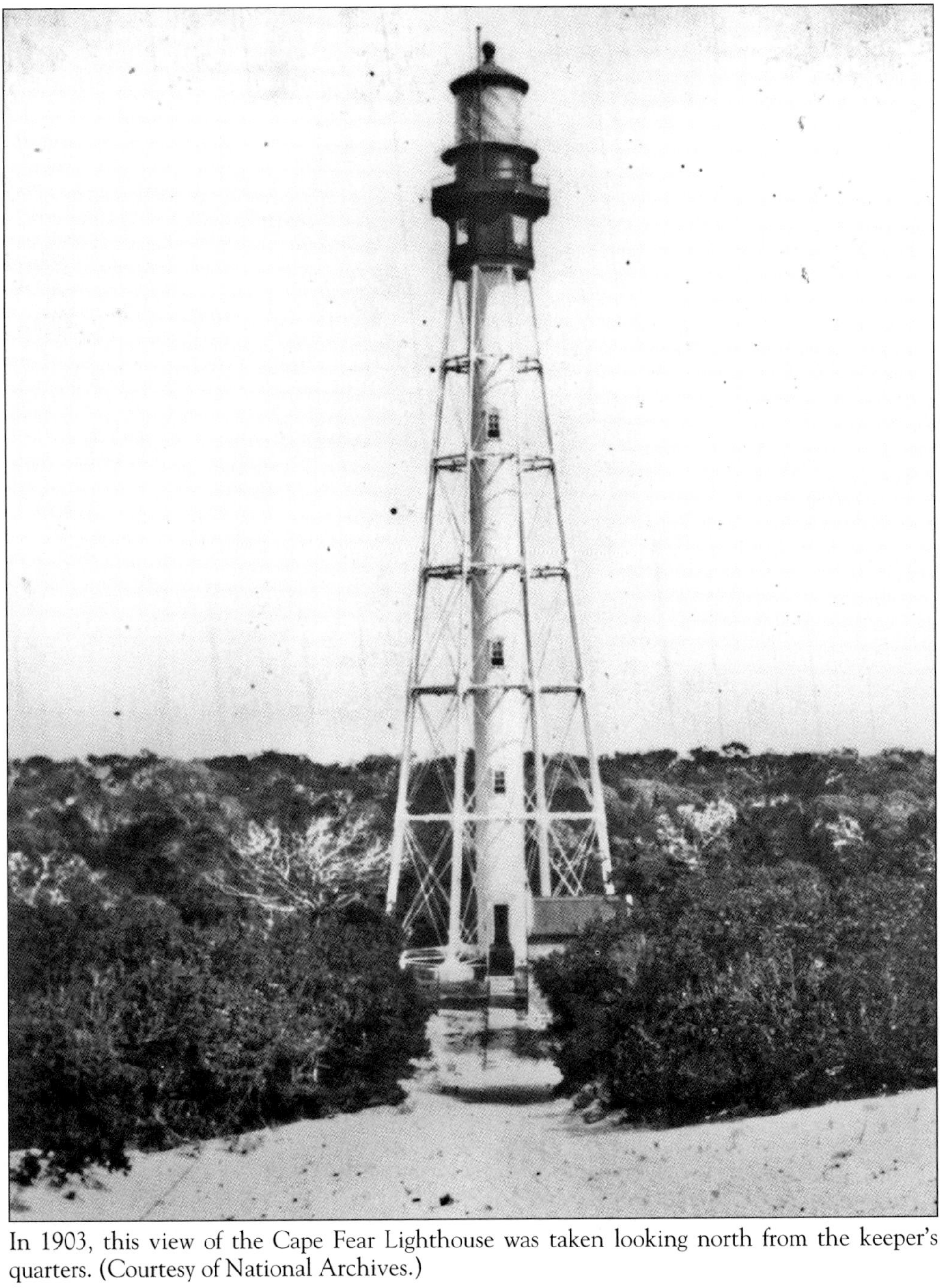

In 1903, this view of the Cape Fear Lighthouse was taken looking north from the keeper's quarters. (Courtesy of National Archives.)

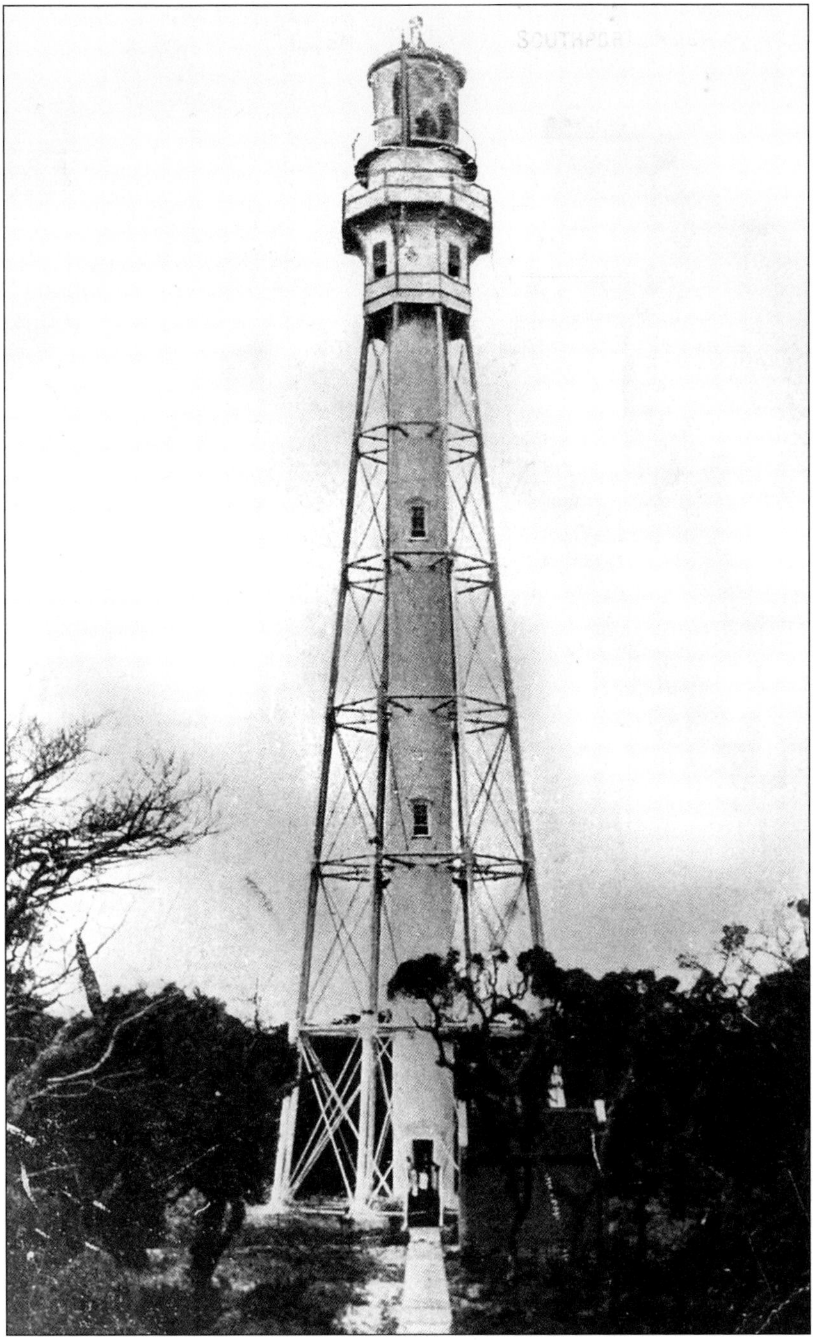

Cape Fear Lighthouse was the only steel skeleton lighthouse constructed along the North Carolina coast. It first went into use on August 31, 1903. Capt. Charlie Swan, keeper of the light, had the privilege of lighting it. For over half a century, the Cape Fear Lighthouse guided mariners into and out of the Cape Fear River and through the treacherous Frying Pan Shoals. By the 1950s, however, its beam was considered inadequate and a new light on Oak Island was built to replace it. On May 15, 1958, the Cape Fear Lighthouse cast its beam for the last time. (Courtesy of National Archives.)

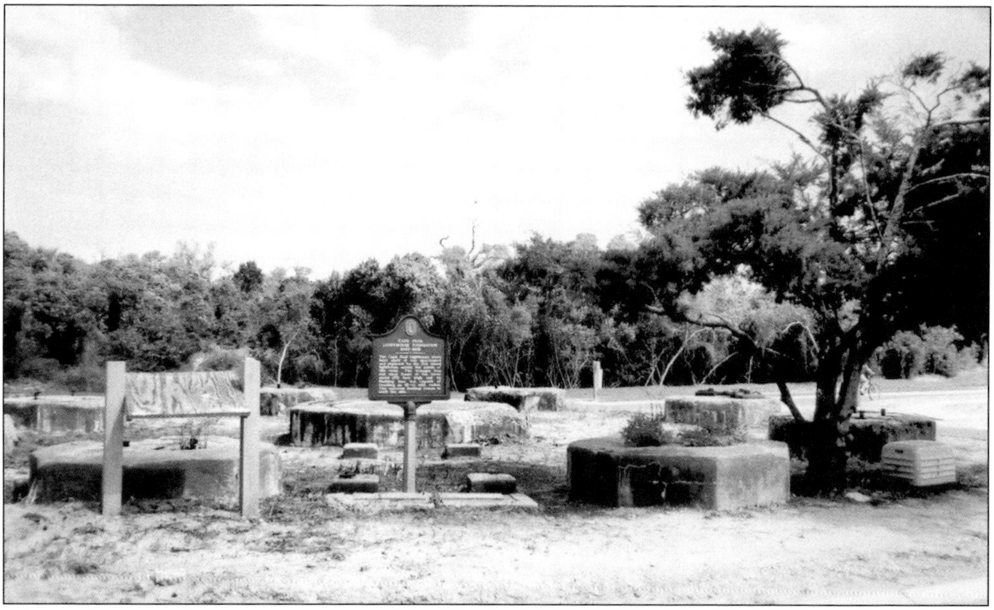

The remains of the Cape Fear Lighthouse are prominently marked out and identified on Bald Head Island.

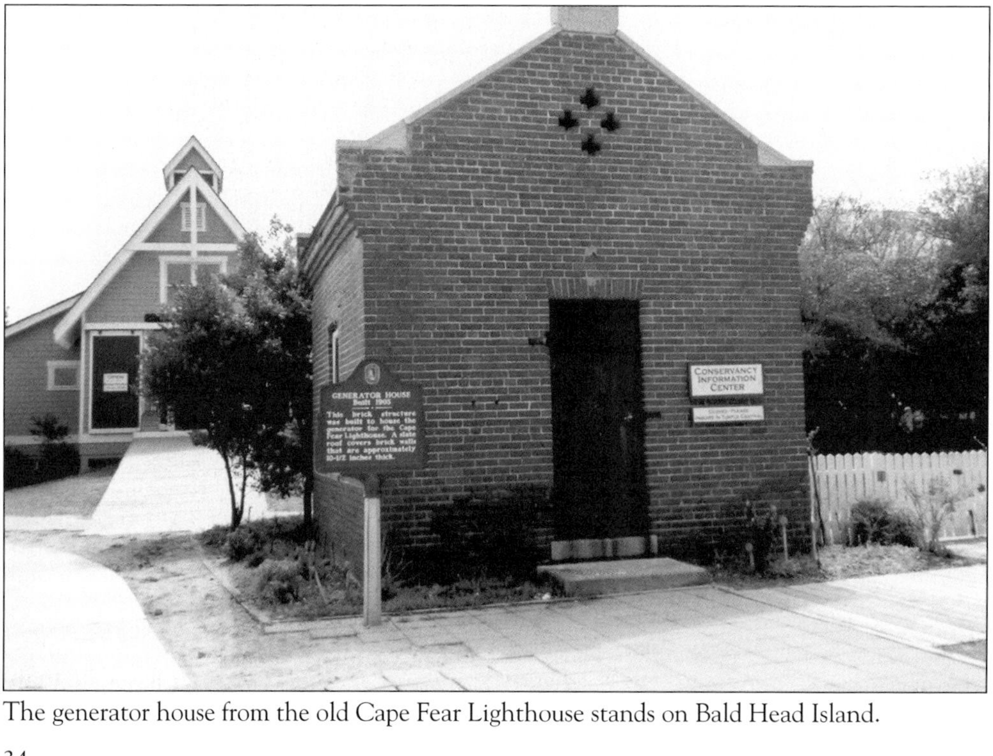

The generator house from the old Cape Fear Lighthouse stands on Bald Head Island.

Four

OAK ISLAND LIGHTHOUSE

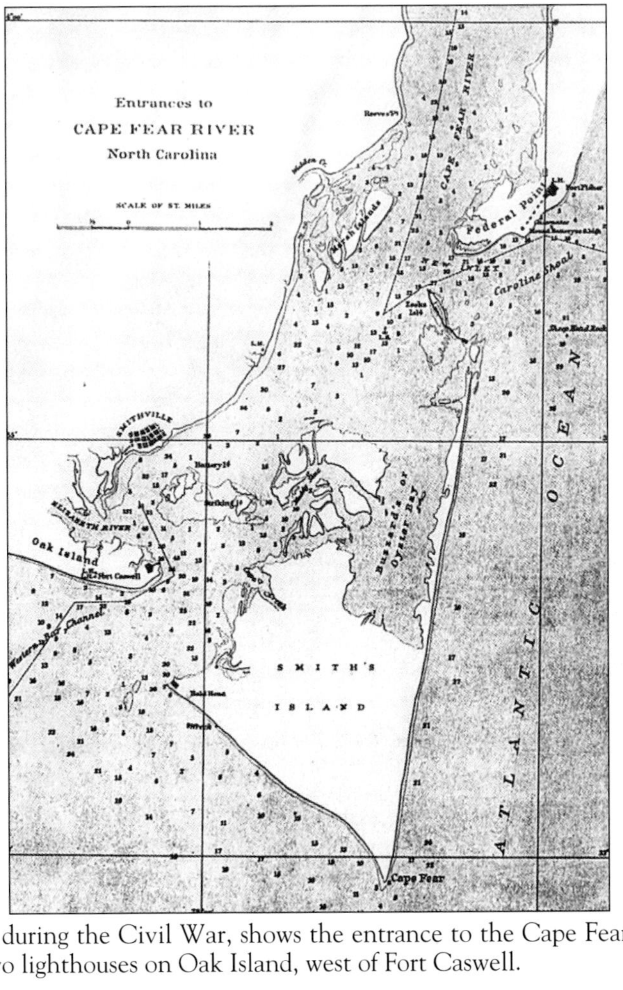

This map, drawn during the Civil War, shows the entrance to the Cape Fear River. Note the location of the two lighthouses on Oak Island, west of Fort Caswell.

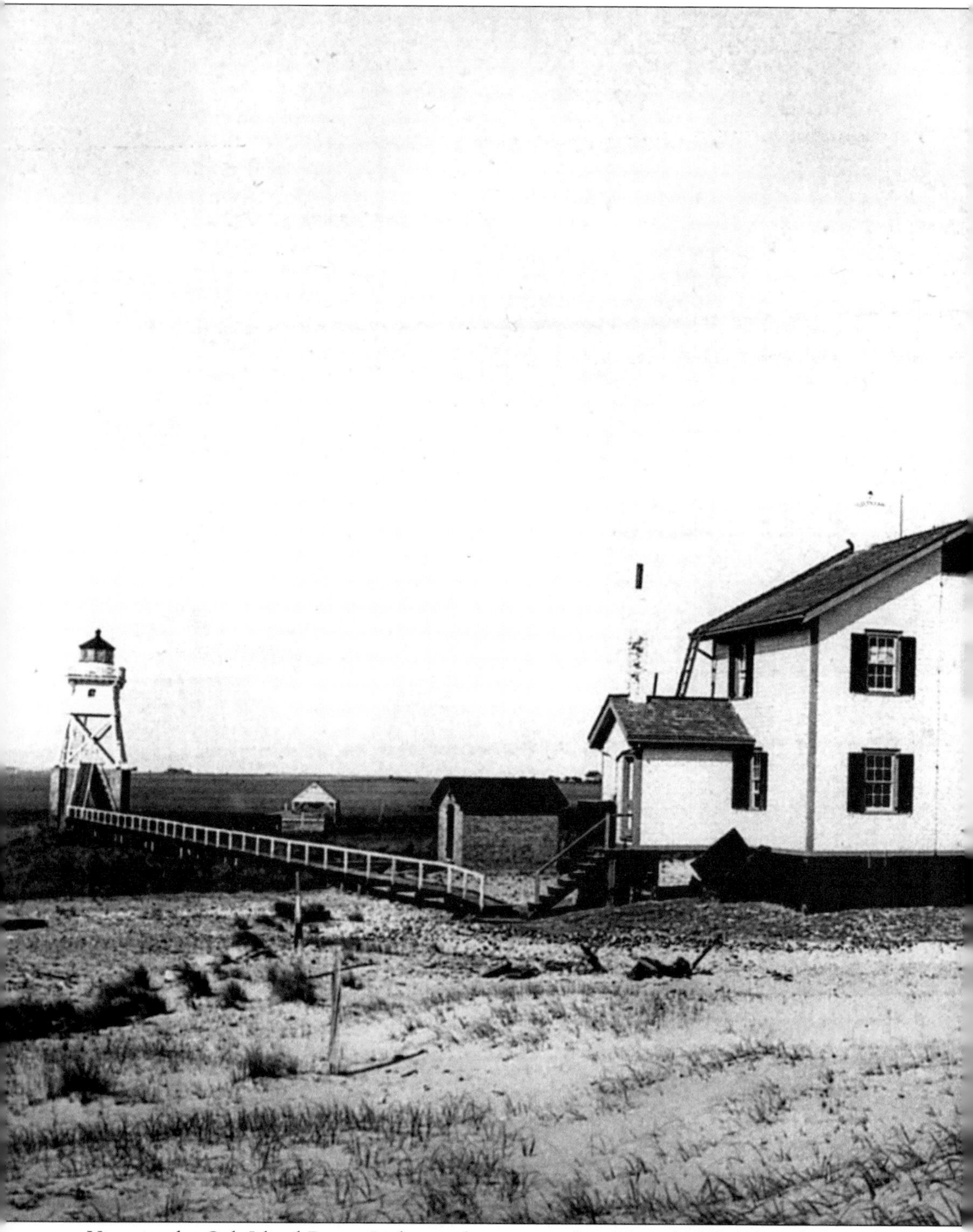

Here are the Oak Island Range Lights as they appeared in May of 1893. These lights, which guided mariners into the entrance of the mouth of the Cape Fear River, replaced an earlier set of range lights that had been constructed concurrently with the Price's Creek Range Lights.

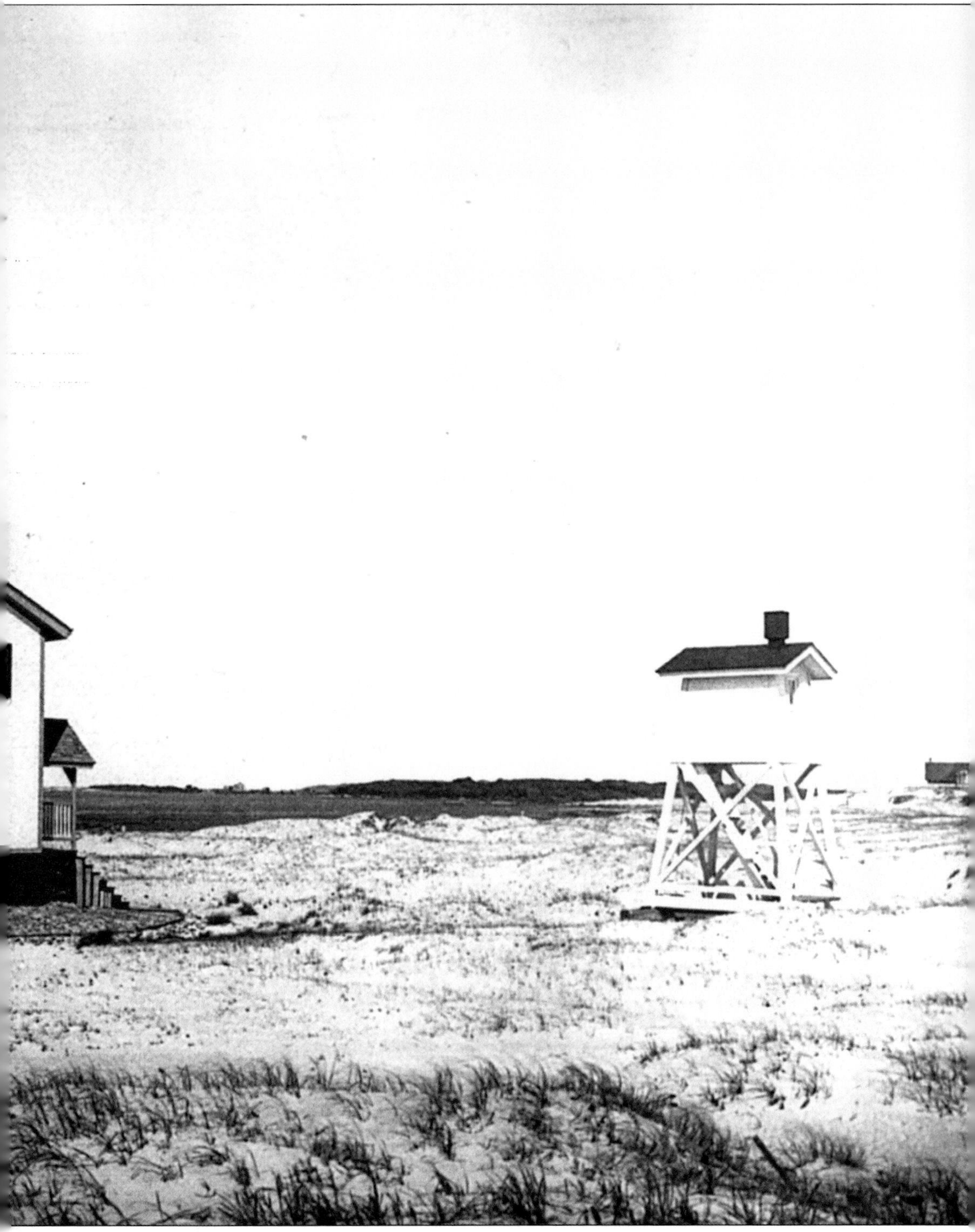

Shortly after this photo was taken, a severe hurricane struck the mouth of Cape Fear and Oak Island was inundated by the storm surge. The range lights were damaged to such an extent that they were not put back into operation. (Courtesy of National Archives.)

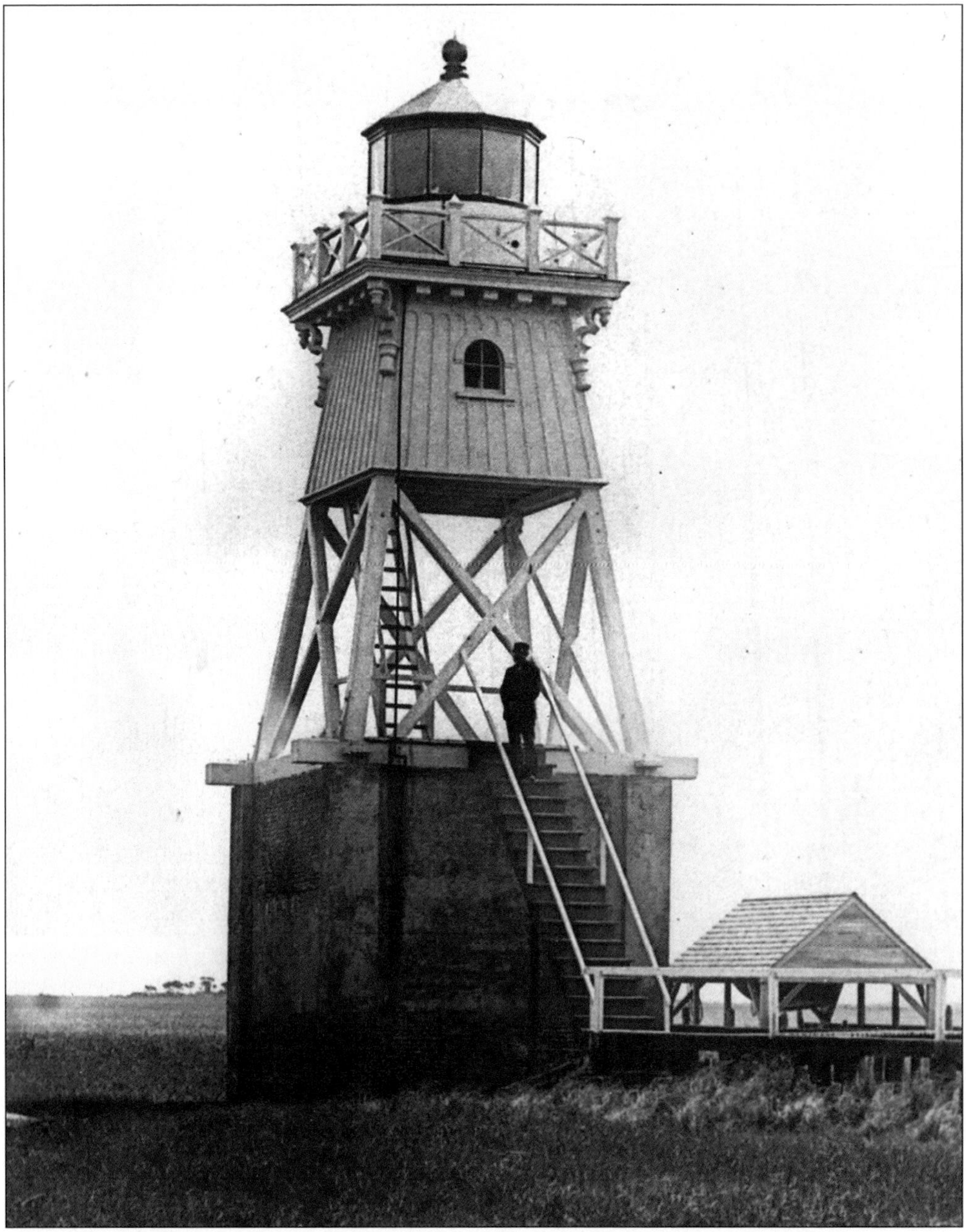

This is the Oak Island Range Rear Light in 1893. The beacon was discontinued on July 31, 1894, but the structure remained a prominent Oak Island landmark until it burned in the 1950s. (Courtesy of National Archives.)

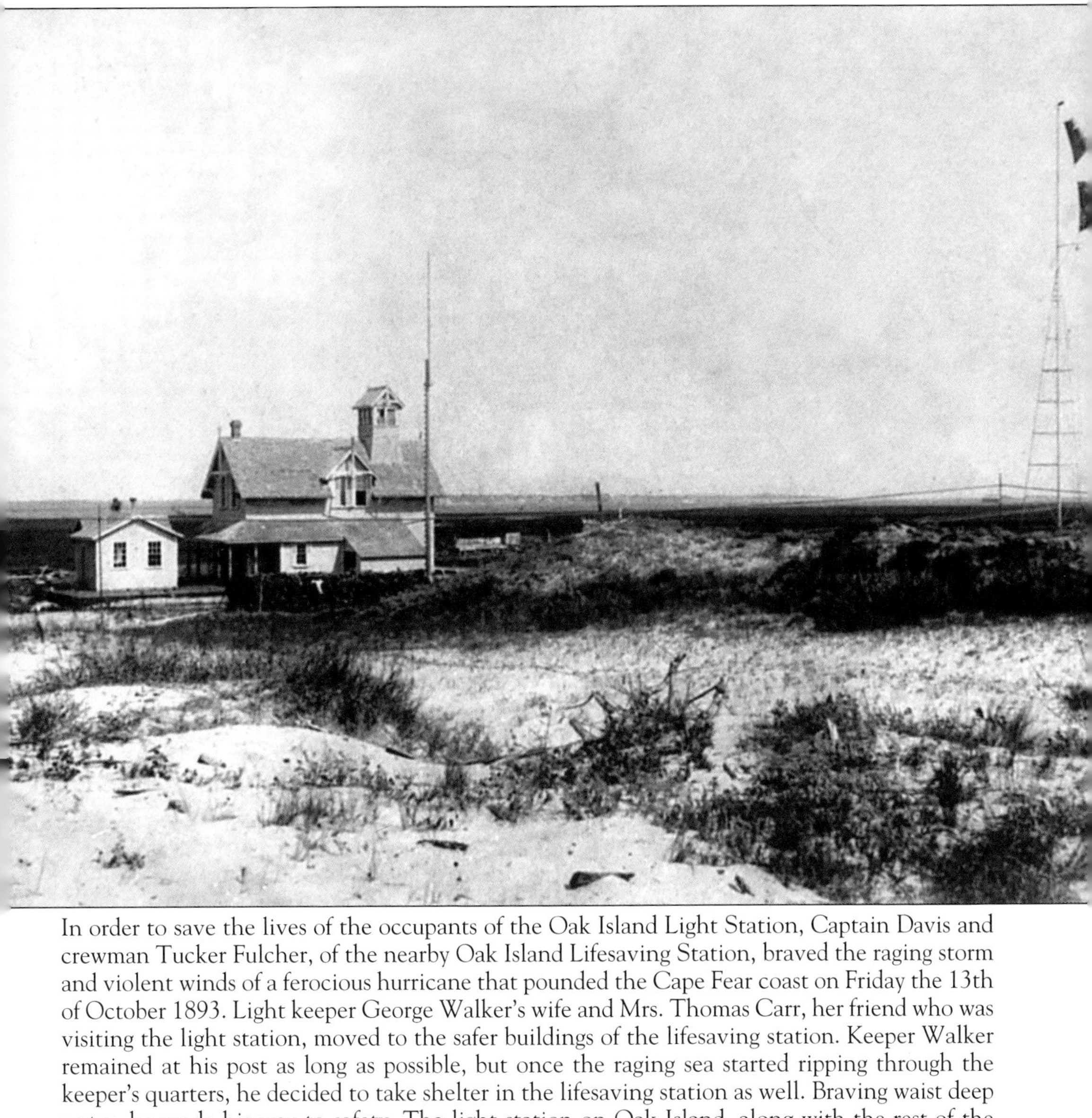

In order to save the lives of the occupants of the Oak Island Light Station, Captain Davis and crewman Tucker Fulcher, of the nearby Oak Island Lifesaving Station, braved the raging storm and violent winds of a ferocious hurricane that pounded the Cape Fear coast on Friday the 13th of October 1893. Light keeper George Walker's wife and Mrs. Thomas Carr, her friend who was visiting the light station, moved to the safer buildings of the lifesaving station. Keeper Walker remained at his post as long as possible, but once the raging sea started ripping through the keeper's quarters, he decided to take shelter in the lifesaving station as well. Braving waist deep water, he made his way to safety. The light station on Oak Island, along with the rest of the island, suffered much damage during this storm. A newspaper account described the damage: "The three water tanks and oil house belonging to the lighthouse were entirely washed away by the storm, also the plank walk from the main dwelling, with the steps up to the light. Some of the oil was carried by the waves across to Southport where it was picked up and afterwards recovered by the keeper." (Courtesy of North Carolina Archives and History.)

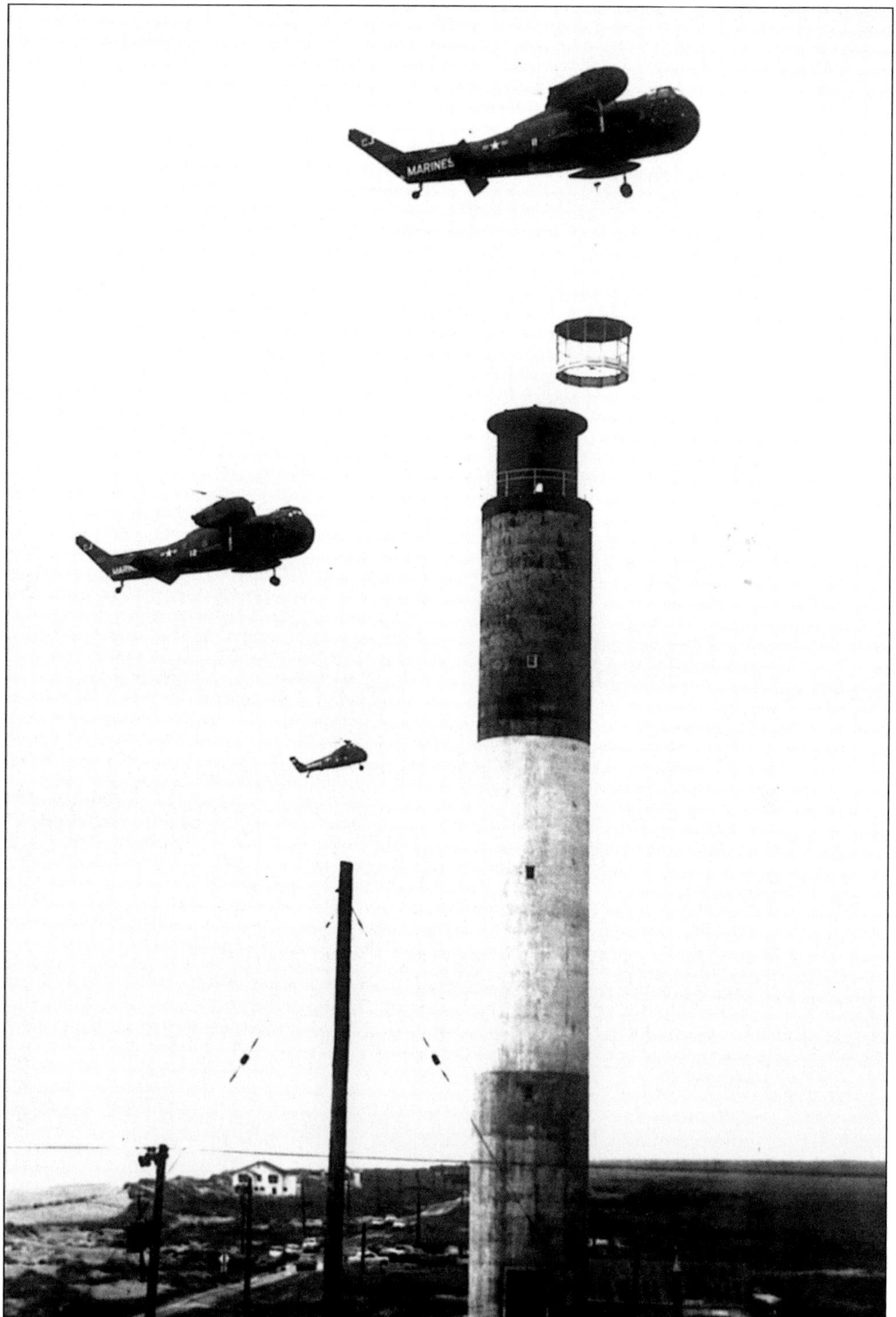

These helicopters are lowering the lantern room atop the Oak Island Lighthouse in December of 1957. (Courtesy of North Carolina Archives and History.)

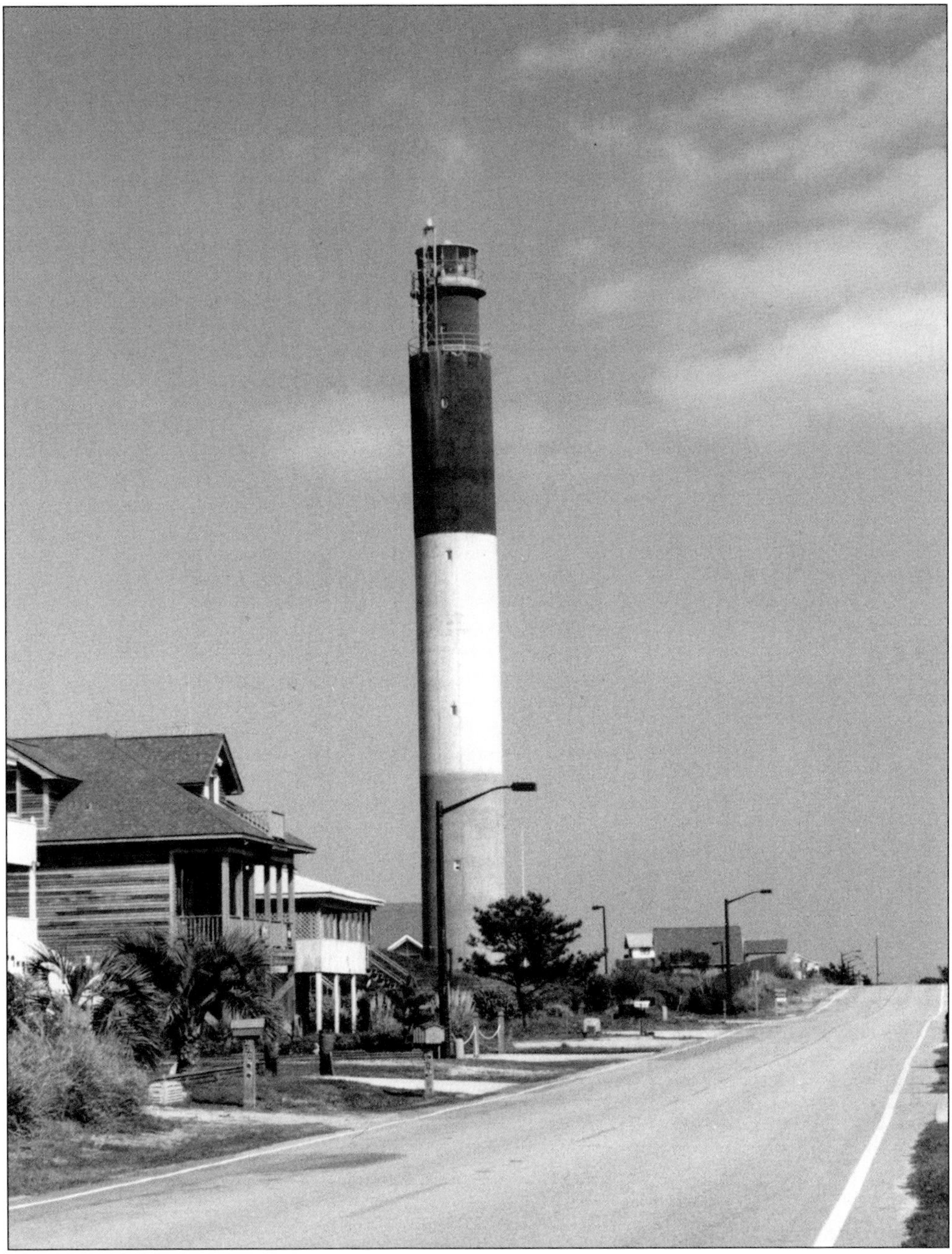

The Oak Island Lighthouse was completed by W.H. Brinkley and Company in 1958. The lighthouse went into operation on May 15, 1958, and was the last lighthouse to be built on the coast of North Carolina. When it was completed, Oak Island had the most powerful light in the United States. This is the only lighthouse in the state built with concrete, using a slip form for construction. Pigment was added to the cement as the tower was built, giving Oak Island its distinctive daymark with gray on the bottom, white in the middle, and black on top. This ingenious method of coloring the tower has saved thousands of taxpayer dollars through the years, as the lighthouse never needs to be repainted. (Photo courtesy Joey Powell)

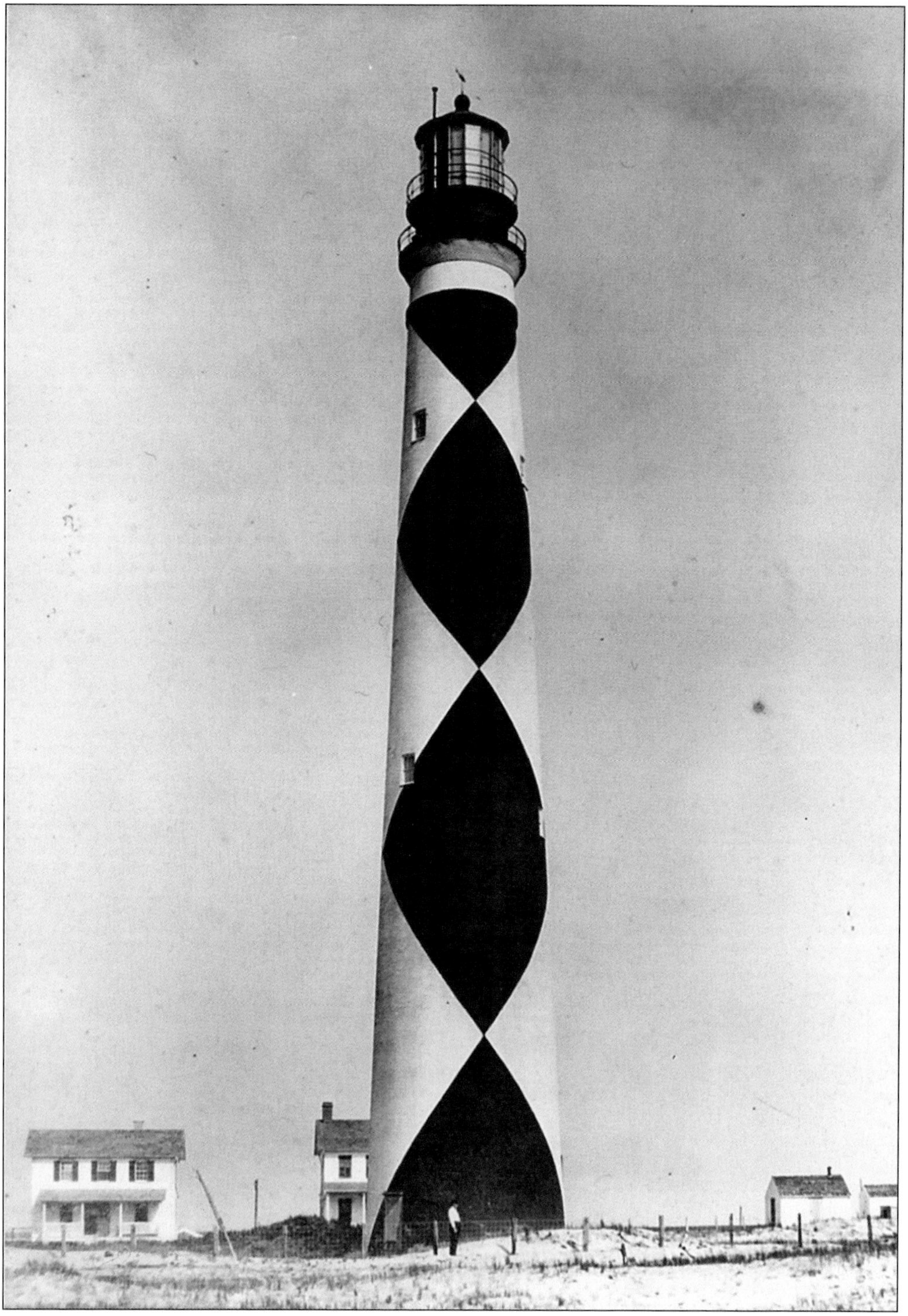

Charles Clifton, keeper of the Cape Lookout Lighthouse, stands in front of the structure *c.* 1910. (Courtesy of the National Park Service, Cape Lookout National Seashore.)

Five
Cape Lookout Lighthouse

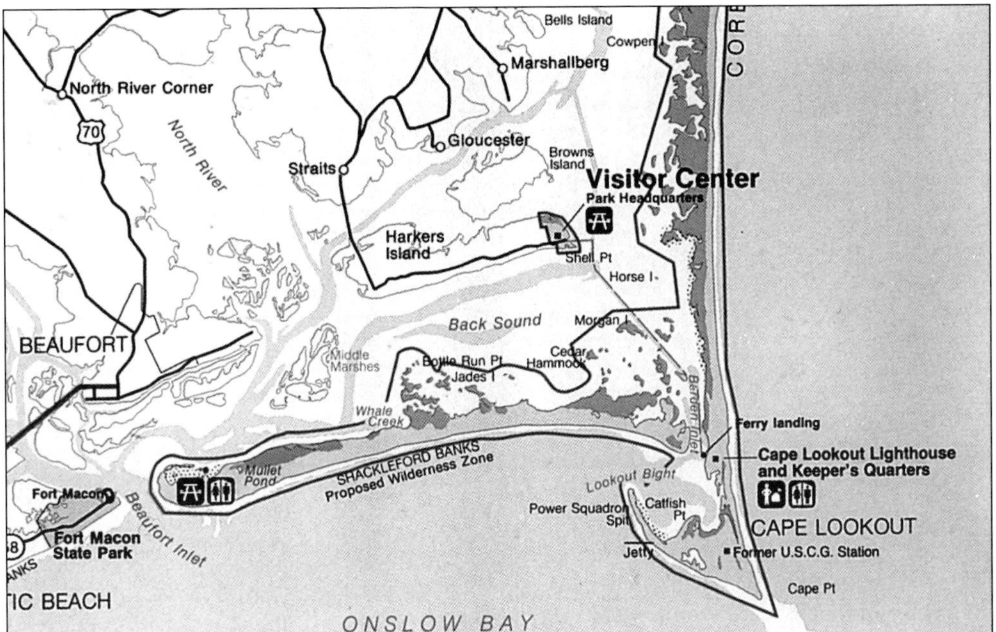

This map shows the location of the Cape Lookout Lighthouse within the Cape Lookout National Seashore. (Courtesy of the National Park Service.)

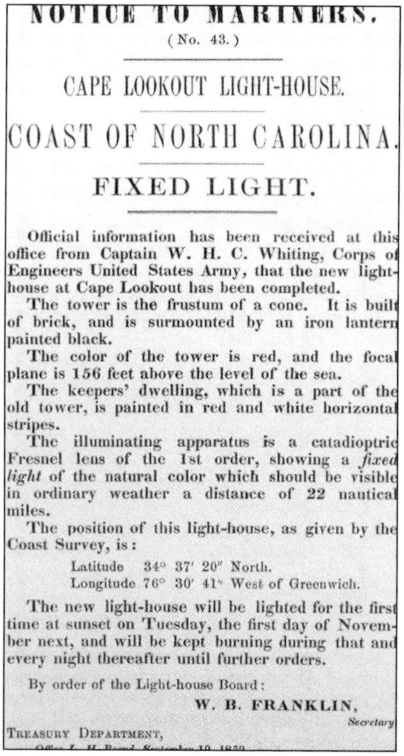

NOTICE TO MARINERS.

(No. 43.)

CAPE LOOKOUT LIGHT-HOUSE.

COAST OF NORTH CAROLINA.

FIXED LIGHT.

Official information has been received at this office from Captain W. H. C. Whiting, Corps of Engineers United States Army, that the new light-house at Cape Lookout has been completed.

The tower is the frustum of a cone. It is built of brick, and is surmounted by an iron lantern painted black.

The color of the tower is red, and the focal plane is 156 feet above the level of the sea.

The keepers' dwelling, which is a part of the old tower, is painted in red and white horizontal stripes.

The illuminating apparatus is a catadioptric Fresnel lens of the 1st order, showing a *fixed light* of the natural color which should be visible in ordinary weather a distance of 22 nautical miles.

The position of this light-house, as given by the Coast Survey, is:

Latitude 34° 37′ 20″ North.
Longitude 76° 30′ 41″ West of Greenwich.

The new light-house will be lighted for the first time at sunset on Tuesday, the first day of November next, and will be kept burning during that and every night thereafter until further orders.

By order of the Light-house Board:

W. B. FRANKLIN,
Secretary

TREASURY DEPARTMENT,

This notice alerted mariners to the completion of the new lighthouse on Cape Lookout in 1859

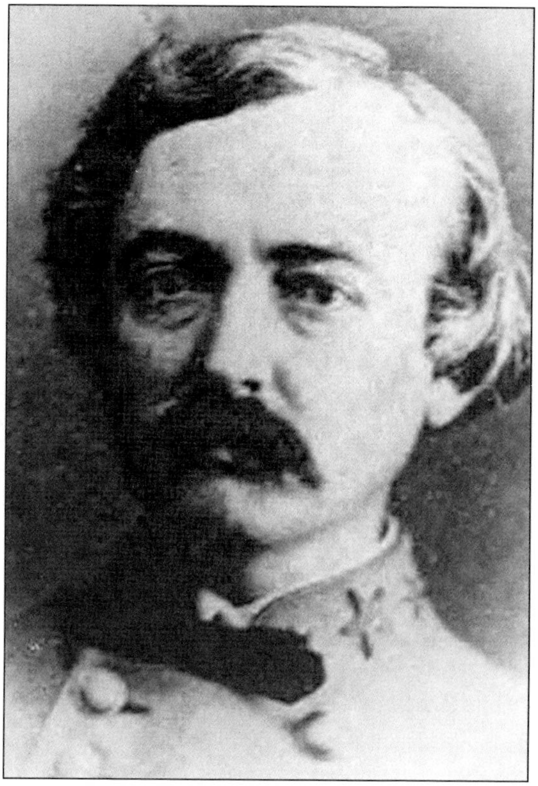

Confederate Gen. W.H.C. Whiting oversaw construction of the Cape Lookout Lighthouse as a captain in the United States Army Corps of Engineers in 1859. He was killed during the battle of Fort Fisher in 1865.

The original Cape Lookout Lighthouse was built in 1812 at a cost of $20,578.54. It stood near where the present-day lighthouse stands and consisted of two structures, one built inside the other. Inside was a brick tower, while the outside was a wooden tower covered with cedar shingles. The tower was painted with red and white horizontal stripes. Blunt's *American Coast Pilot* for 1842 provides the following description of this light: "Cape Lookout light-house is painted with red and white stripes horizontally, and can be seen 16 or 18 miles, and resembles a ship under sail. It contains a fixed light, elevated 100 feet above the level of the sea. The house is surrounded by a small growth of trees, from which a bold sand beach extends in a S.E. direction, about 3 miles, in the centre of which are small hillocks of sand. This light, although seen clearly all night, until near the approach of day, cannot then be discerned, owing, it is thought, to a mist that rises between the vessel and the lamps. It is judged imprudent to approach the shoals of Lookout in the night nearer than 7 fathoms on the east, or 10 on the west side." (Courtesy of the National Park Service, Cape Lookout National Seashore.)

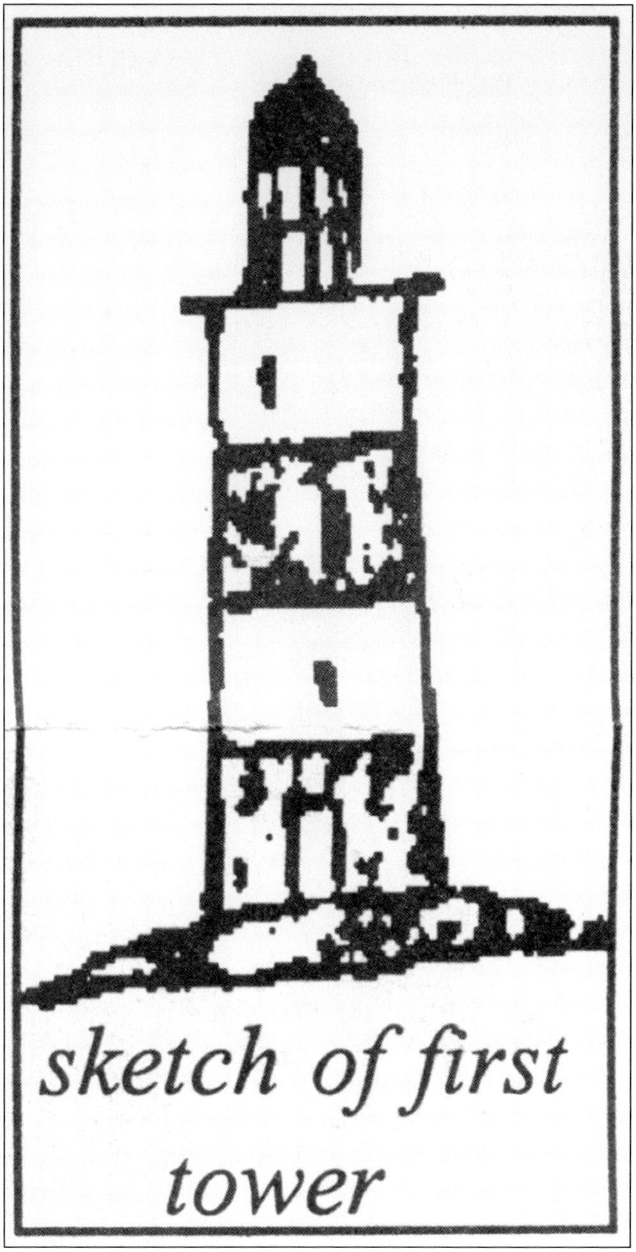

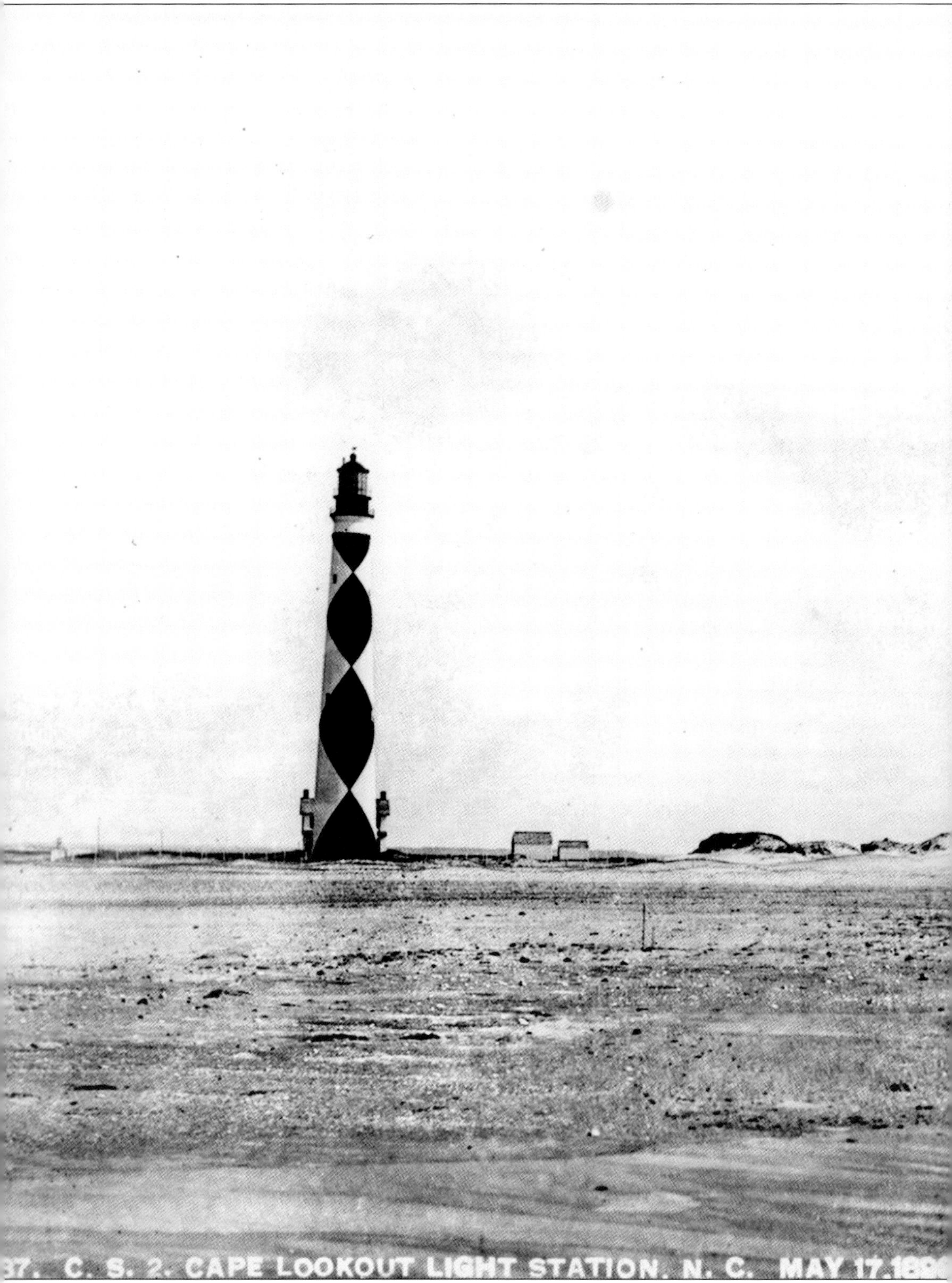
37. C. S. 2. CAPE LOOKOUT LIGHT STATION. N. C. MAY 17.18

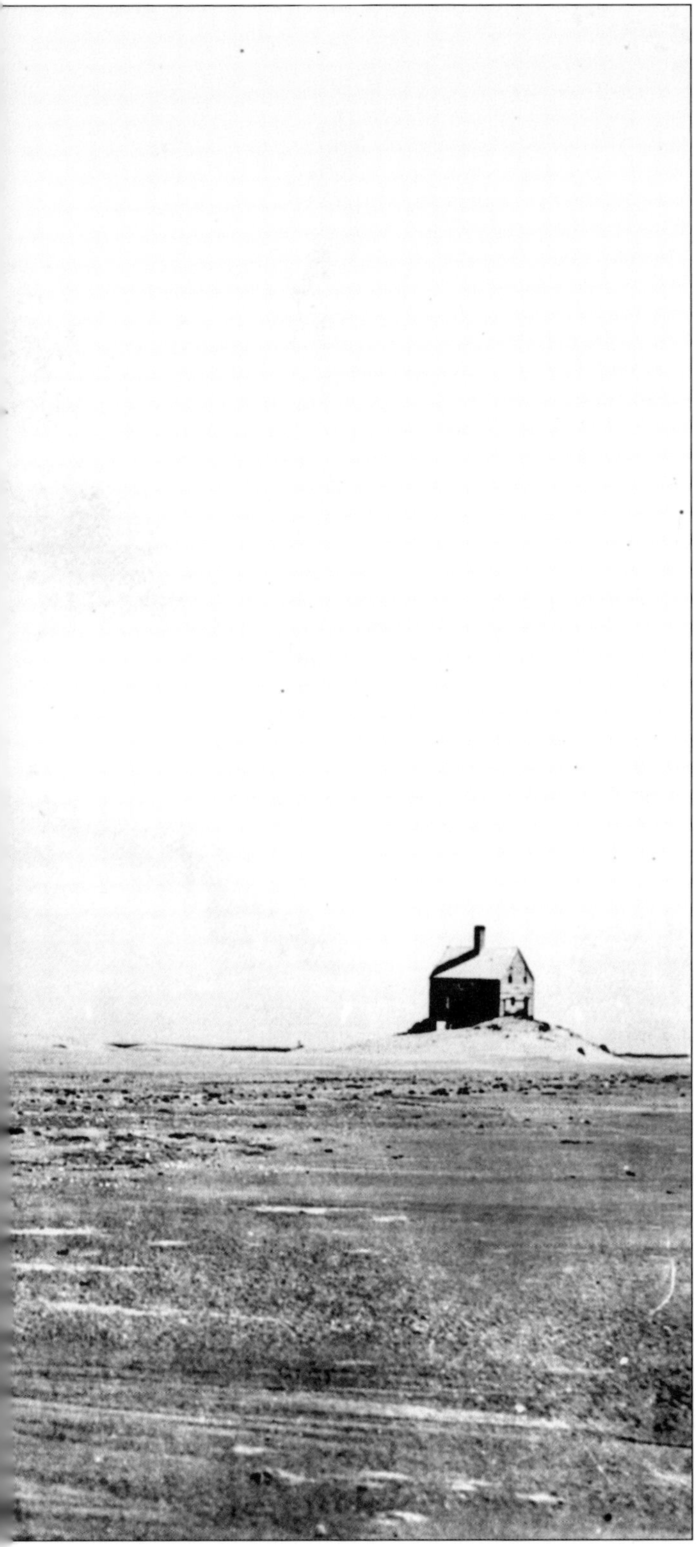

This is Cape Lookout Light Station as it appeared on May 17, 1893. The old building far to the right of the lighthouse is thought to be the original keeper's quarters, built for the light keepers of the first Cape Lookout Lighthouse. (Courtesy of National Archives.)

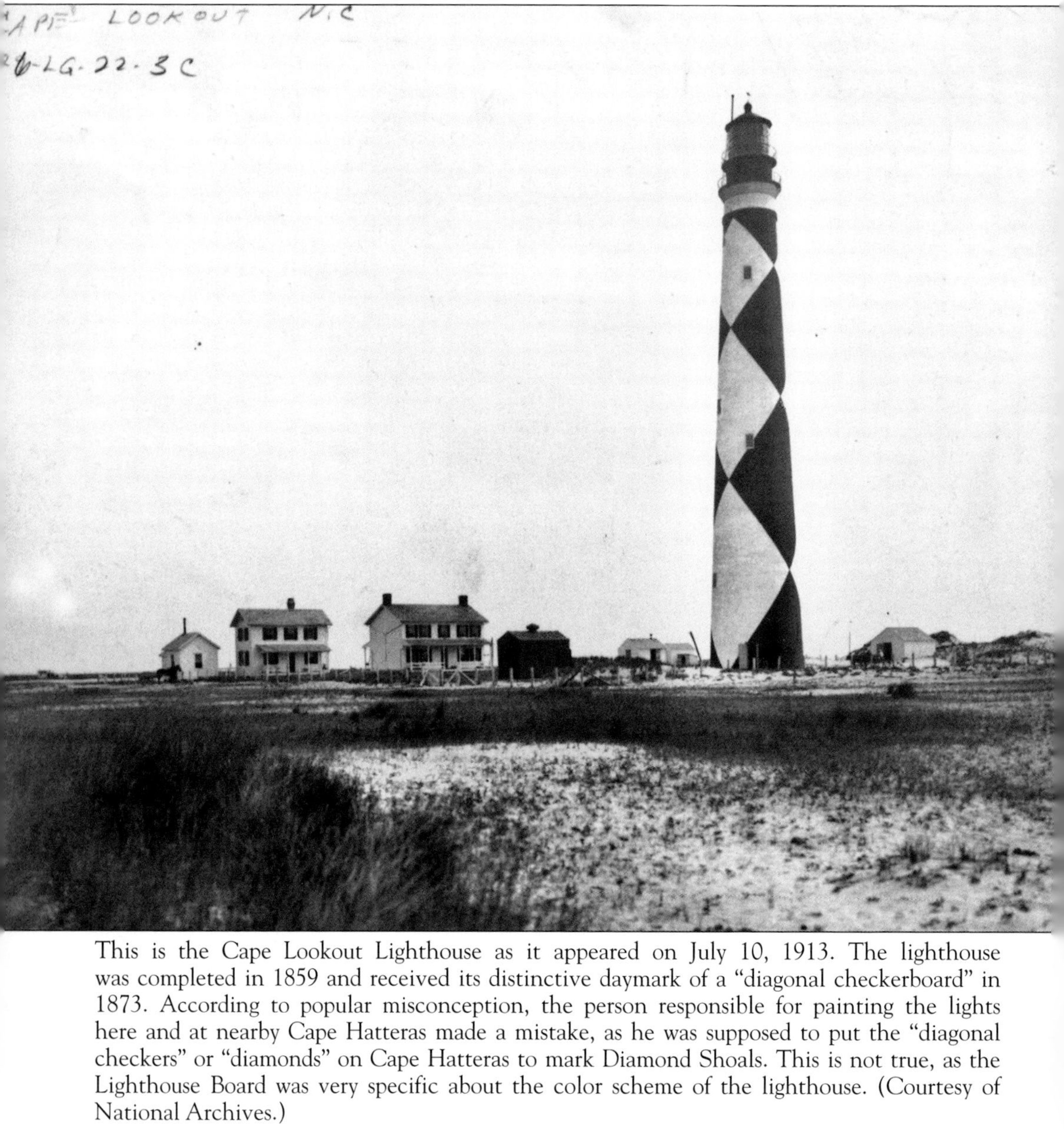

This is the Cape Lookout Lighthouse as it appeared on July 10, 1913. The lighthouse was completed in 1859 and received its distinctive daymark of a "diagonal checkerboard" in 1873. According to popular misconception, the person responsible for painting the lights here and at nearby Cape Hatteras made a mistake, as he was supposed to put the "diagonal checkers" or "diamonds" on Cape Hatteras to mark Diamond Shoals. This is not true, as the Lighthouse Board was very specific about the color scheme of the lighthouse. (Courtesy of National Archives.)

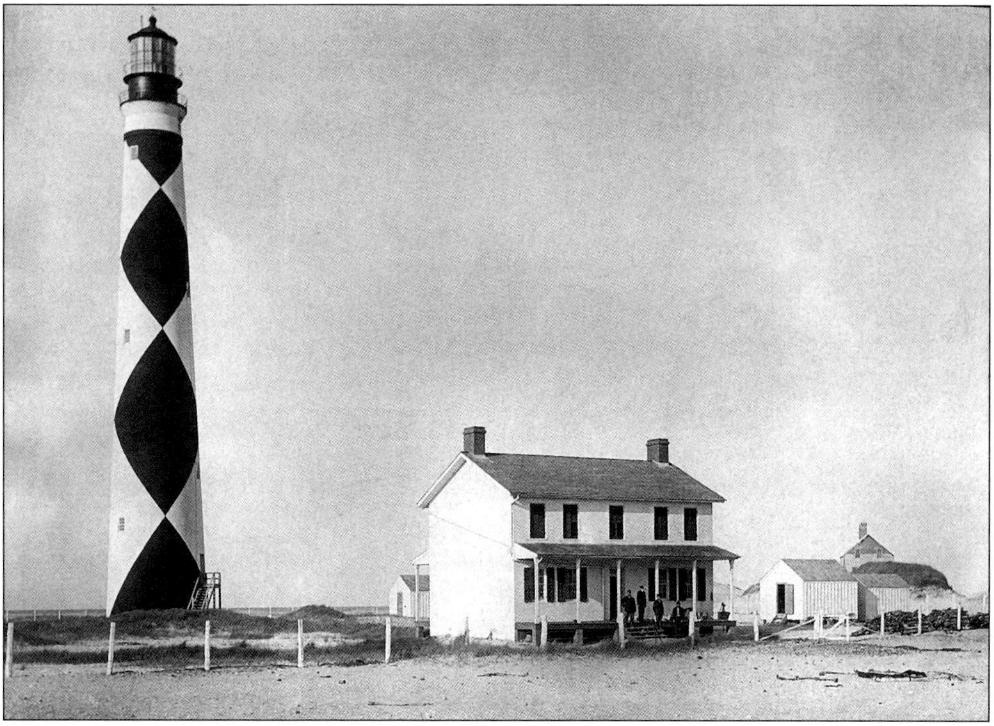
Here is a picture of the Cape Lookout Lighthouse *c.* 1890. (Courtesy of National Archives.)

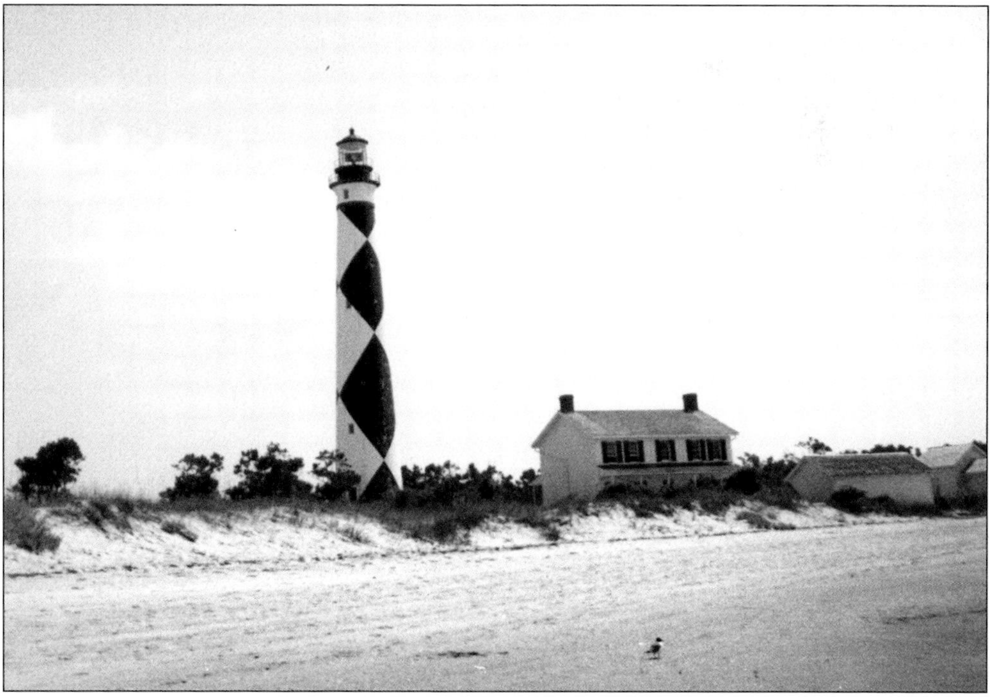
The National Park Service maintains a museum inside the assistant keeper's quarters, which are adjacent to the Cape Lookout Lighthouse.

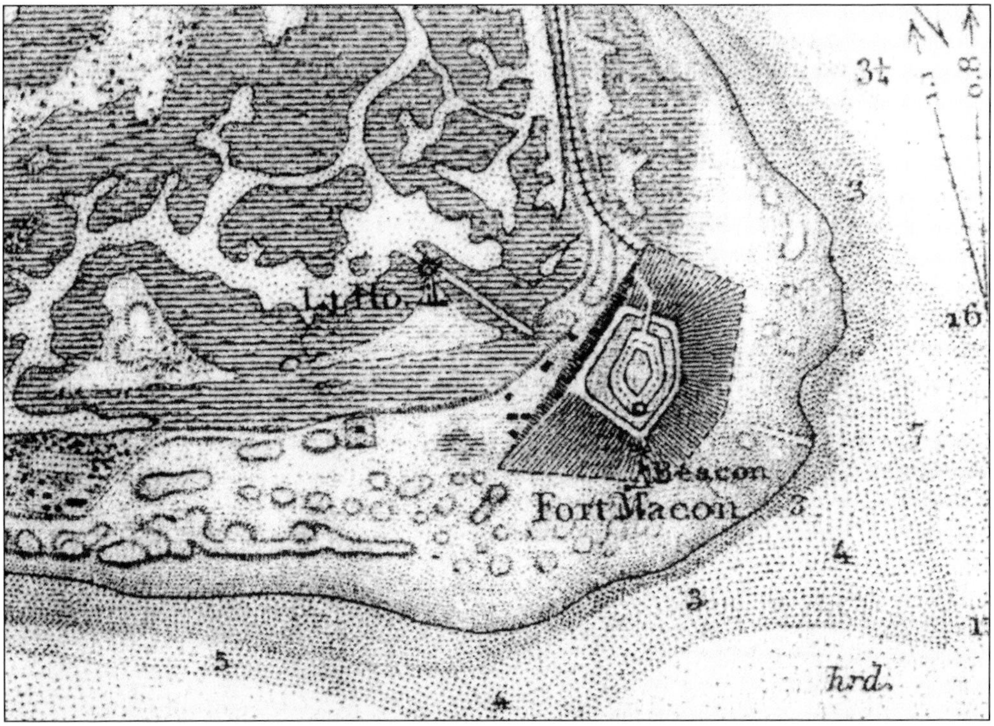

In 1852, Congress appropriated $5,000 to construct a lighthouse near Fort Macon, marking the entrance to Beaufort Inlet. The light, known as the Bogue Banks Lighthouse, went into operation on May 20, 1855. The map above is taken from a nautical chart prepared in 1857. It shows the location of the lighthouse, as well as the accompanying range light. According to this chart, the brick lighthouse stood 50 feet tall and contained a fixed light that was visible 12.5 miles out to sea. According to historian Paul Branch of Fort Macon State Park, Confederate soldiers tore down the Bogue Banks Lighthouse and the Fort Macon Beacon in late March of 1862. They needed to remove the structures, as the towers interfered with the gunners' field of fire. (Courtesy of North Carolina Archives and History.)

Six
LIGHTSHIPS AND LIGHT TOWERS

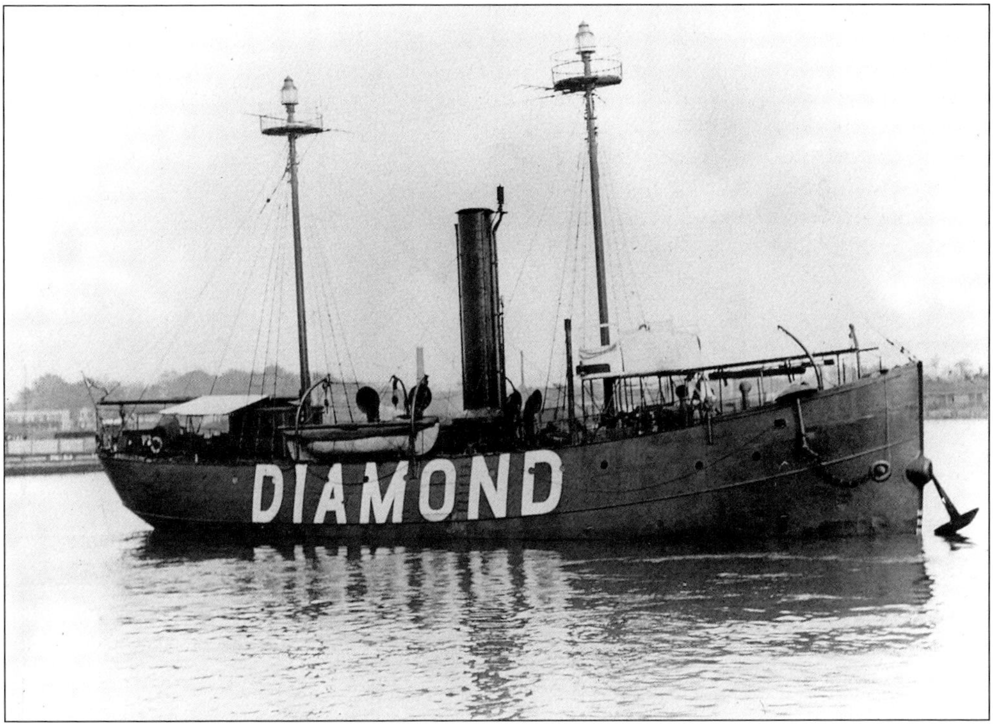

The second *Diamond Shoals* Lightship took up its station in Diamond Shoals in 1897. Another lightship served in these treacherous waters from 1824 through 1827, when she was wrecked in a hurricane. (Courtesy of the United States Coast Guard.)

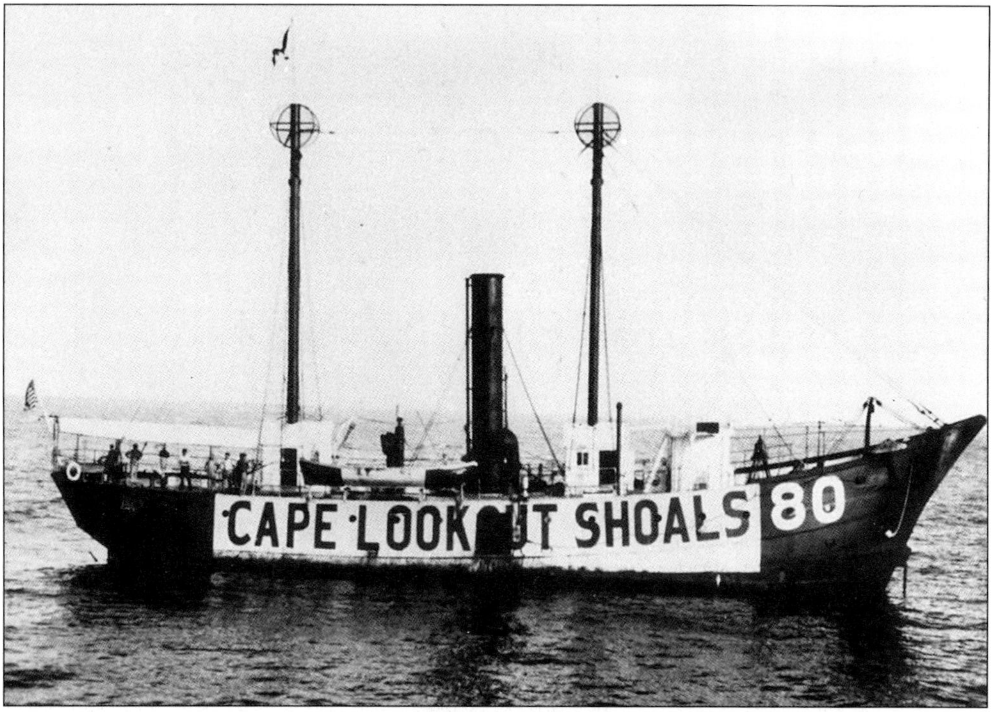

The *Cape Lookout Shoals* Lightship spent nearly 30 eventful years stationed in the turbulent waters of Cape Lookout Shoals. (Courtesy of the National Park Service, Cape Lookout National Seashore.)

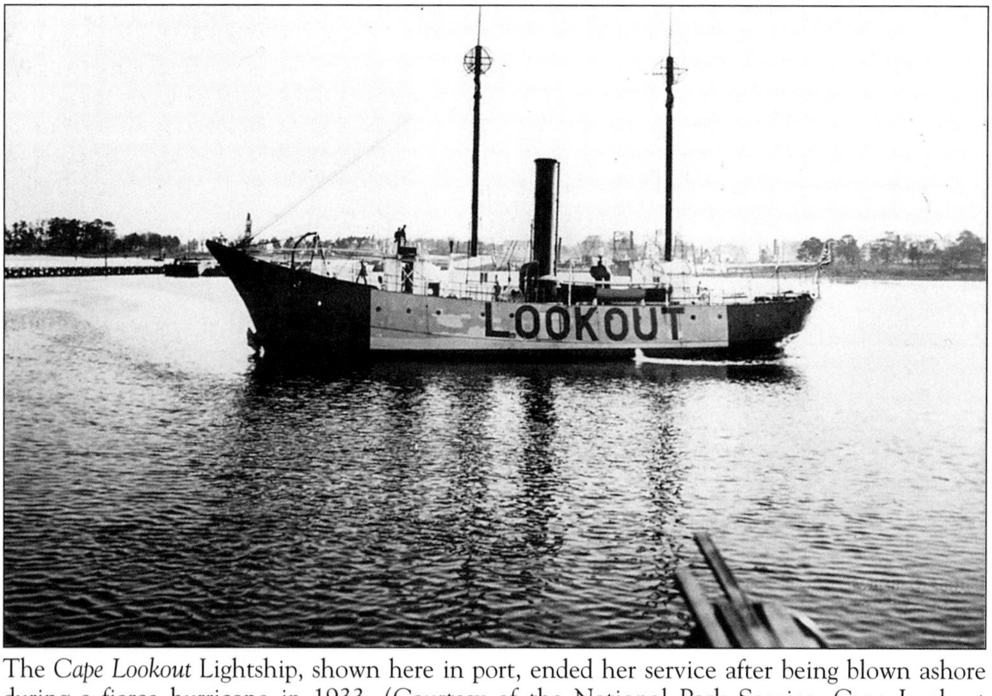

The *Cape Lookout* Lightship, shown here in port, ended her service after being blown ashore during a fierce hurricane in 1933. (Courtesy of the National Park Service, Cape Lookout National Seashore.)

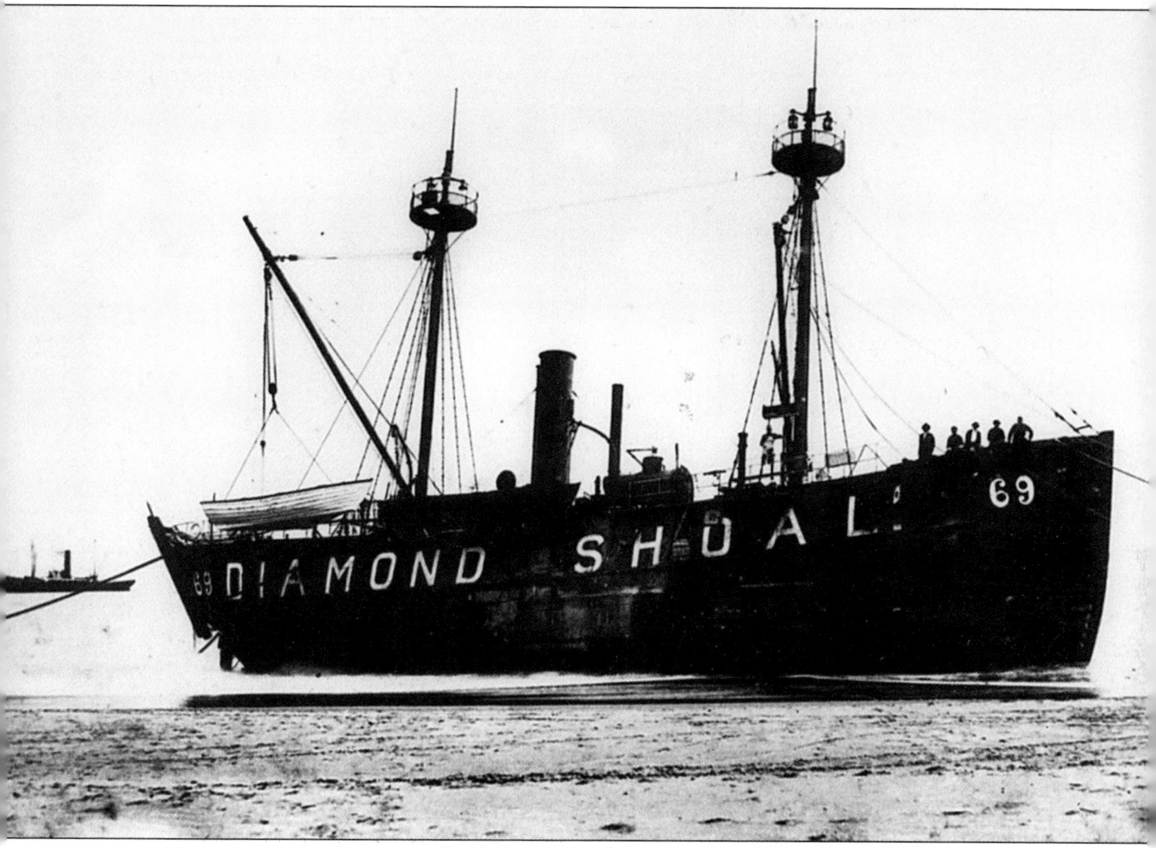

Diamond Shoals Lightship was tossed up onto the shores of the Outer Banks during the San Ciriaco Hurricane in August of 1899. This hurricane was one of the most ferocious hurricanes to ever brush the Outer Banks and was keenly felt by the inhabitants of the sandy barrier islands. In fact, this hurricane cut a swath of destruction from the West Indies to the coast of France. Weather observer S.L. Dosher noted that the winds were howling at nearly 140 miles per hour when the anemometer blew away. This occurred before the storm had reached peak intensity at Hatteras. One can only imagine what wind speed records would have been set had the mechanism held up. (Courtesy of North Carolina Archives and History.)

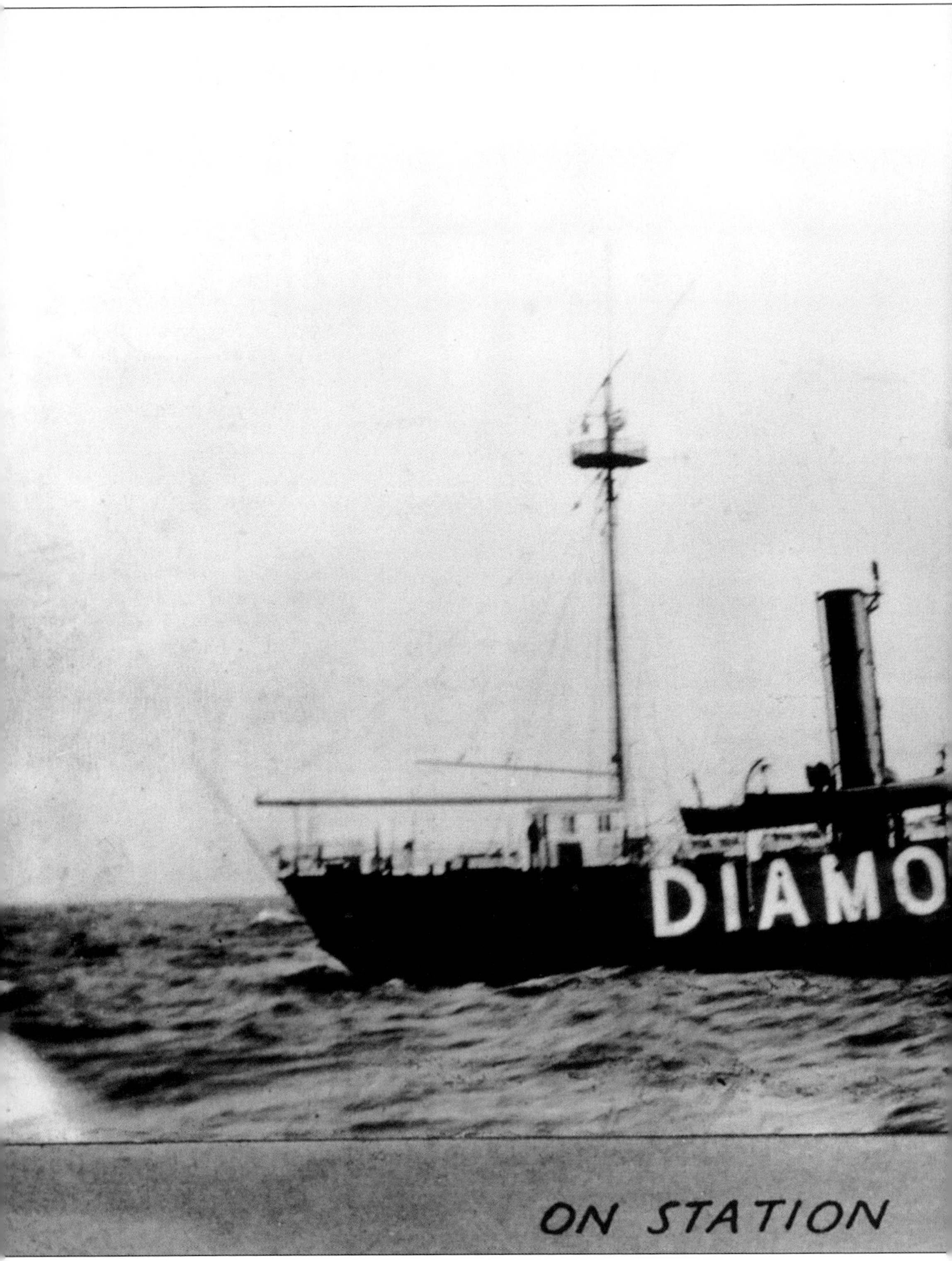

ON STATION

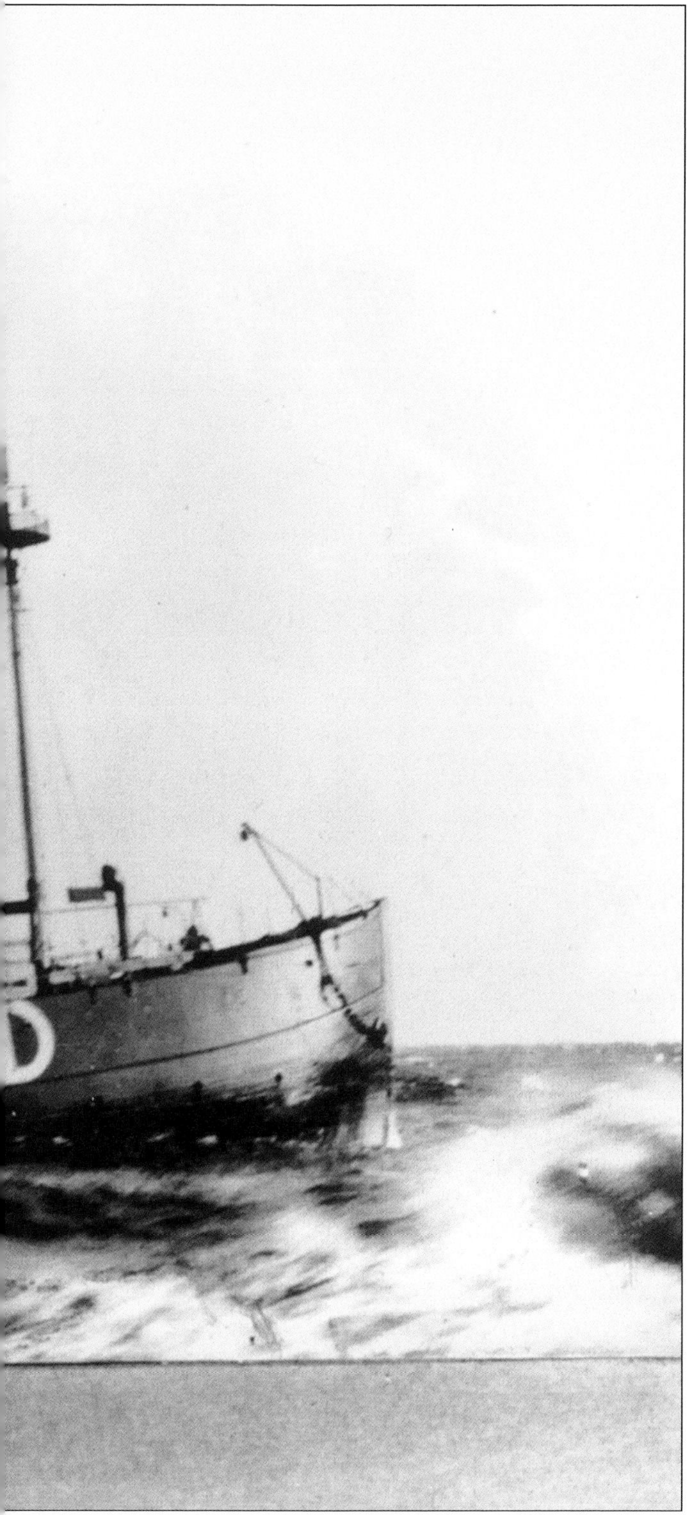

The *Diamond Shoals* Lightship was sunk by the U-140 on August 6, 1918. The lightship drew the fire of Fregattenkapitan Waldemar Kophamel, a German commander, by wiring the news of an attack the U-boat had made upon a nearby freighter. The U-140 fired six shots at the lightship at approximately 3:25 p.m., from a distance of nearly two miles. Two of the shots passed between the mainmast and the smokestack, two passed near the antenna, and two landed on the port side of the boat. Within five minutes, the crewmen of the stricken craft were rowing for safety in their lifeboat. Figuring that he had silenced the problem vessel, Fregattenkapitan Kophamel went off in pursuit of other game. Once their work was completed, the Germans returned to Diamond Shoals to finish off the lightship. It took seven more shots to sink the stubborn craft. A Coast Guard report later noted, "At the time the last shots were fired, the lightship's men included the mate (in charge), engineer, cook, three firemen, four seamen and two radio operators, the latter Navy personnel. All escaped without injury. While the lightship was sunk, reports indicated that the wireless message she had sent out resulted in about 25 other vessels taking refuge in Lookout Bight and escaping possible attack. (Courtesy of the United States Coast Guard.)

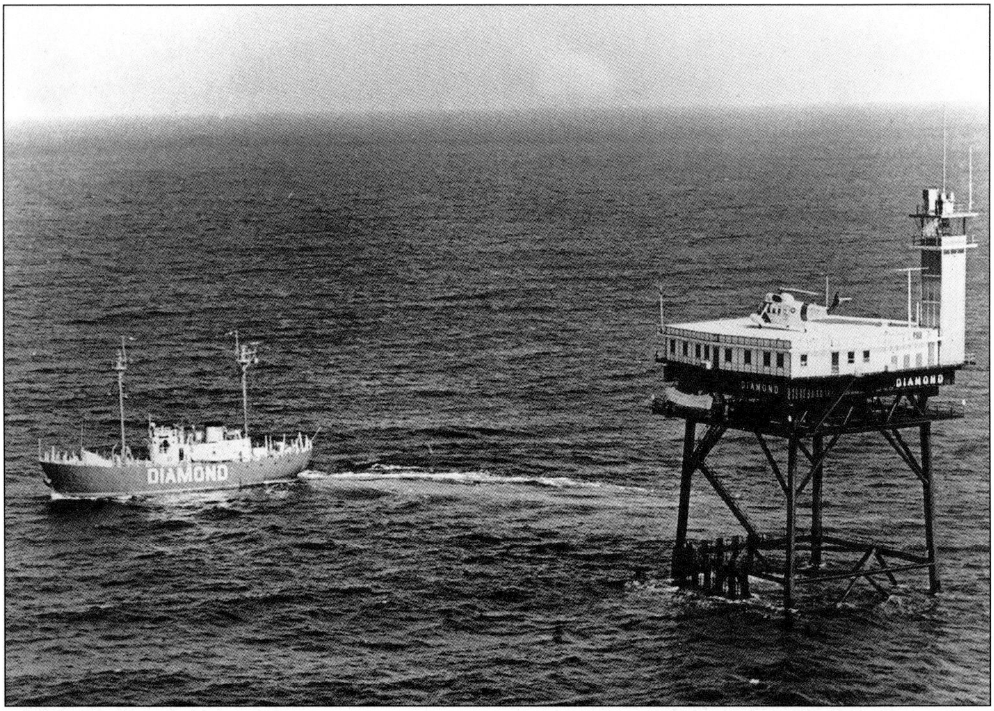

The *Diamond Shoals* Light Tower replaced the *Diamond Shoals* Lightship in 1967. The tower, which was operational until the early part of the 21st century, stood 54 feet above the level of the sea, and was visible 17 miles away. (Courtesy of the United States Coast Guard.)

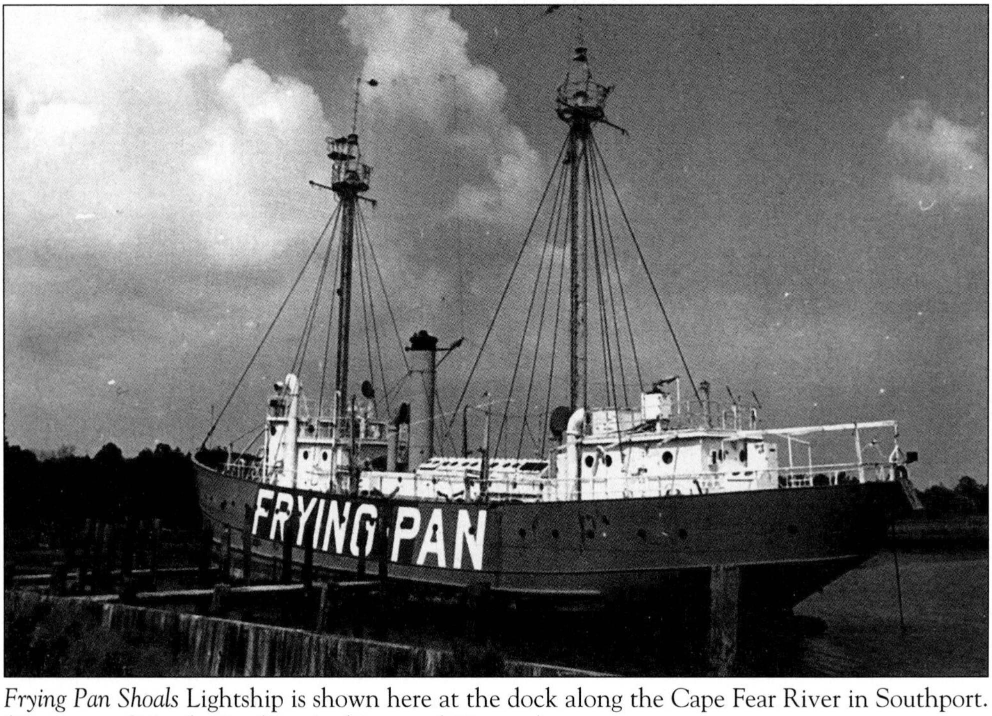

Frying Pan Shoals Lightship is shown here at the dock along the Cape Fear River in Southport. (Courtesy of North Carolina Archives and History.)

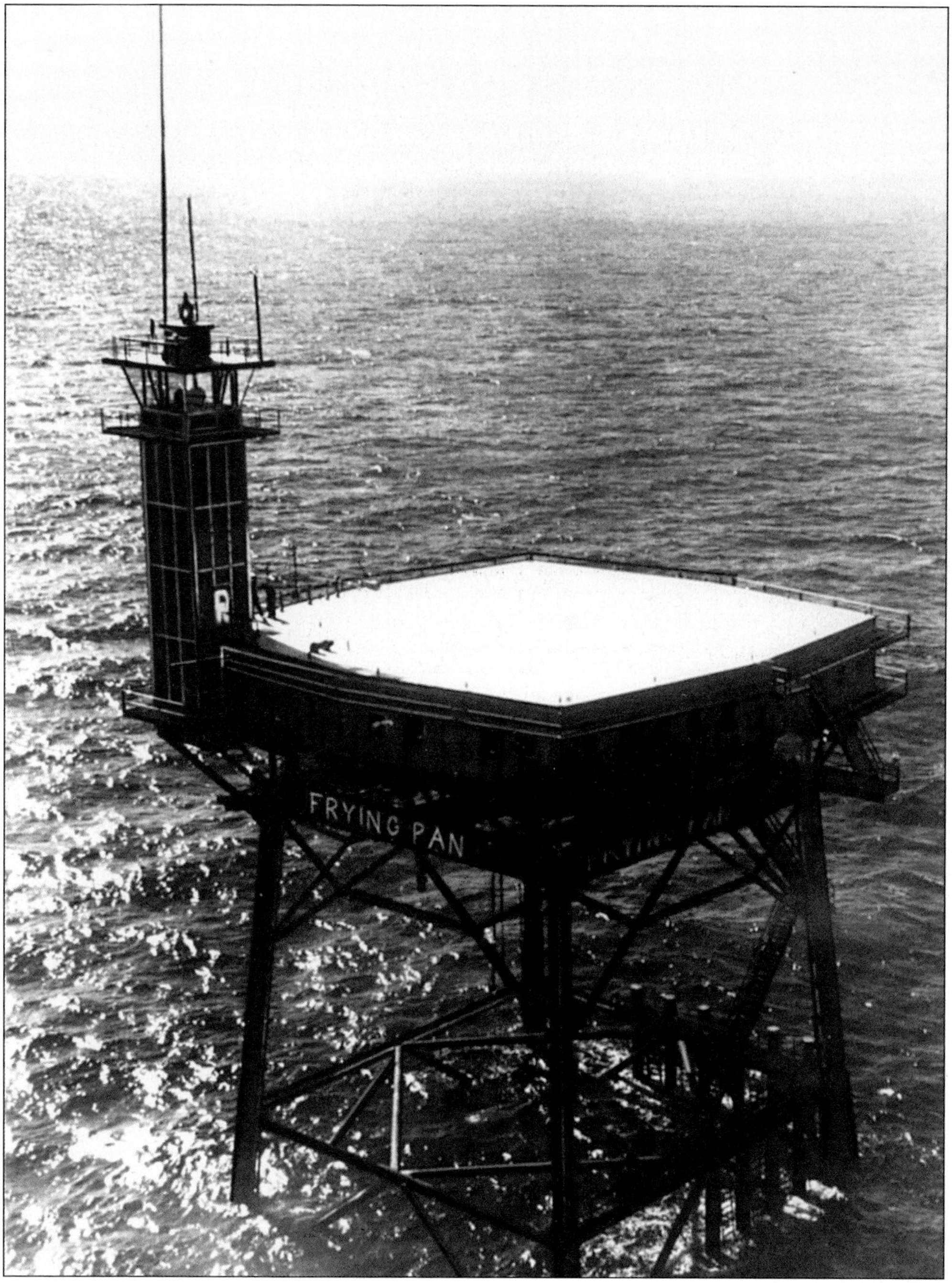

Frying Pan Shoals Light Tower was placed in the Frying Pan Shoals in 1964. A structure known as a Texas tower, this modified oil drilling platform was prefabricated in Louisiana and towed into position. The legs of the tower were driven nearly 300 feet into the seafloor to help the building hold its position, even during the worst of weather. The station was originally manned by a crew of six Coast Guardsmen, but has been automated since 1977. The Coast Guard plans to discontinue this navigational aid. (Courtesy of North Carolina Archives and History.)

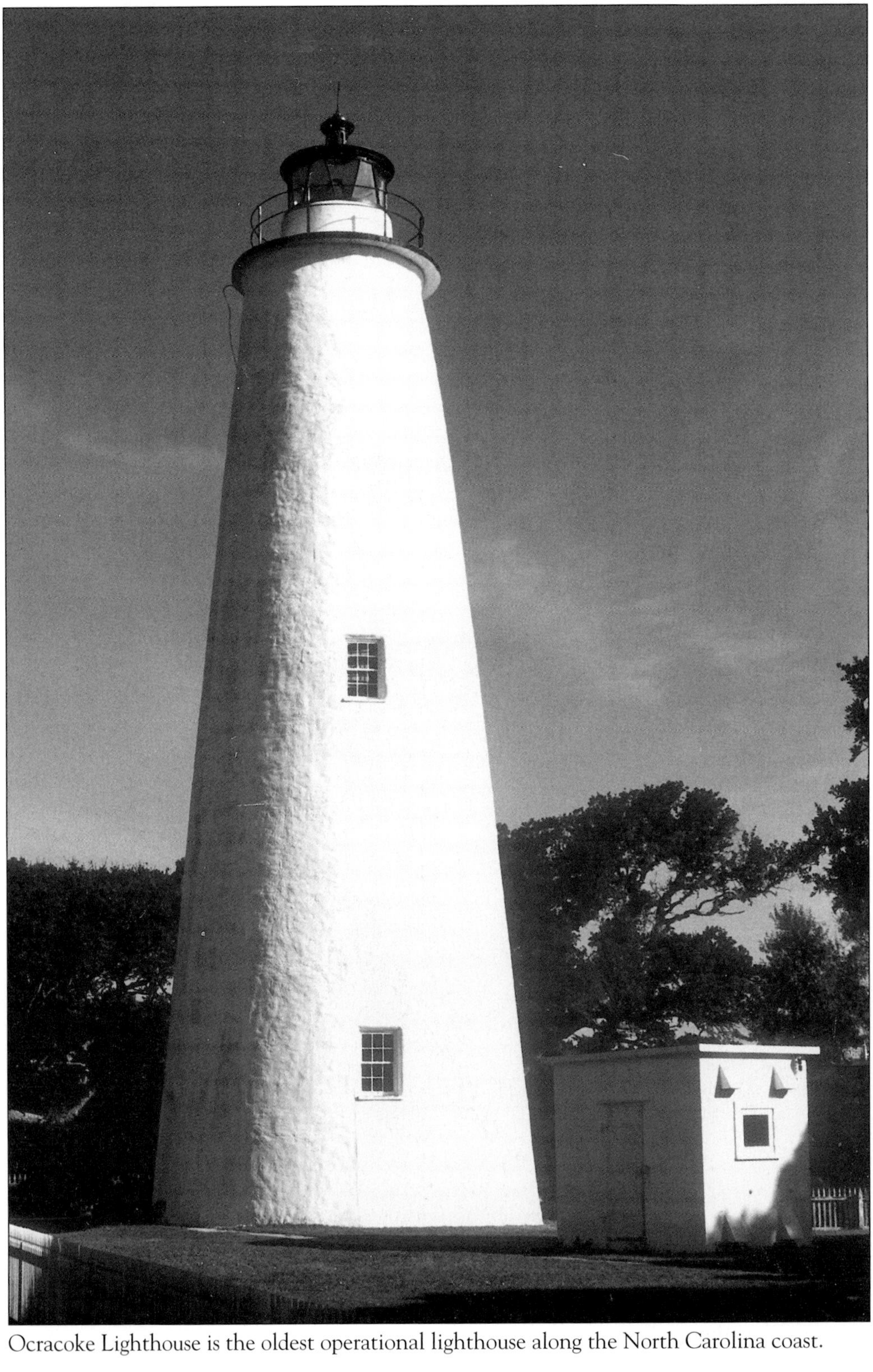

Ocracoke Lighthouse is the oldest operational lighthouse along the North Carolina coast.

Seven
OCRACOKE LIGHTHOUSE

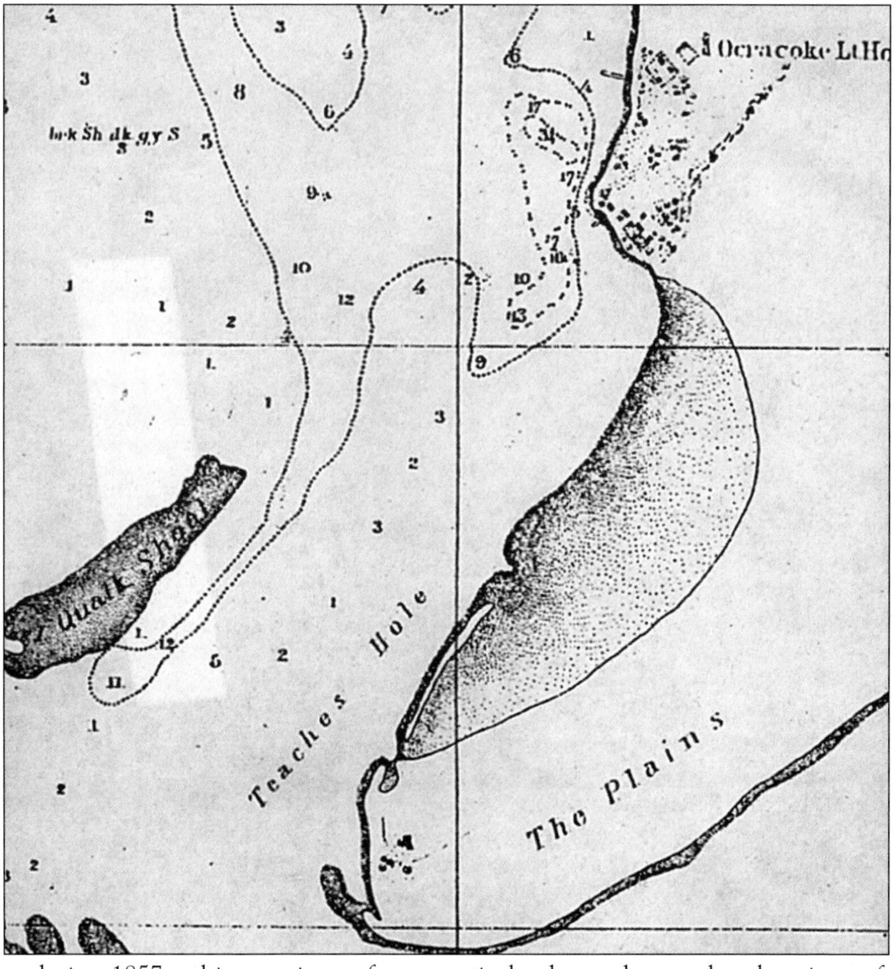

Released in 1857, this portion of a nautical chart shows the location of the Ocracoke Lighthouse.

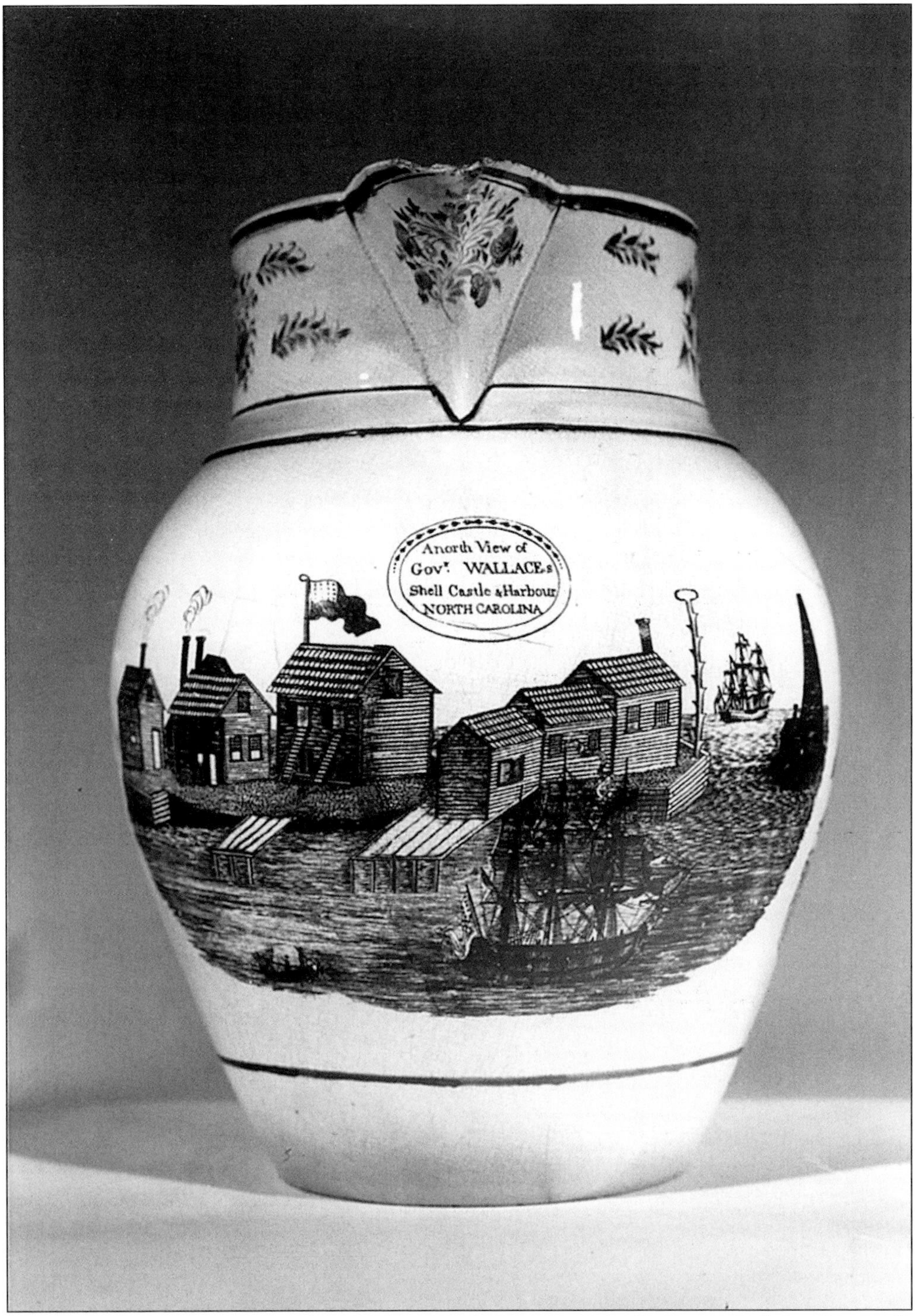

The painting on this pitcher shows the once thriving port facilities at Shell Castle, inside Ocracoke Inlet. The lighthouse, shown on the far right, was erected by the federal government here *c.* 1800 and served as a prominent landmark until it was destroyed by lightning in 1818. (Courtesy of North Carolina Archives and History.)

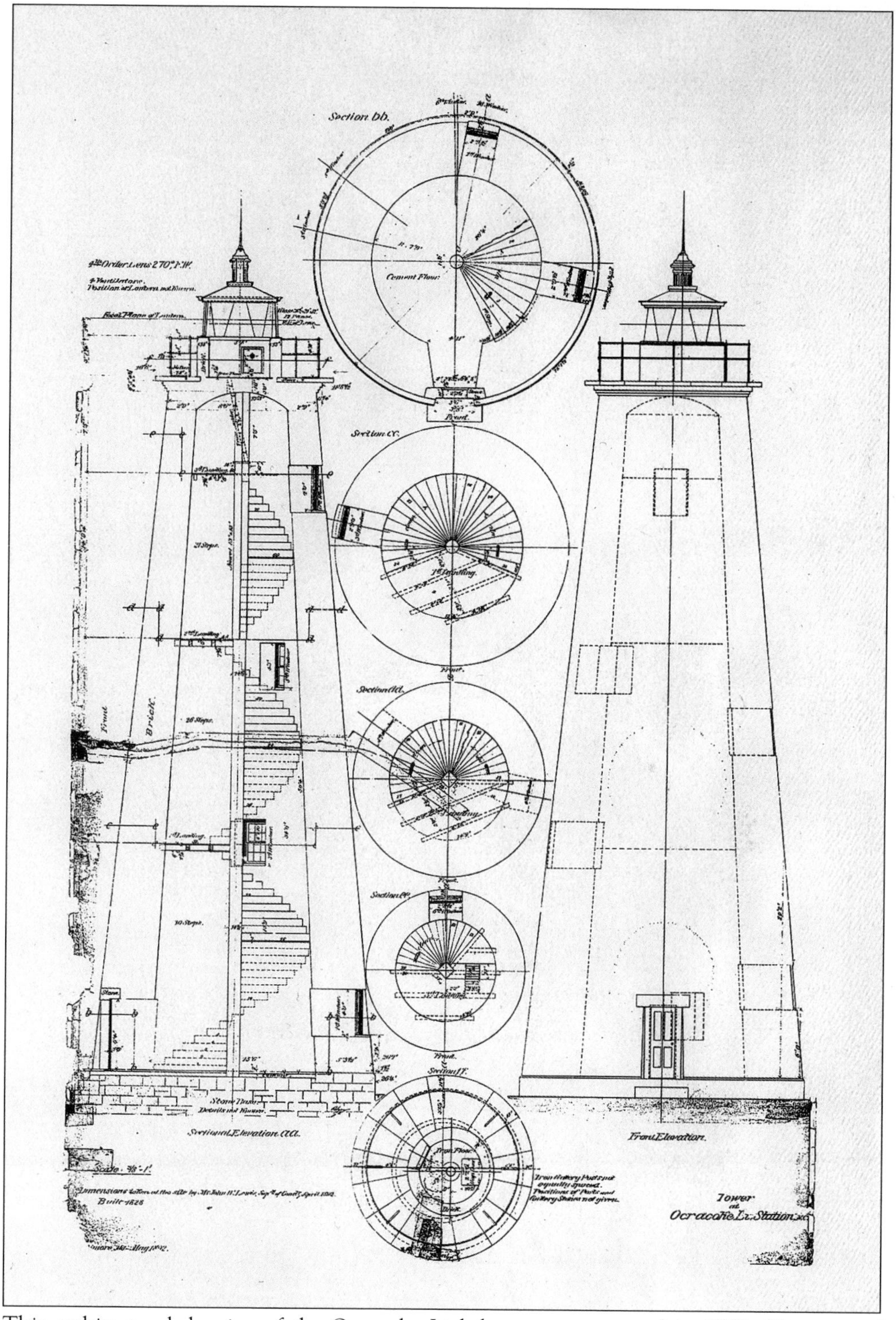

This architectural drawing of the Ocracoke Lighthouse was prepared in 1892. (Courtesy of National Archives.)

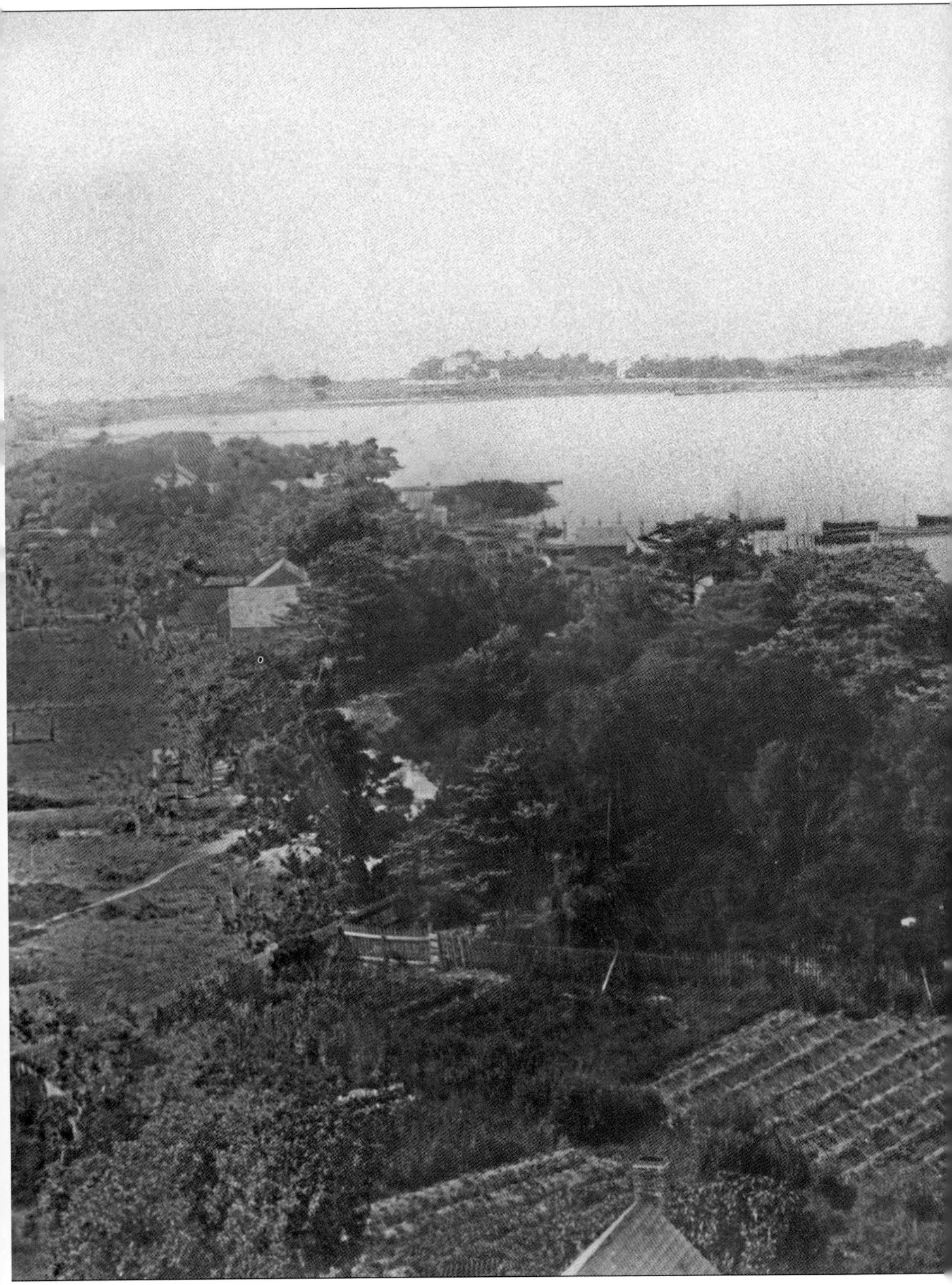

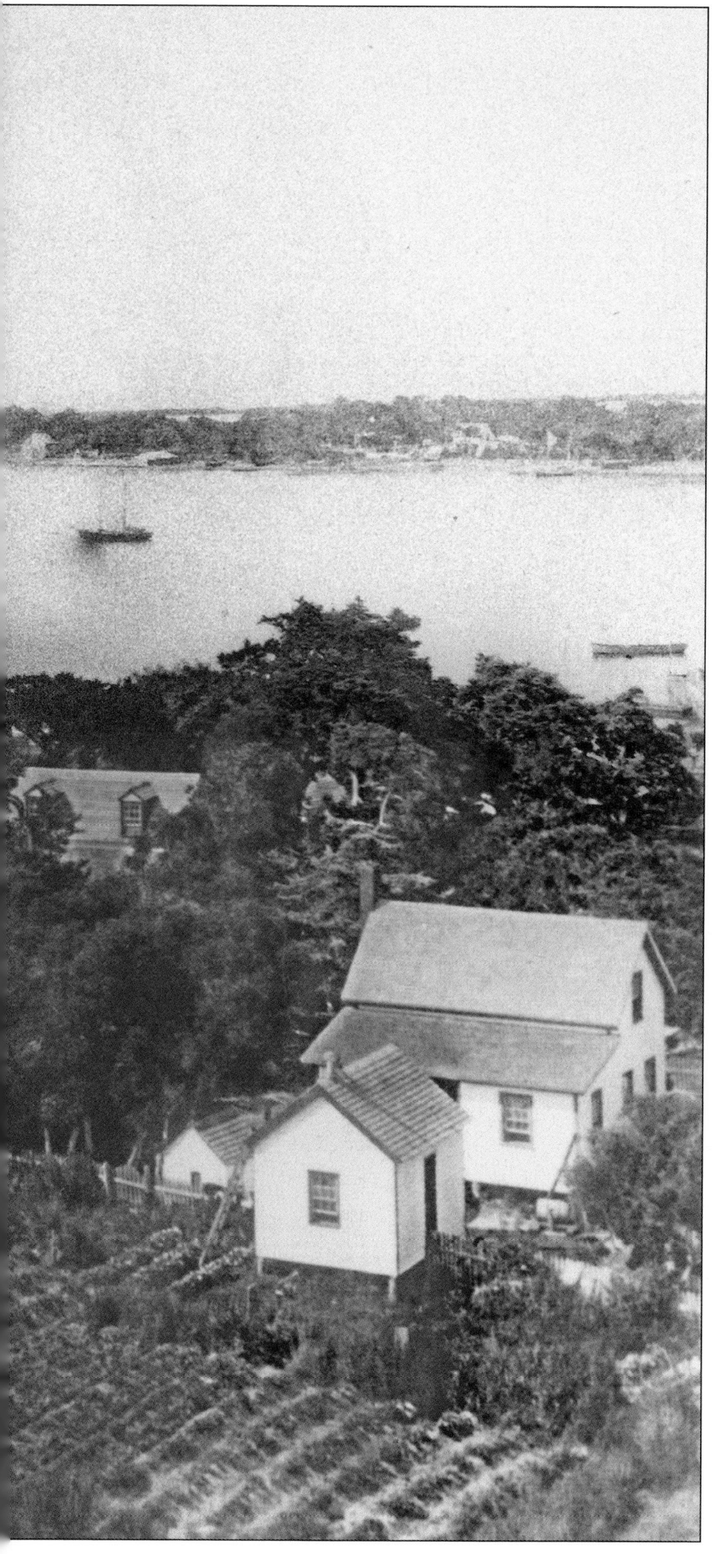

This panoramic view of Silver Lake and Ocracoke was taken from the top of the lighthouse in1890. (Courtesy of North Carolina Archives and History.)

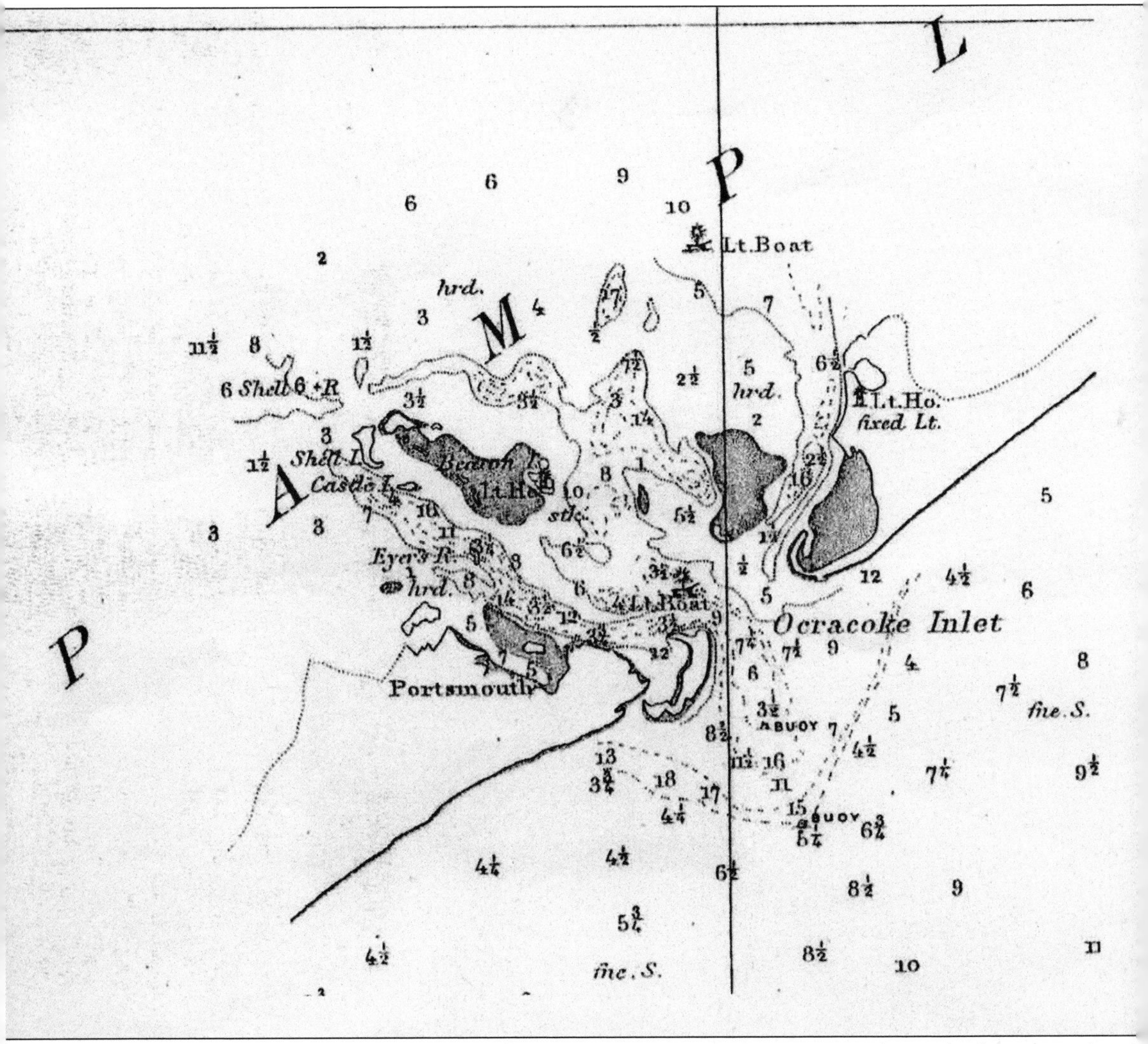

This nautical chart, prepared by the United States Coast Survey in 1856, shows the location of the Ocracoke Lighthouse, as well as several other lights that helped guide mariners through Ocracoke Inlet. (Courtesy of North Carolina Archives and History.)

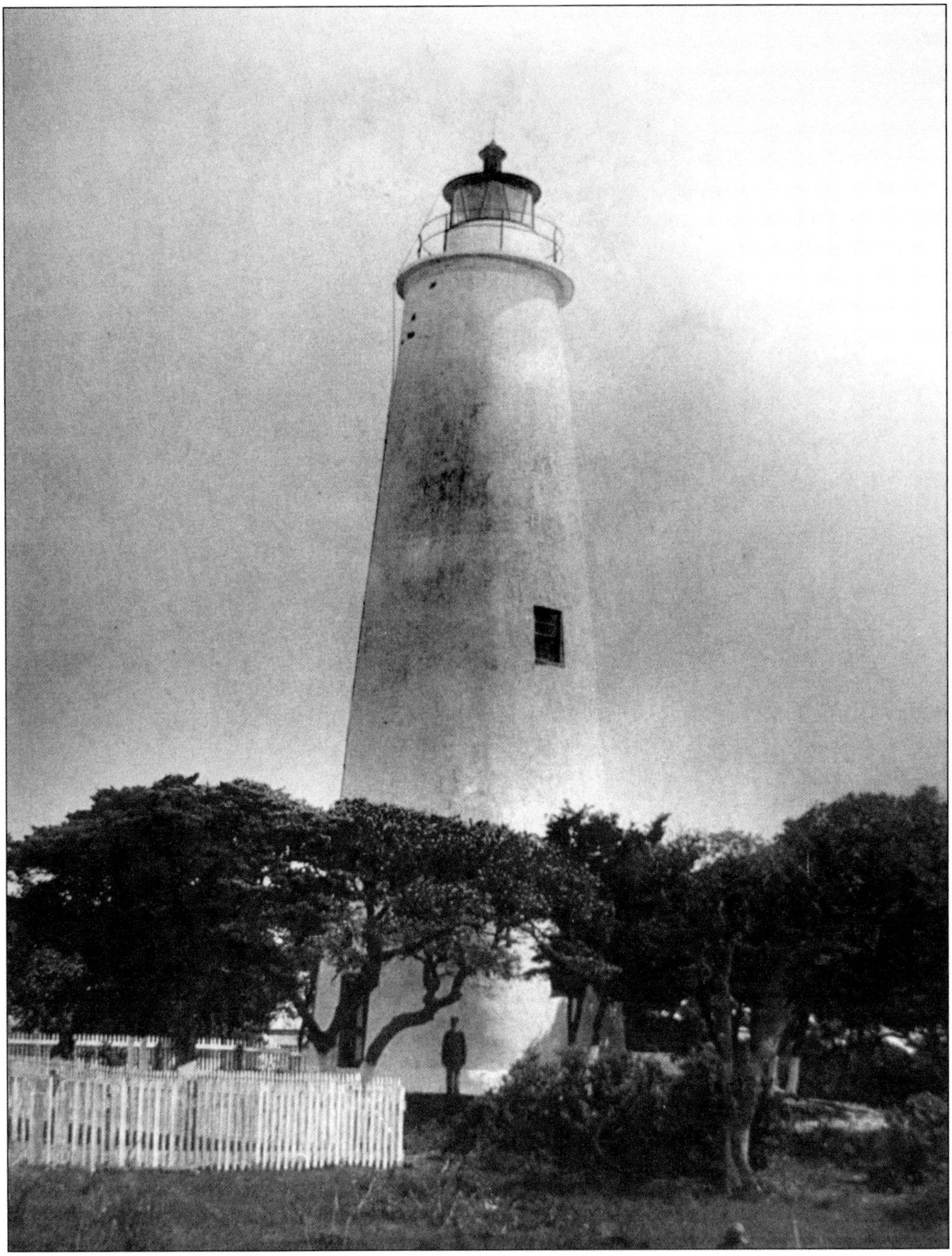

This is the Ocracoke Lighthouse as it appeared on May 24, 1893. (Courtesy of the United States Coast Guard.)

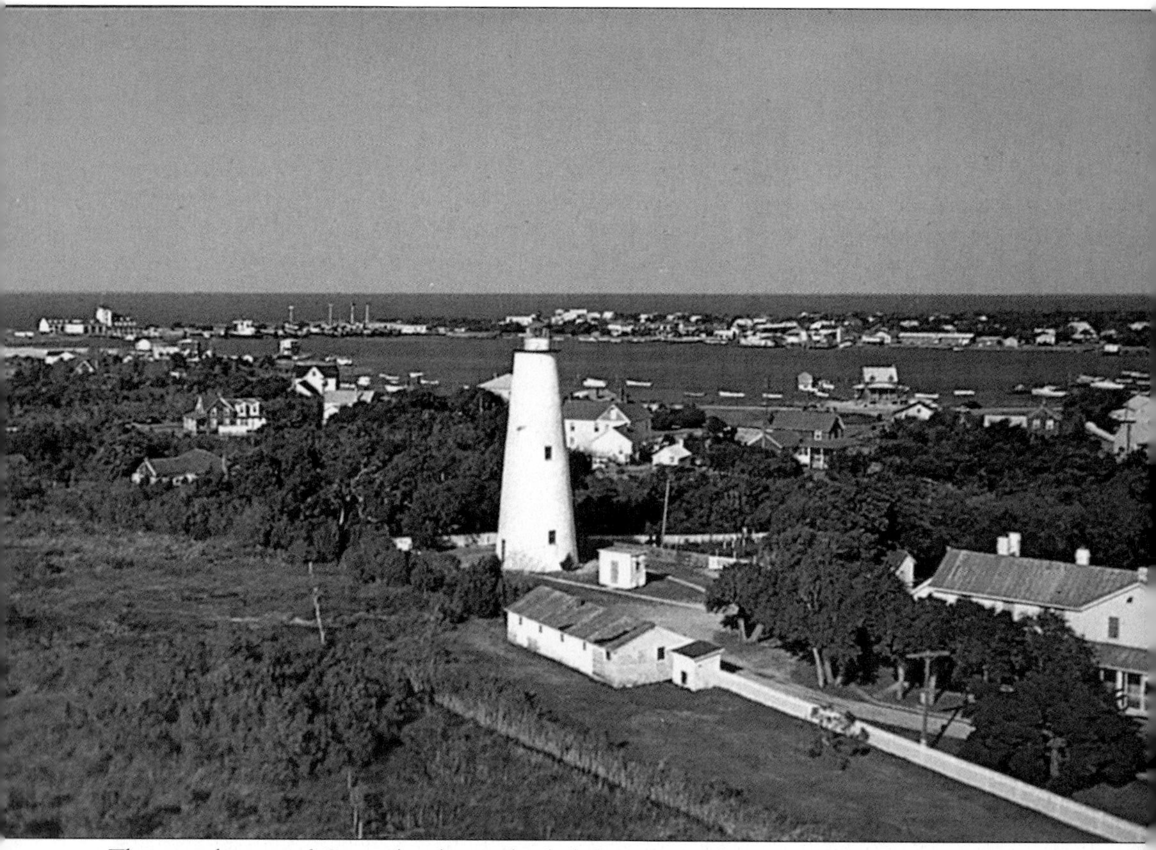

This aerial view of Ocracoke shows the lighthouse in relation to Silver Lake. (Courtesy of North Carolina Archives and History.)

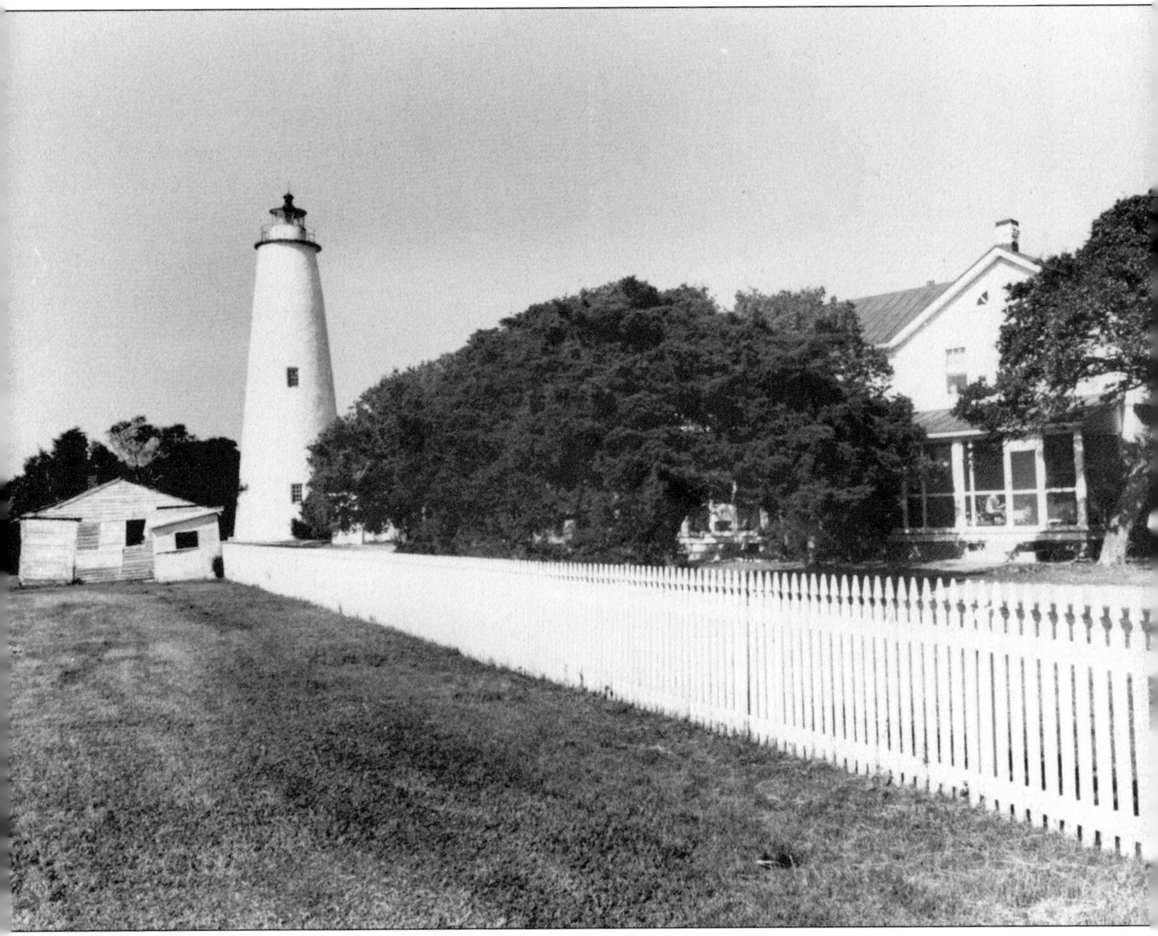

Ocracoke Lighthouse is now owned by the National Park Service and jointly managed by the United States Coast Guard. The grounds to the lighthouse are open to the public, though the inside of the structure and the keeper's quarters are off limits. (Courtesy of Outer Banks History Center.)

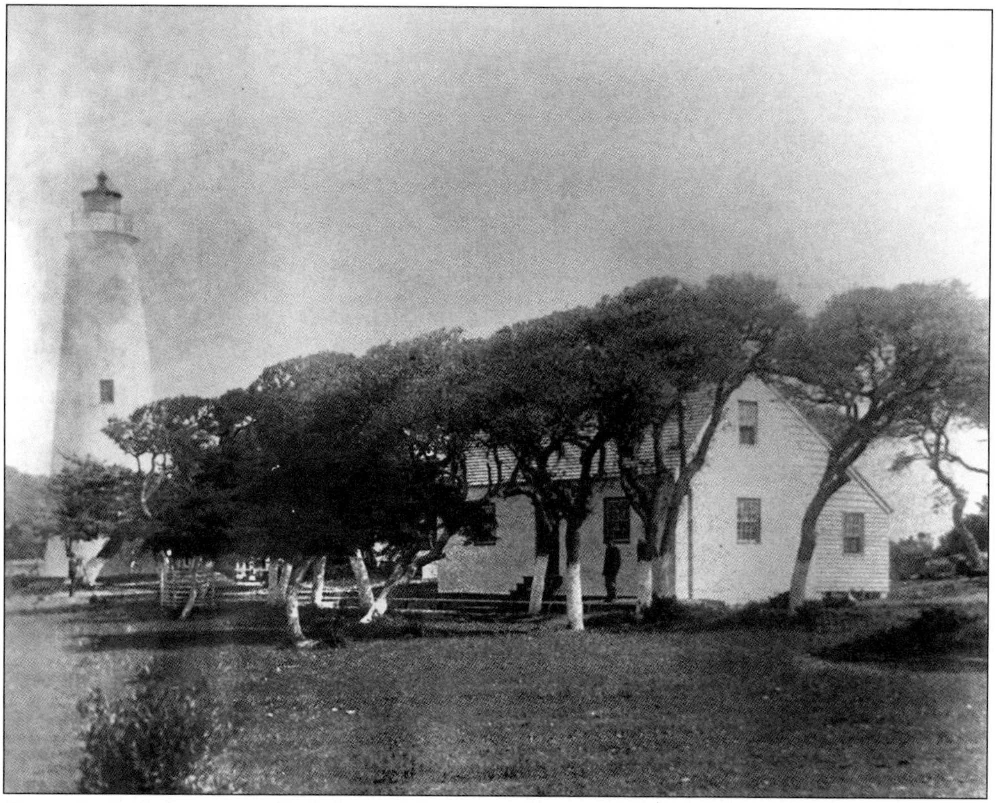

Ocracoke Lighthouse was built by Noah Porter of Massachusetts, who also built the keeper's quarters. Although Congress had appropriated $20,000 to build the structure, Porter did the job for well under budget, completing it for $11,359.35. (Courtesy of Outer Banks History Center.)

Eight

Lighthouses of Cape Hatteras

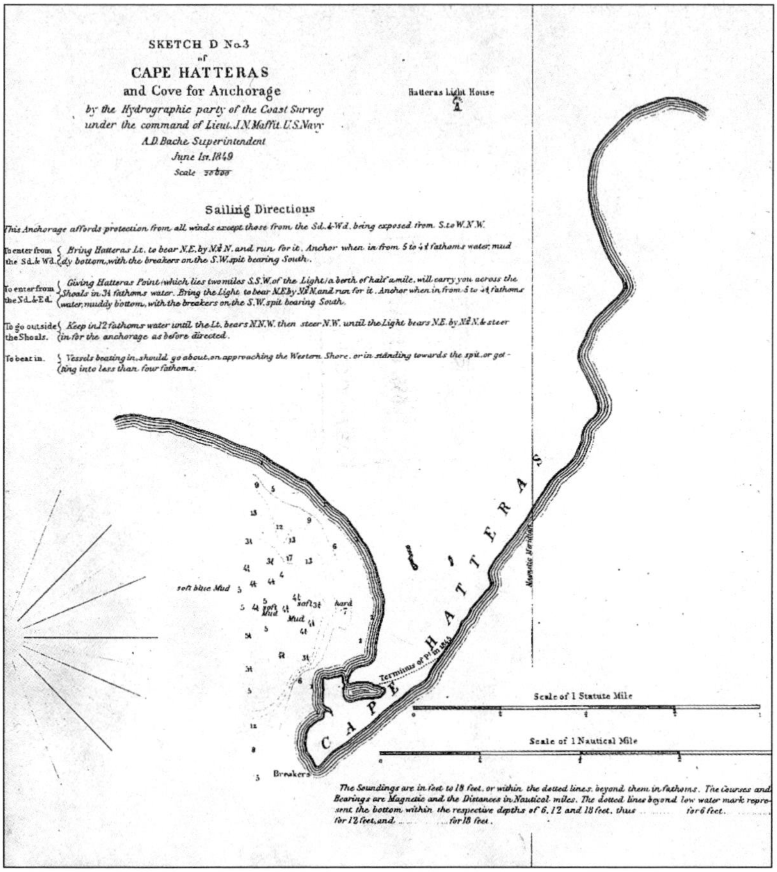

Prepared in 1849, this nautical chart shows the location of the first Cape Hatteras Lighthouse. (Courtesy of North Carolina Archives and History.)

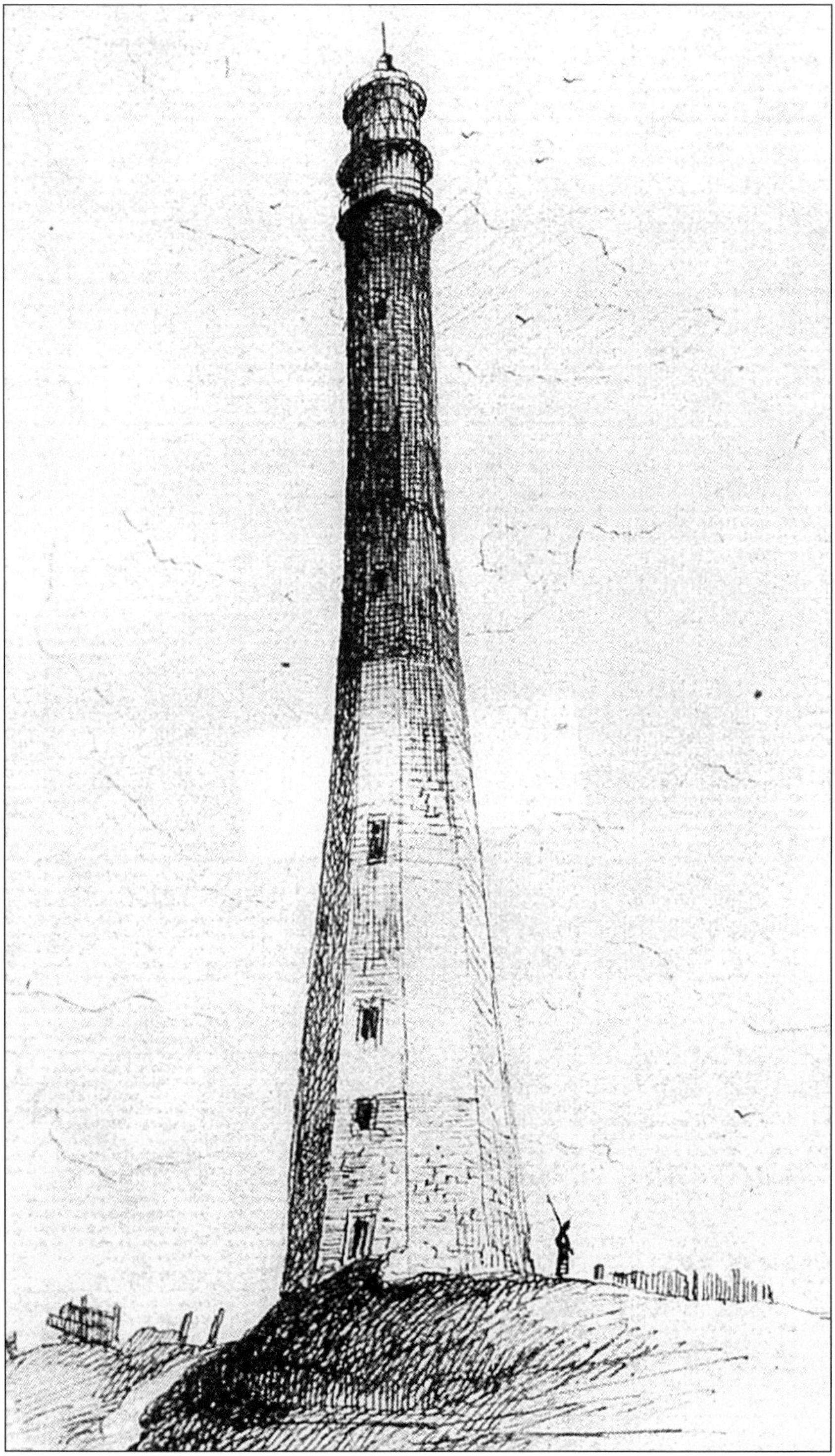

This sketch of the Cape Hatteras Lighthouse was made by a Union soldier in 1863. (Courtesy of North Carolina Archives and History.)

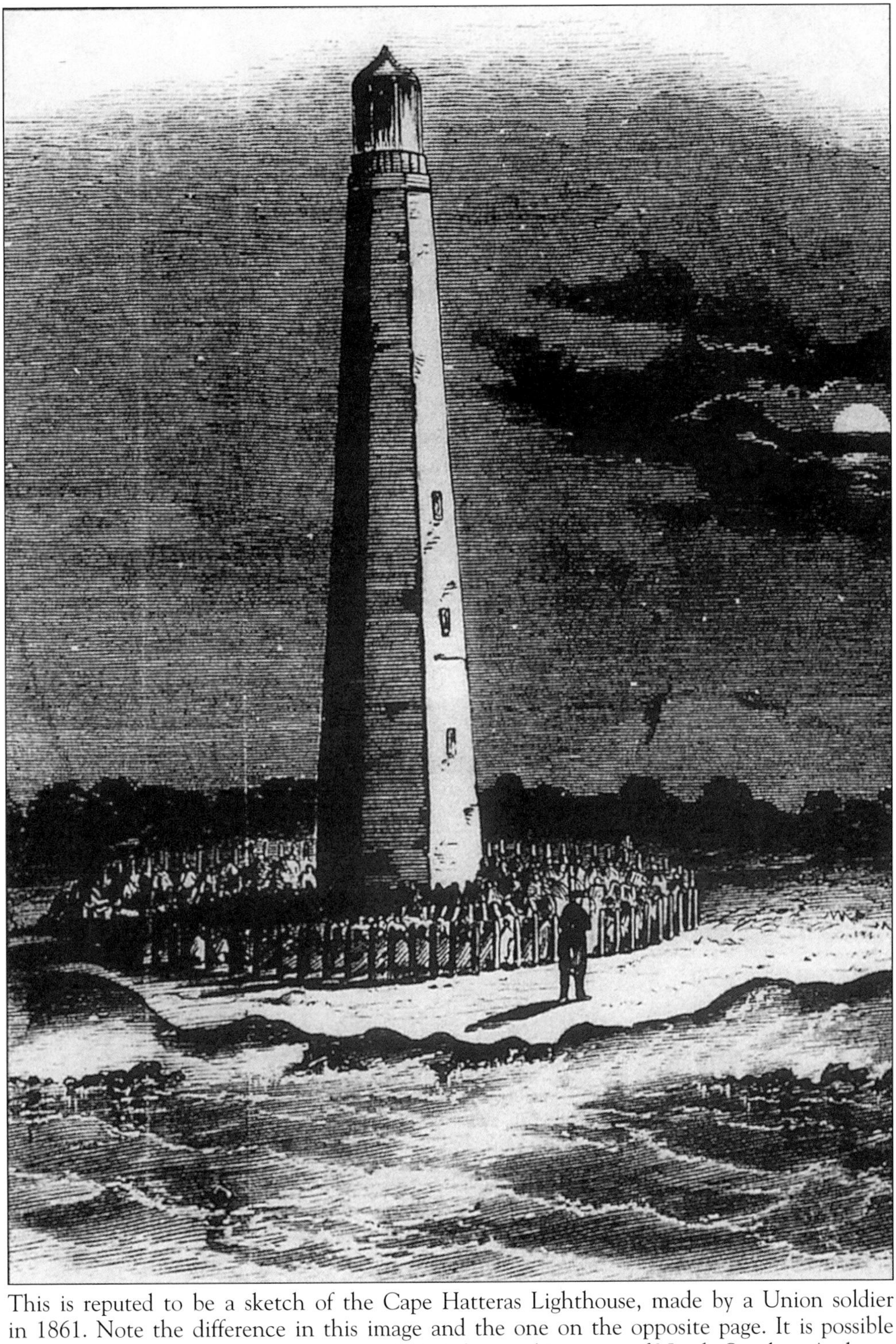

This is reputed to be a sketch of the Cape Hatteras Lighthouse, made by a Union soldier in 1861. Note the difference in this image and the one on the opposite page. It is possible that this is a view of another Outer Banks lighthouse. (Courtesy of North Carolina Archives and History.)

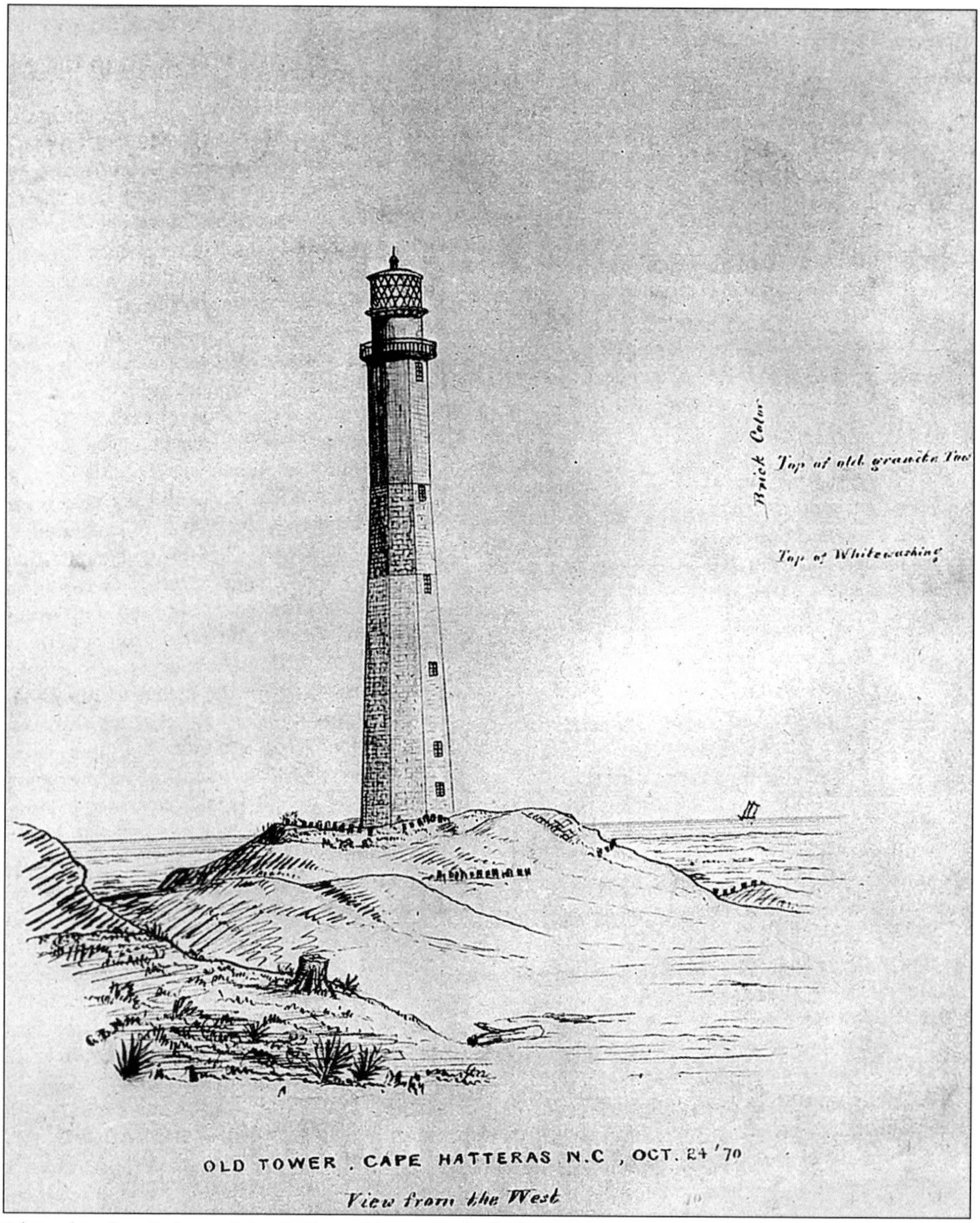

This sketch of the original Cape Hatteras Lighthouse was made on October 24, 1870, by George B. Nicholson, assistant engineer of the Fifth Lighthouse District. Completed in 1802, this lighthouse stood 100 feet above the ground and was constructed with white stone on the bottom and red stone on top. In 1806, William Tatham described it as an "architectural eyesore" and suggested painting it red. Note similarities between this sketch and the sketch made in 1863 (page 70). Now note the total lack of similarity with the lighthouse shown in the image sketched in 1861. Are these the same structures? In 1854, an addition was made to the tower, raising its height to 150 feet. (Courtesy of National Archives.)

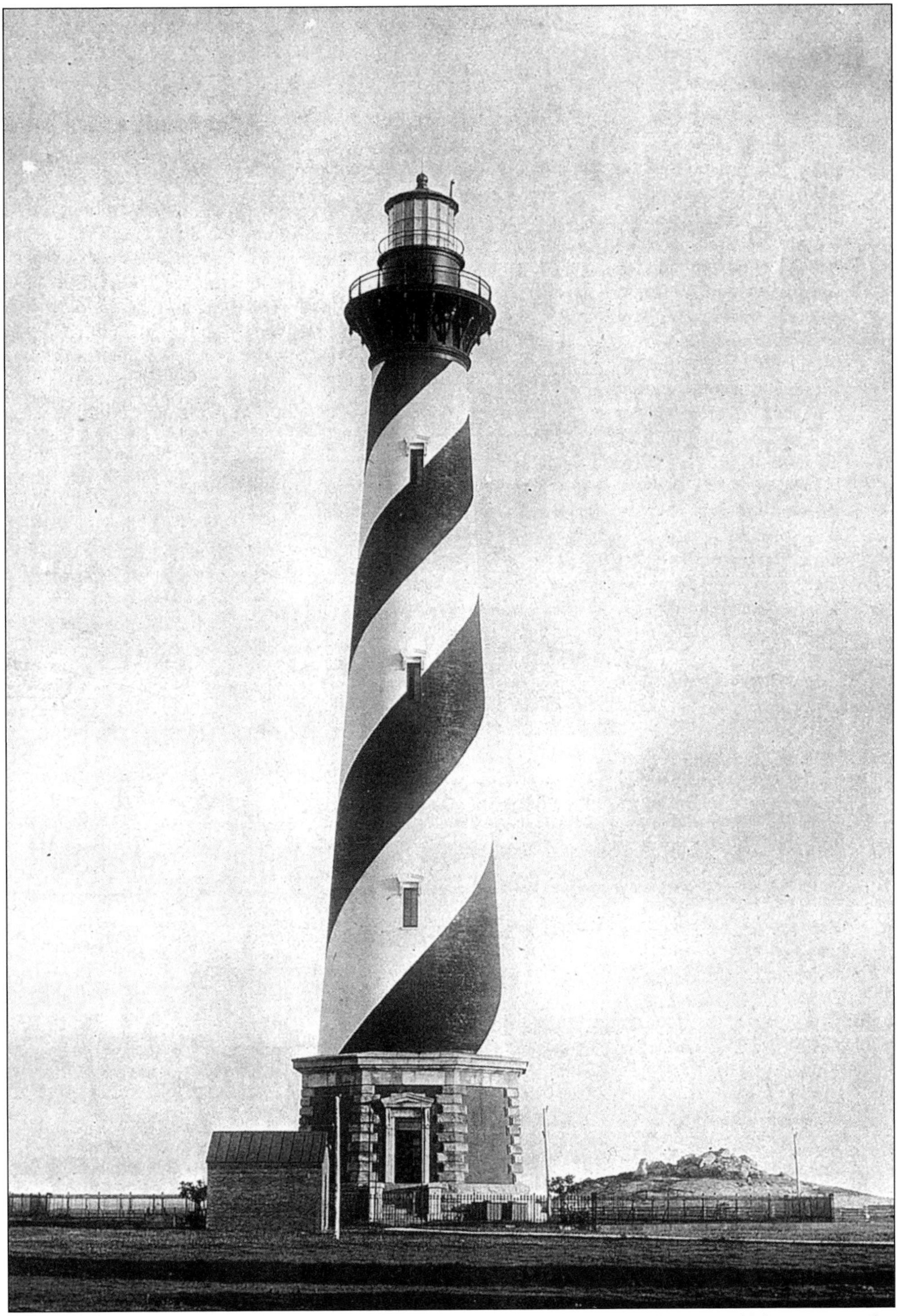

The first Cape Hatteras Lighthouse was destroyed in 1871. The piles of rubble seen in the background of this photo are the remains of the first tower. (Courtesy of North Carolina Archives and History.)

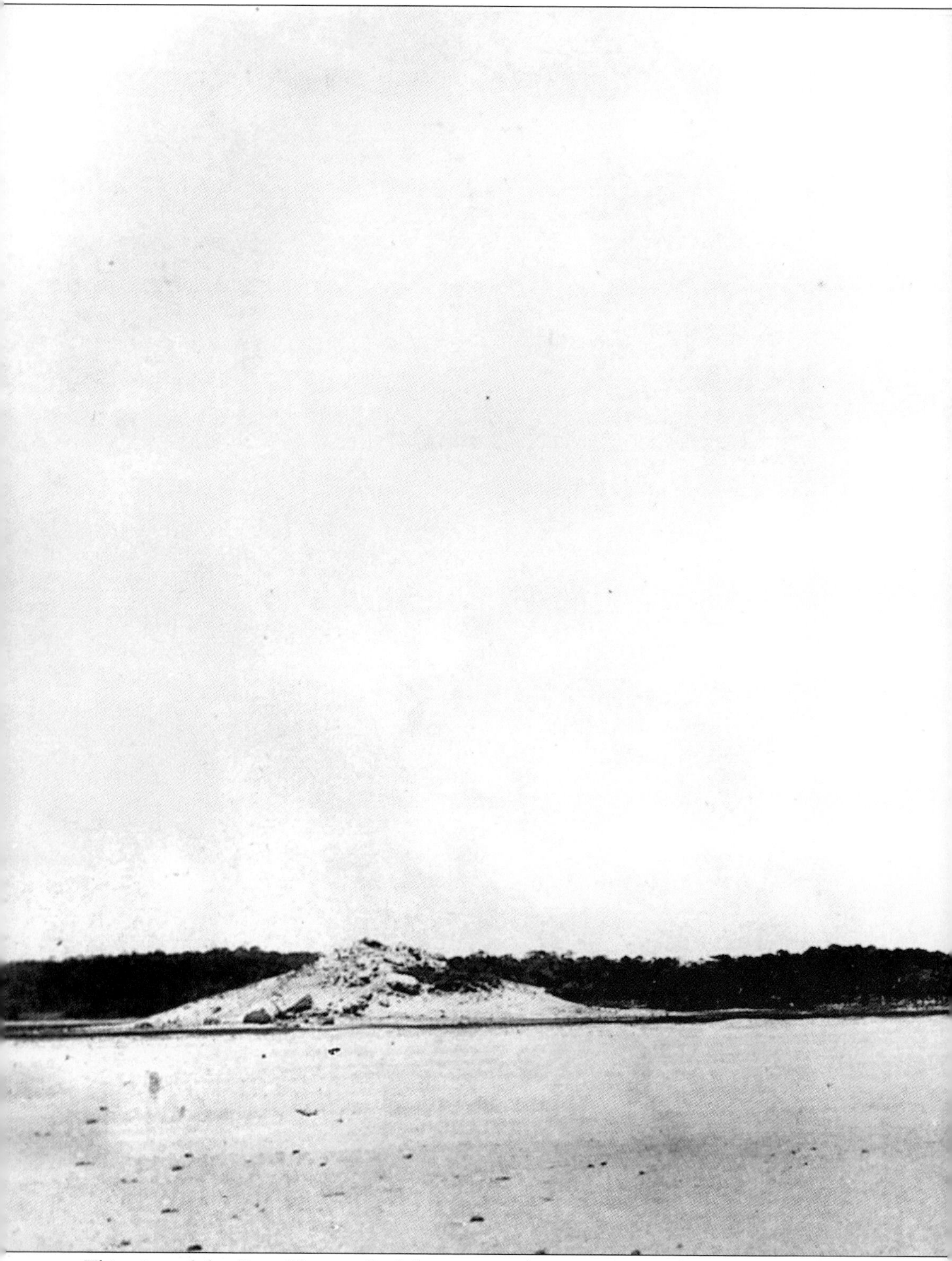

This view of the Cape Hatteras Lighthouse was taken May 30, 1893. Note the width of the

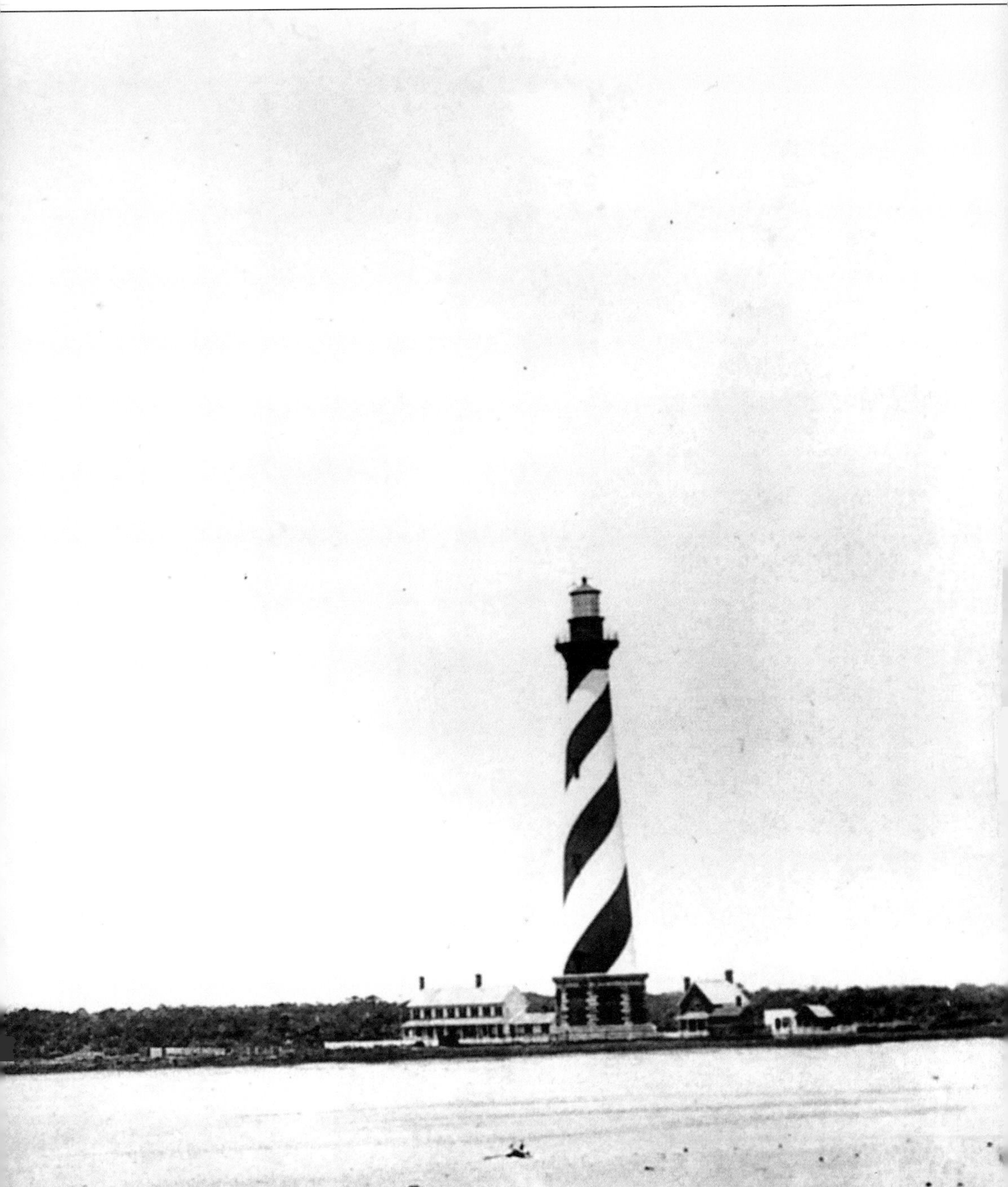

beach in front of the lighthouse. (Courtesy of the United States Coast Guard.)

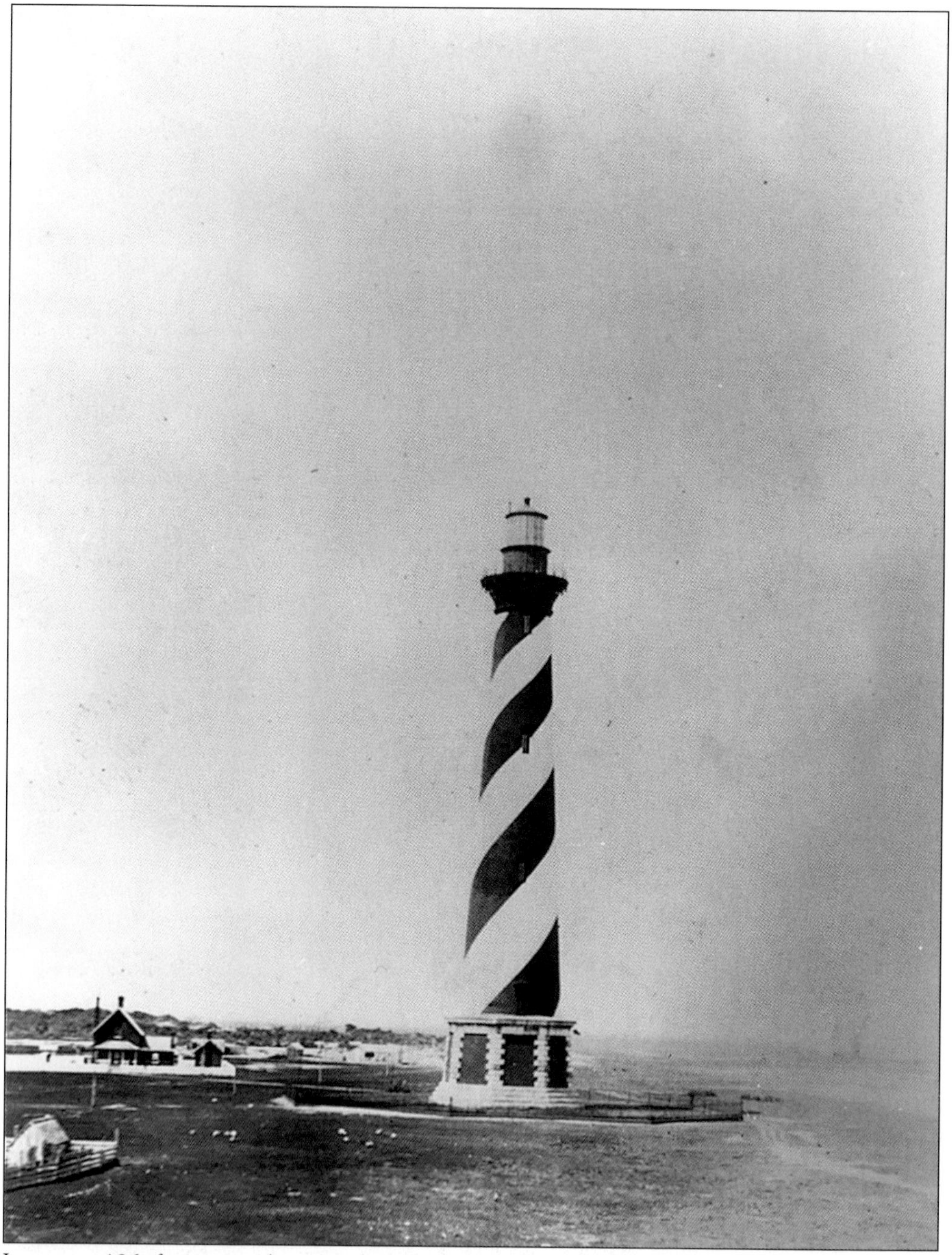

Looming 196 feet into the air, the Cape Hatteras Lighthouse, shown here in a 1900 photograph, is the tallest lighthouse in the United States. The tower was built in 1870. Because of the persistent threat of erosion of the beach, the Cape Hatteras Lighthouse was moved to a new location in 1999. The move took 23 days, and placed the lighthouse 2,900 feet to the southwest of its previous location. (Courtesy of the United States Coast Guard.)

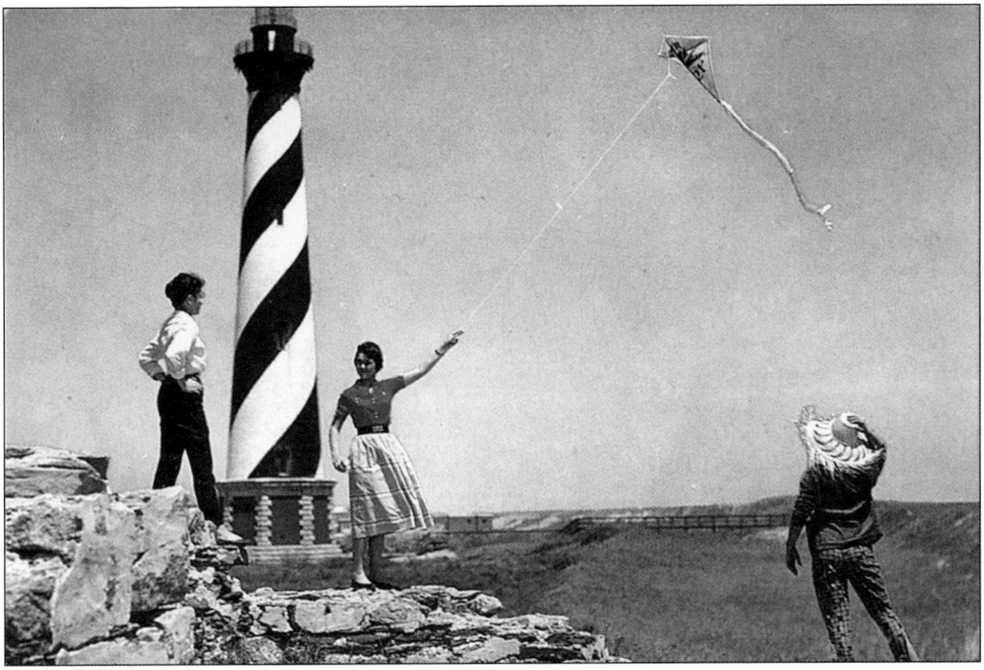

This old postcard shows three ladies flying a kite near the Cape Lookout Lighthouse.

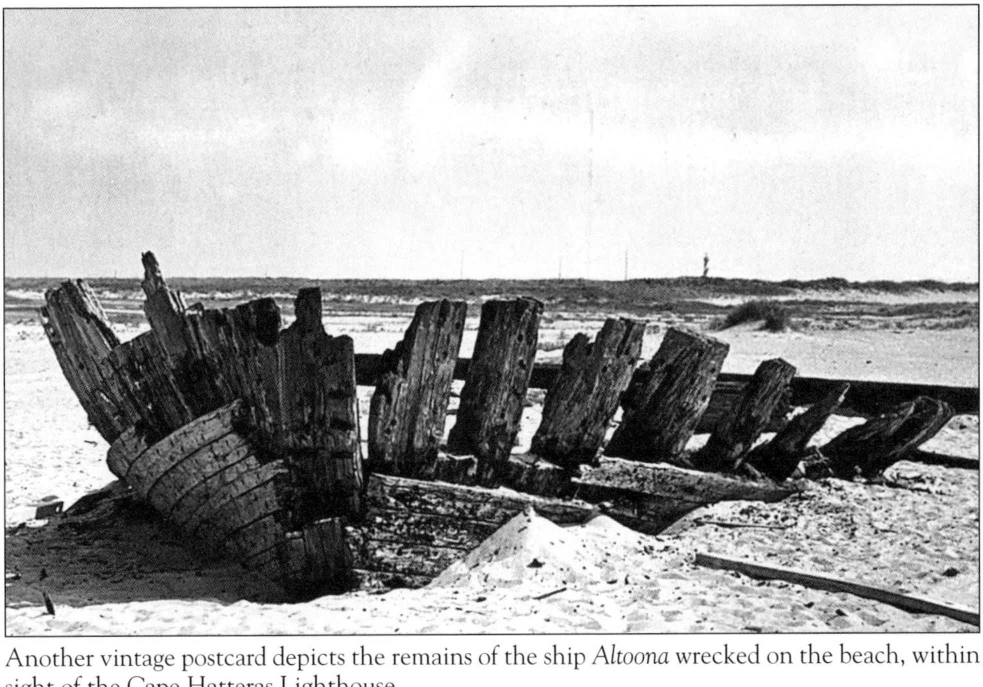

Another vintage postcard depicts the remains of the ship *Altoona* wrecked on the beach, within sight of the Cape Hatteras Lighthouse.

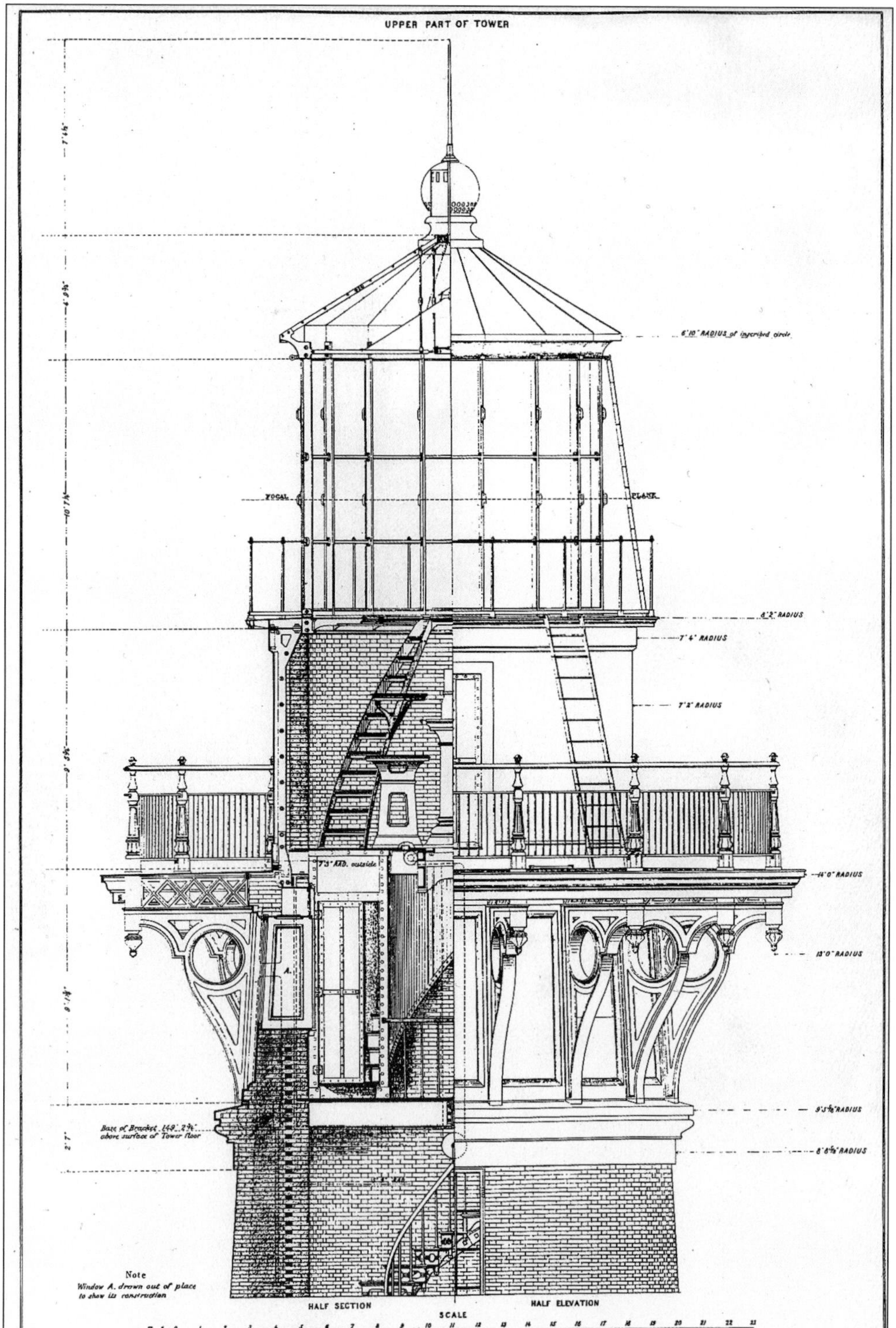

This is an architectural drawing of the lantern room of the Cape Lookout Lighthouse. (Courtesy of National Archives.)

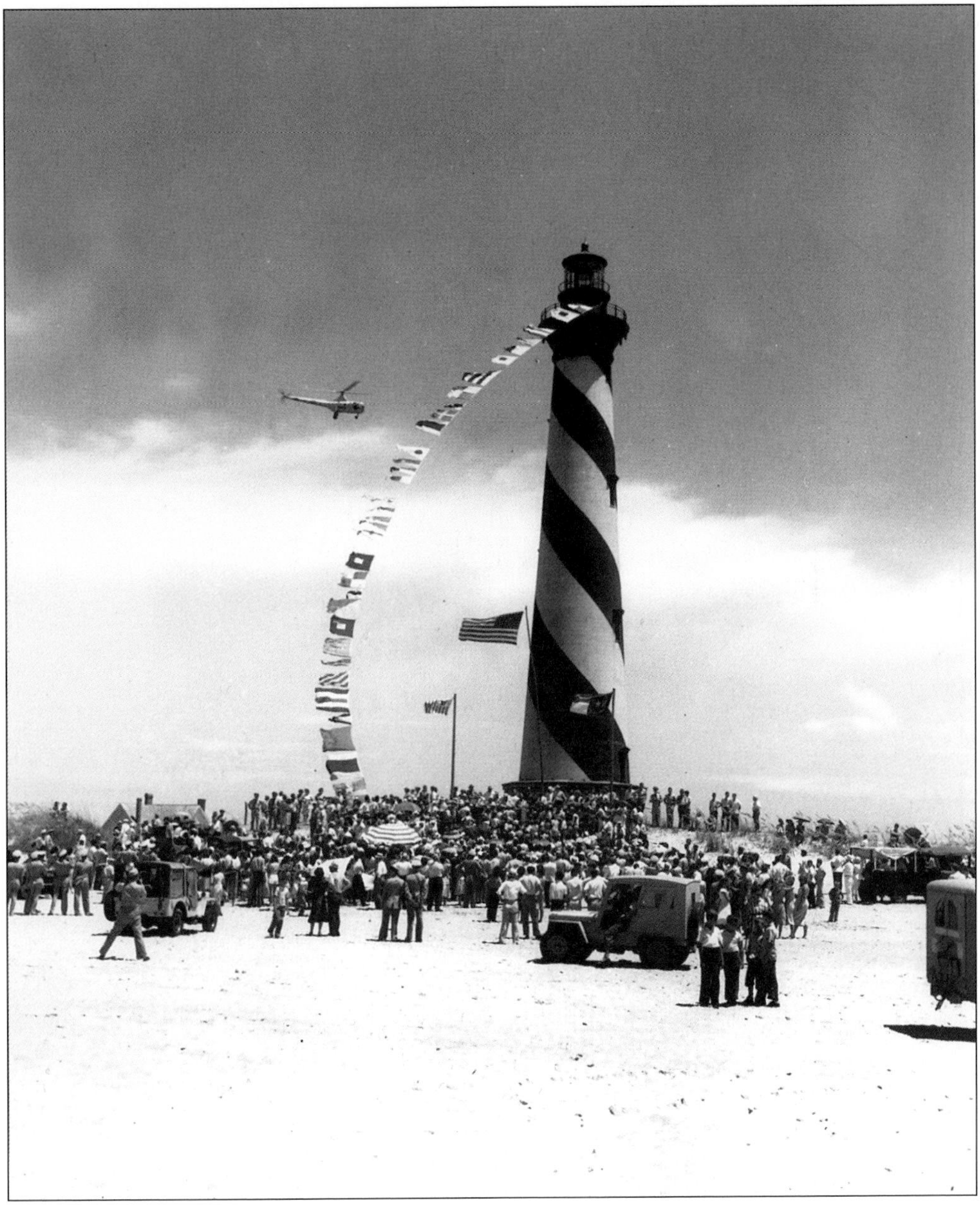

This Coast Guard Day celebration took place at the Cape Hatteras Lighthouse in 1948. (Courtesy of North Carolina Archives and History.)

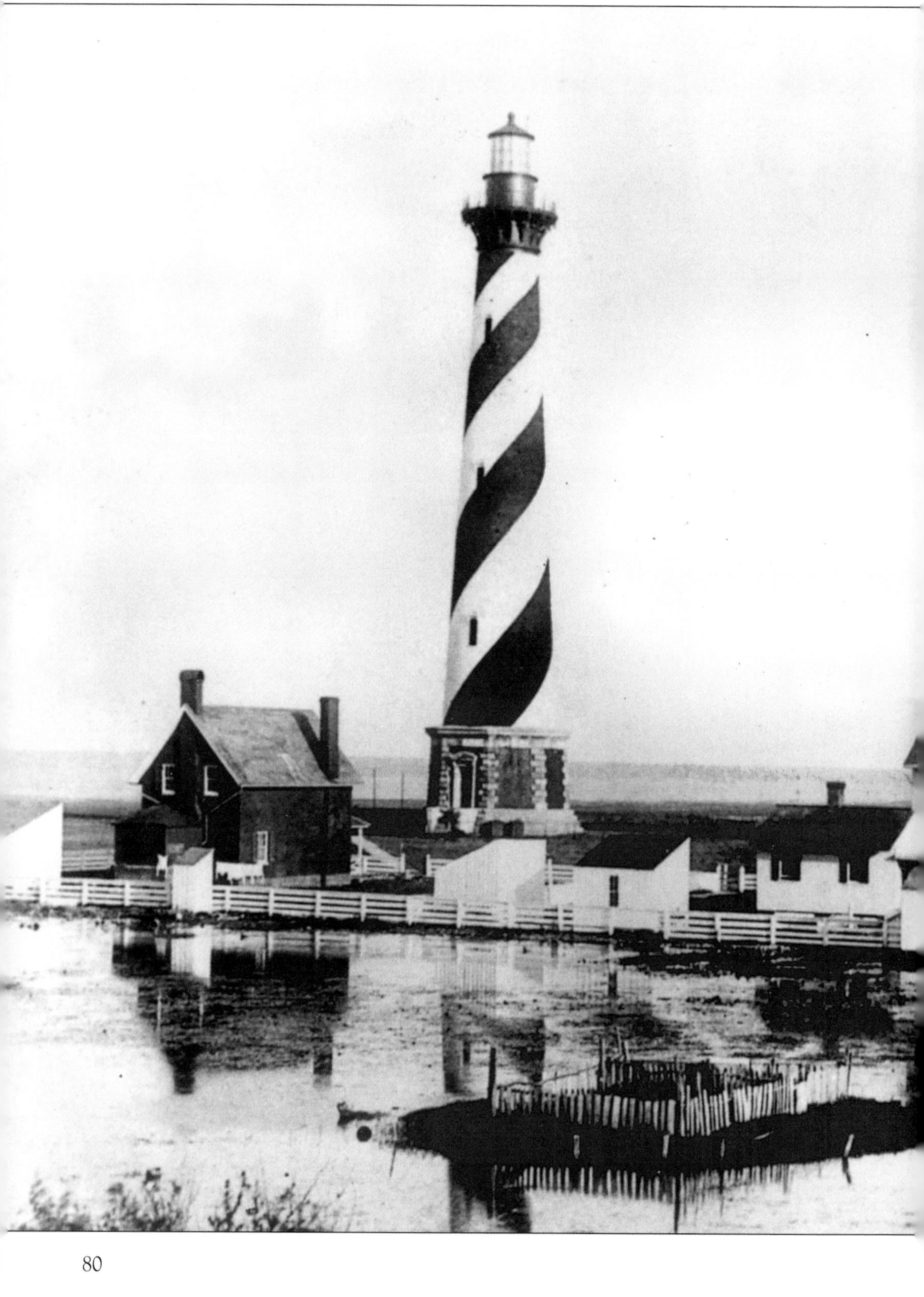

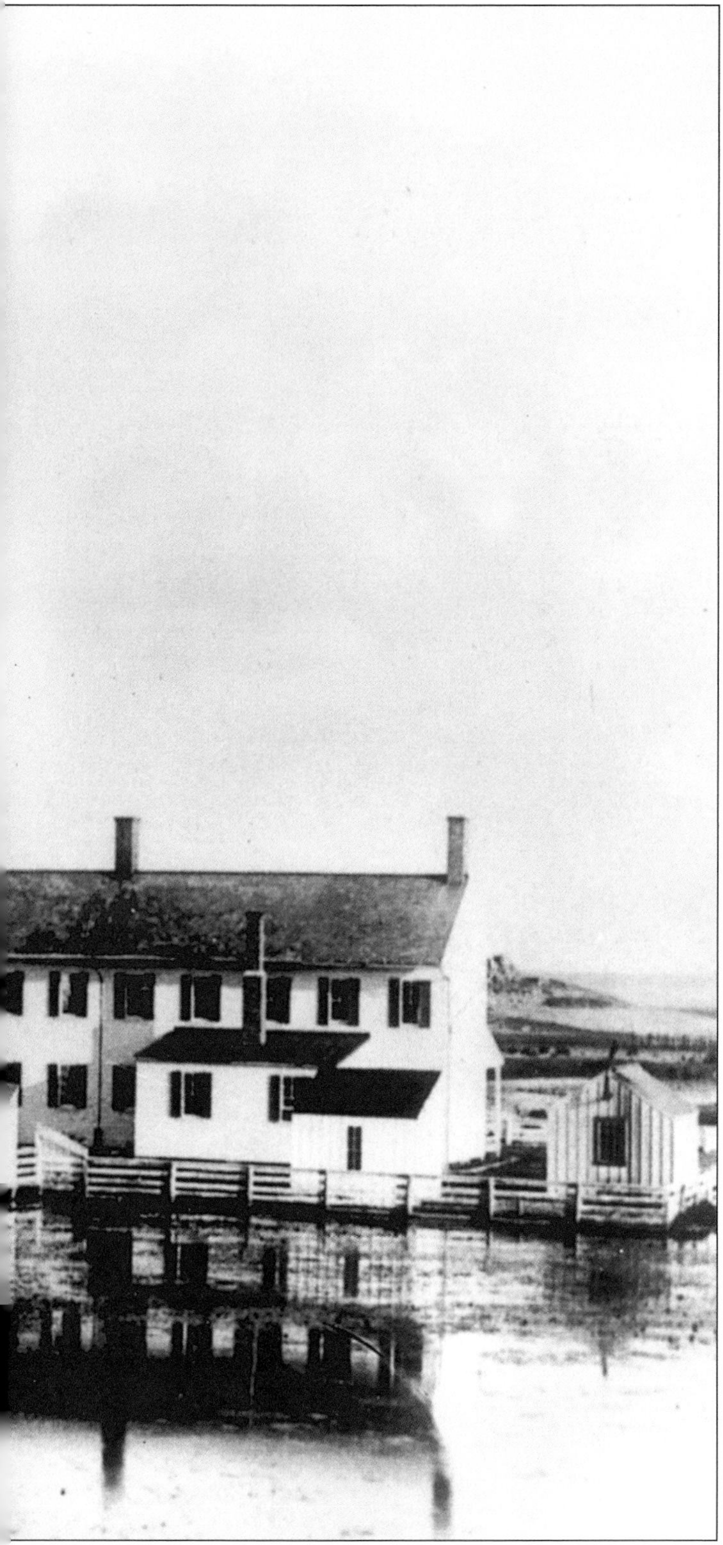

This photo depicts the Cape Hatteras Lighthouse and keeper's quarters. Note the ponds behind the dwelling houses. These standing bodies of water were excellent breeding grounds for mosquitoes. (Courtesy of National Archives.)

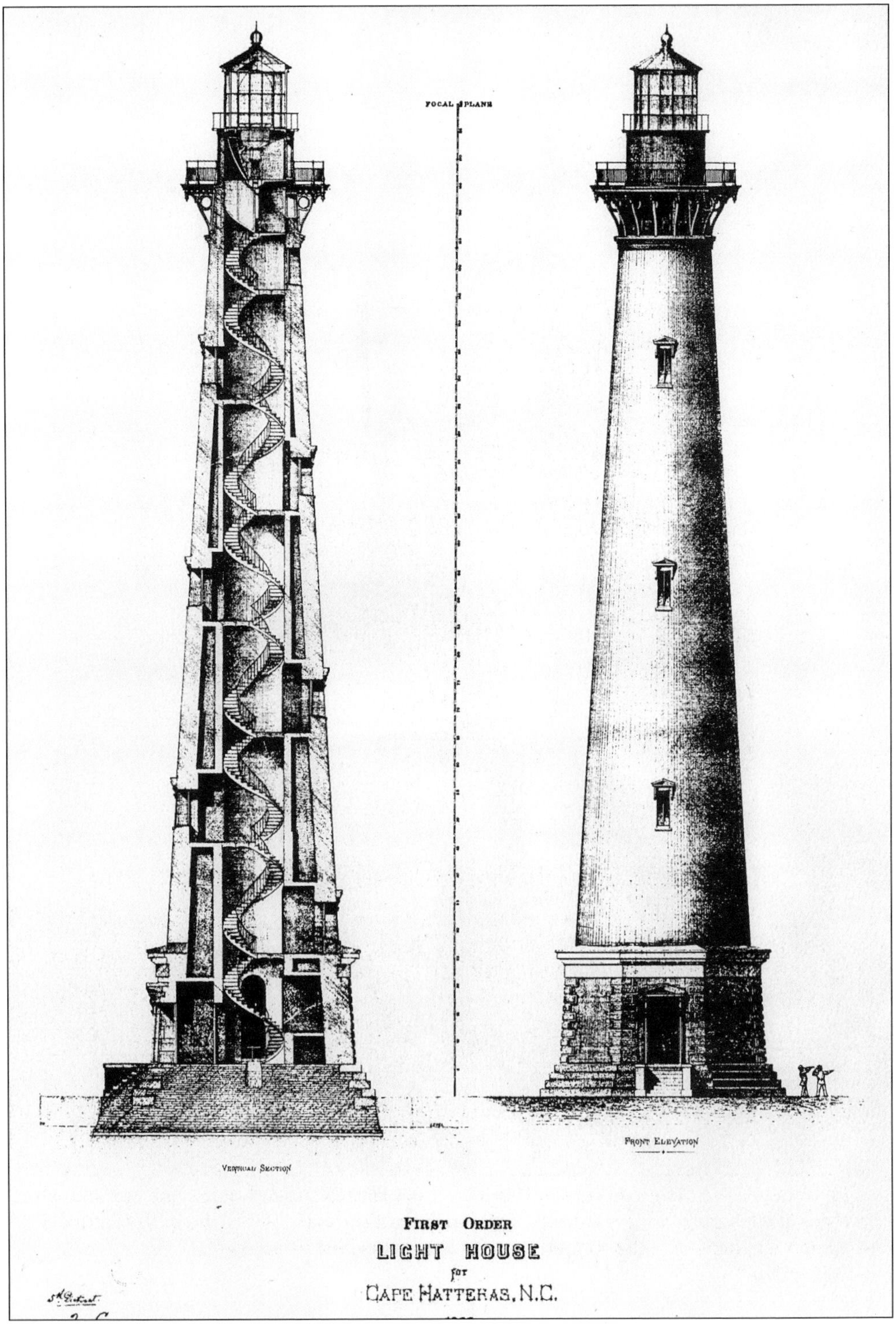

An architectural drawing of the Cape Hatteras Lighthouse was prepared in 1869. (Courtesy of National Archives.)

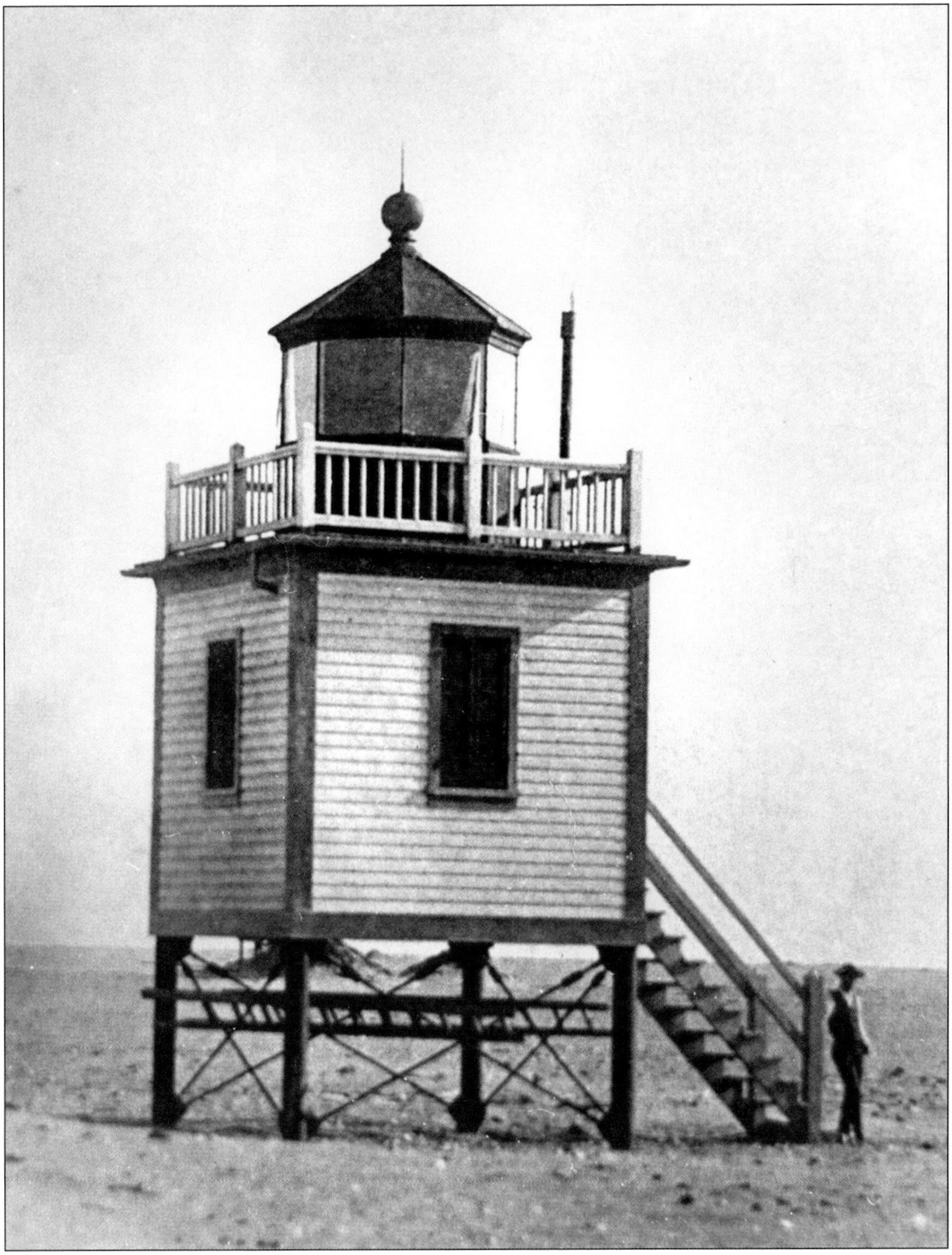

The Hatteras Beacon Light stood south of the Cape Hatteras Lighthouse. The red and white structure guided local mariners around Cape Point until the early part of the 20th century. This photograph was taken *c.* 1890. (Courtesy of Outer Banks History Center.)

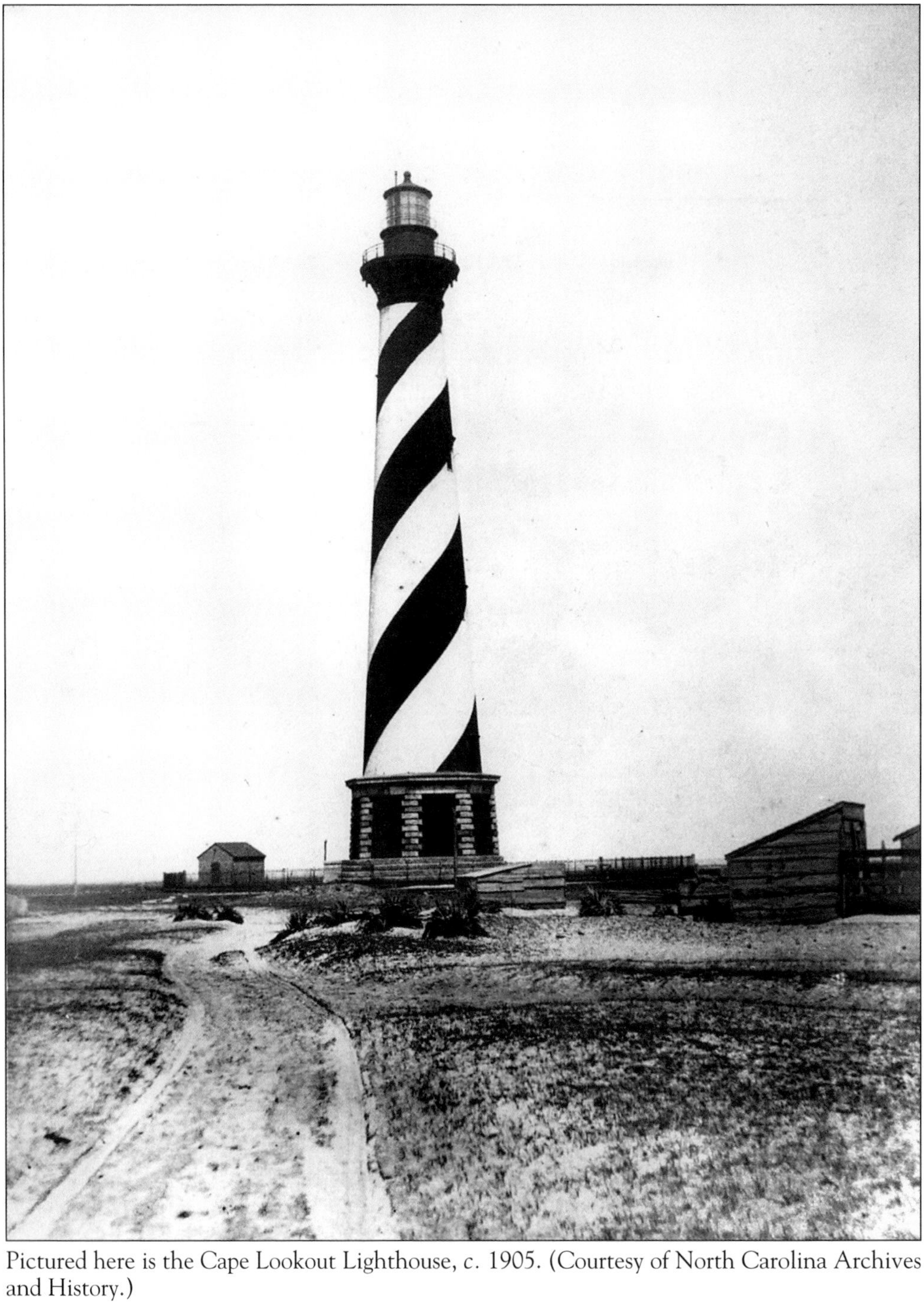

Pictured here is the Cape Lookout Lighthouse, *c.* 1905. (Courtesy of North Carolina Archives and History.)

Nine

Bodie Island Lighthouse

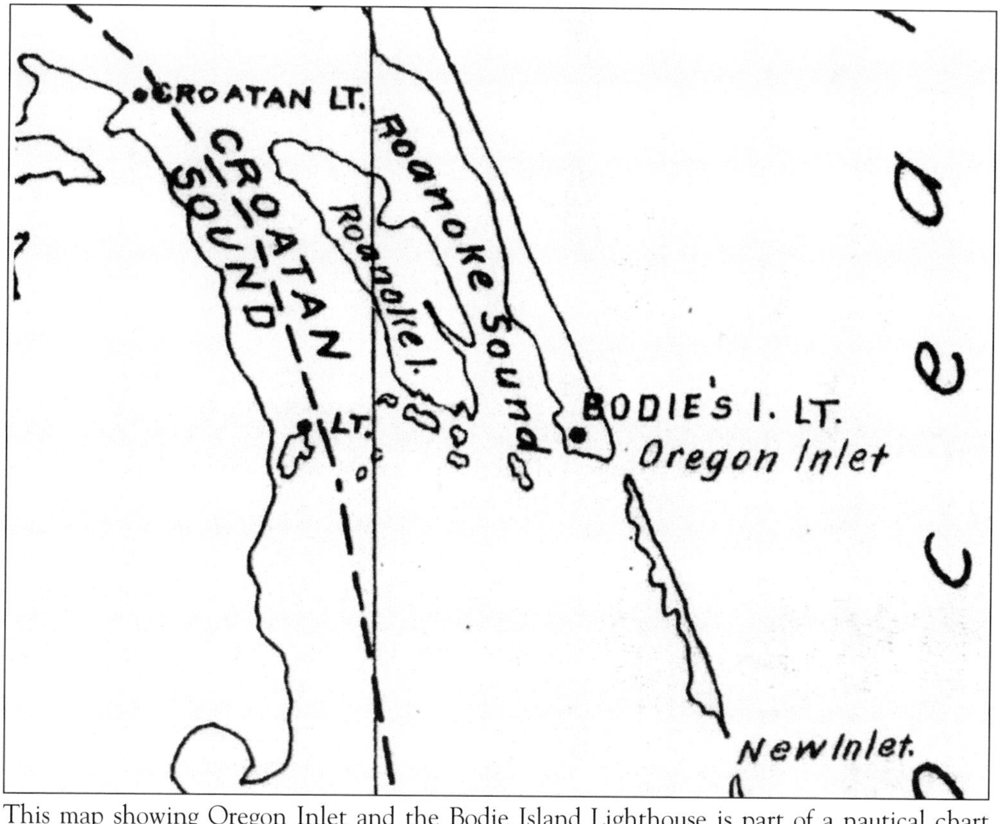

This map showing Oregon Inlet and the Bodie Island Lighthouse is part of a nautical chart drawn in 1900. The Bodie Island Lighthouse was located on the south side of the inlet. The first two Bodie Island Lighthouses were built on this site. The first one was built in 1847, but an unsecured foundation resulted in the tower's leaning out of plumb and the lighthouse had to be abandoned. In 1859, the second lighthouse on this spot was built on a more secure foundation. It was in operation for only a short time, however, as Confederate soldiers blew the tower up in 1861 to keep it from falling into enemy hands. The third tower was built on the north side of the inlet.

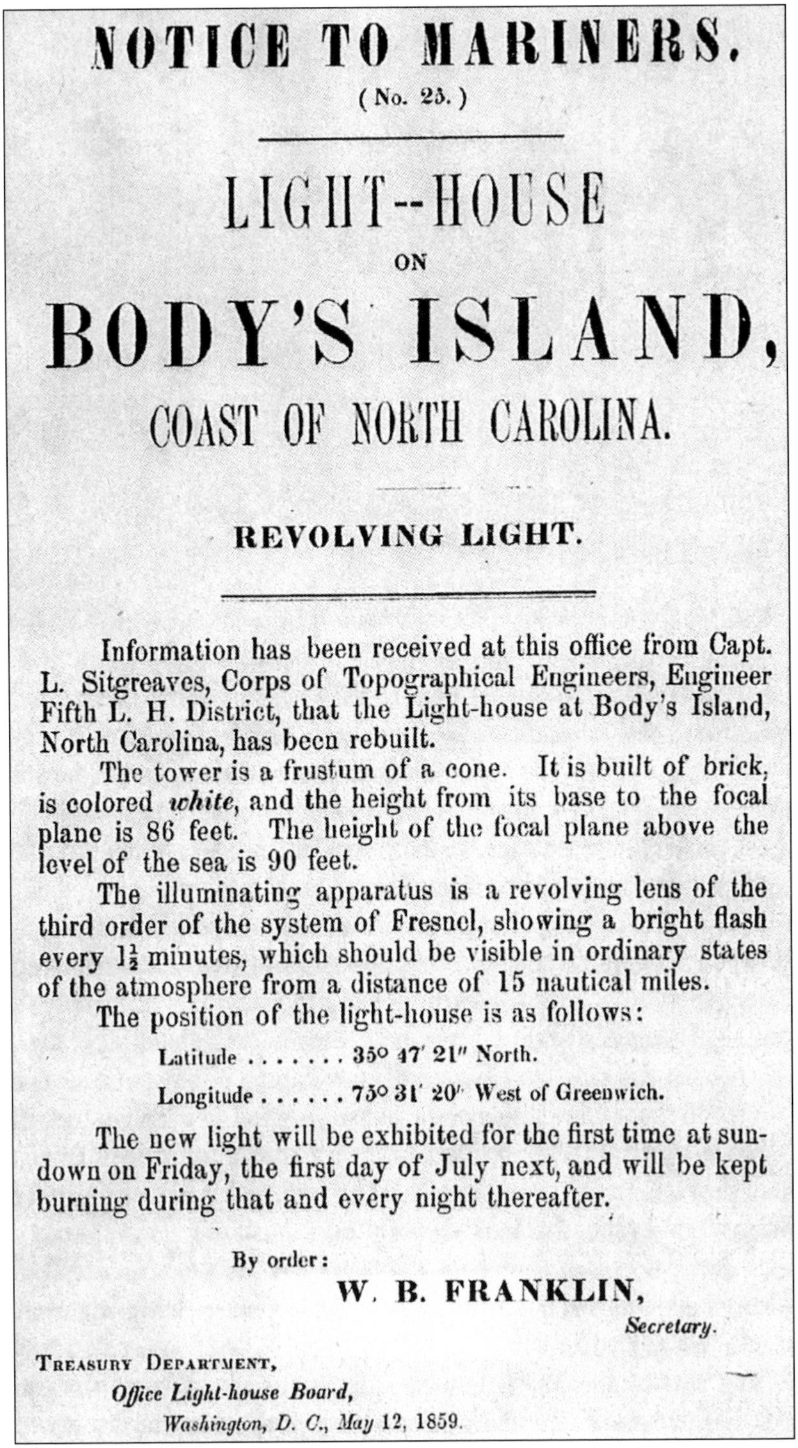

NOTICE TO MARINERS.

(No. 25.)

LIGHT--HOUSE

ON

BODY'S ISLAND,

COAST OF NORTH CAROLINA.

REVOLVING LIGHT.

Information has been received at this office from Capt. L. Sitgreaves, Corps of Topographical Engineers, Engineer Fifth L. H. District, that the Light-house at Body's Island, North Carolina, has been rebuilt.

The tower is a frustum of a cone. It is built of brick, is colored *white*, and the height from its base to the focal plane is 86 feet. The height of the focal plane above the level of the sea is 90 feet.

The illuminating apparatus is a revolving lens of the third order of the system of Fresnel, showing a bright flash every 1½ minutes, which should be visible in ordinary states of the atmosphere from a distance of 15 nautical miles.

The position of the light-house is as follows:

Latitude . . . . 35° 47′ 21″ North.

Longitude . . . . . . 75° 31′ 20″ West of Greenwich.

The new light will be exhibited for the first time at sundown on Friday, the first day of July next, and will be kept burning during that and every night thereafter.

By order:

W. B. FRANKLIN,

Secretary.

TREASURY DEPARTMENT,

Office Light-house Board,

Washington, D. C., May 12, 1859.

This mariner notice was released in May 1859, informing the public of the new lighthouse that was to go into operation at sundown on July 1, 1859. The tower was destroyed during the Civil War.

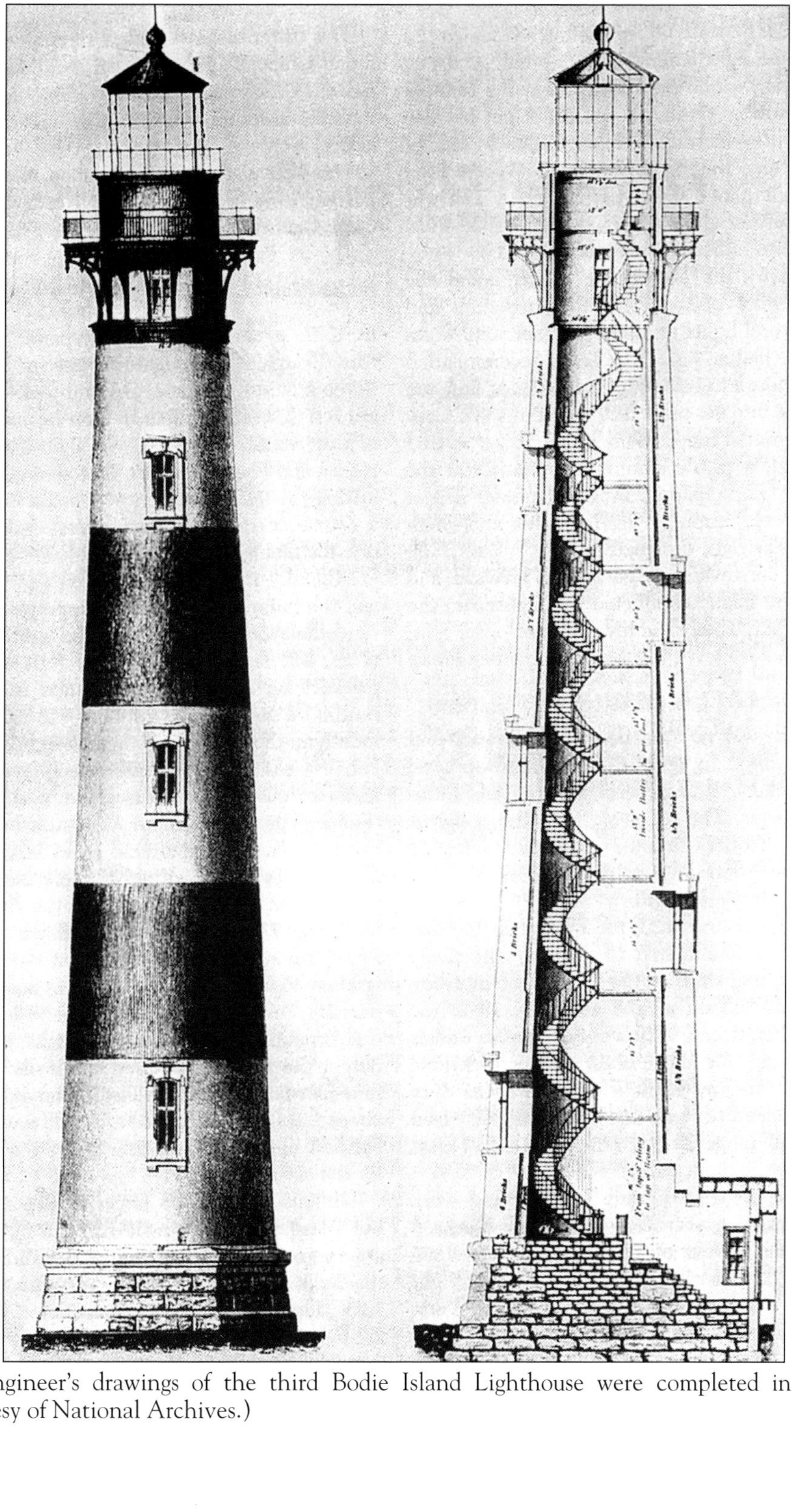

This engineer's drawings of the third Bodie Island Lighthouse were completed in 1872. (Courtesy of National Archives.)

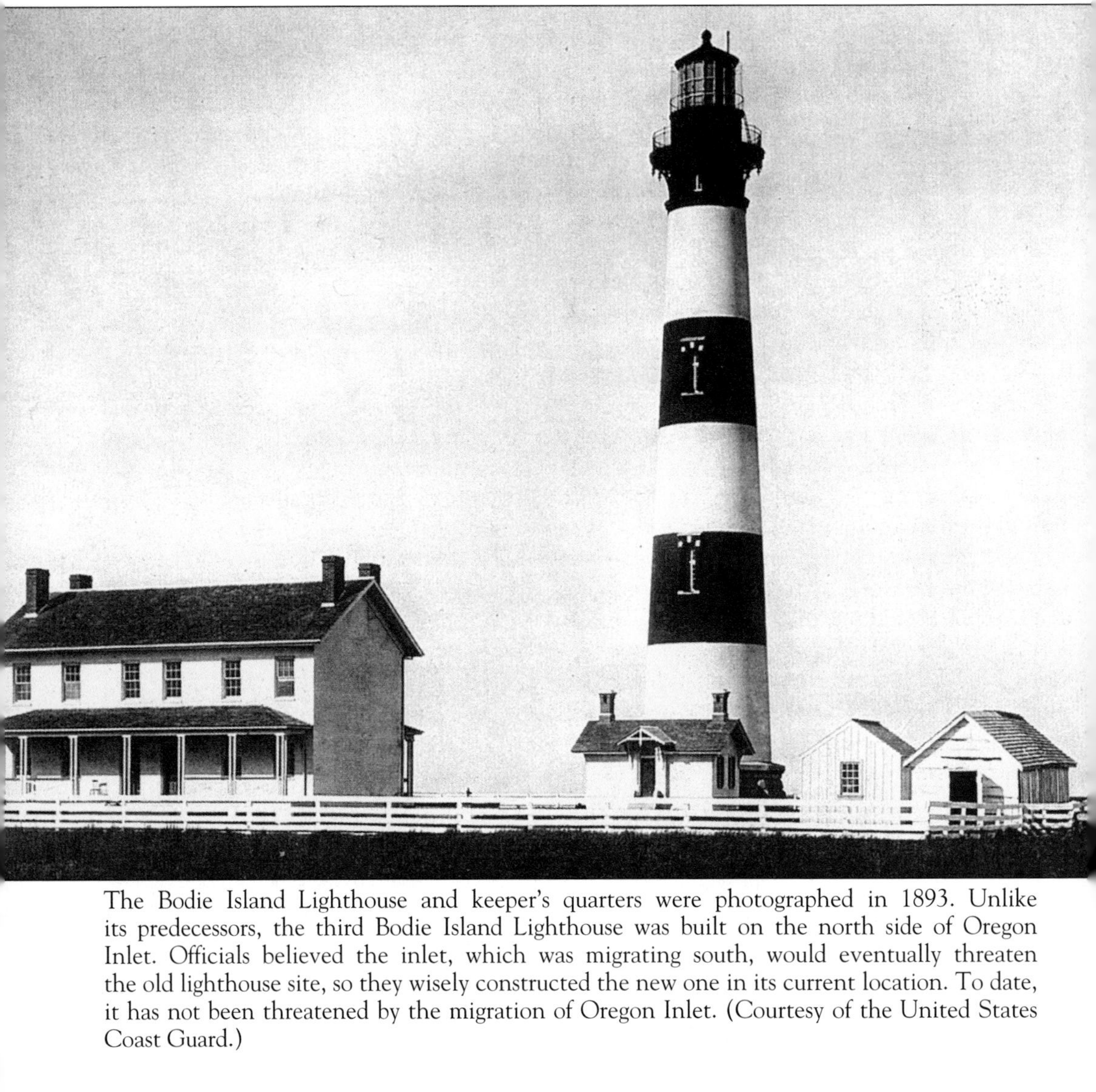

The Bodie Island Lighthouse and keeper's quarters were photographed in 1893. Unlike its predecessors, the third Bodie Island Lighthouse was built on the north side of Oregon Inlet. Officials believed the inlet, which was migrating south, would eventually threaten the old lighthouse site, so they wisely constructed the new one in its current location. To date, it has not been threatened by the migration of Oregon Inlet. (Courtesy of the United States Coast Guard.)

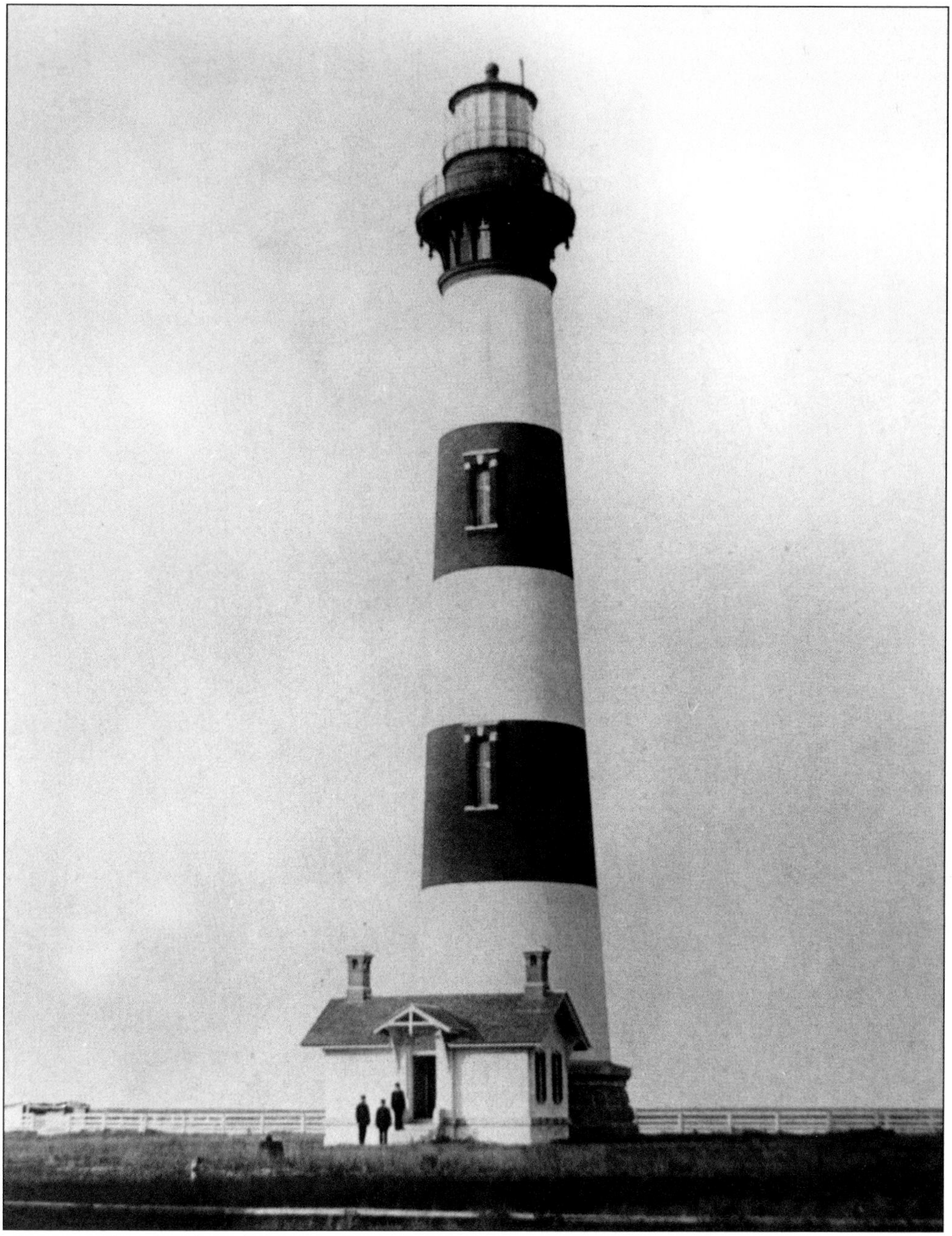
This is Bodie Island in the 1890s. (Courtesy of Outer Banks History Center.)

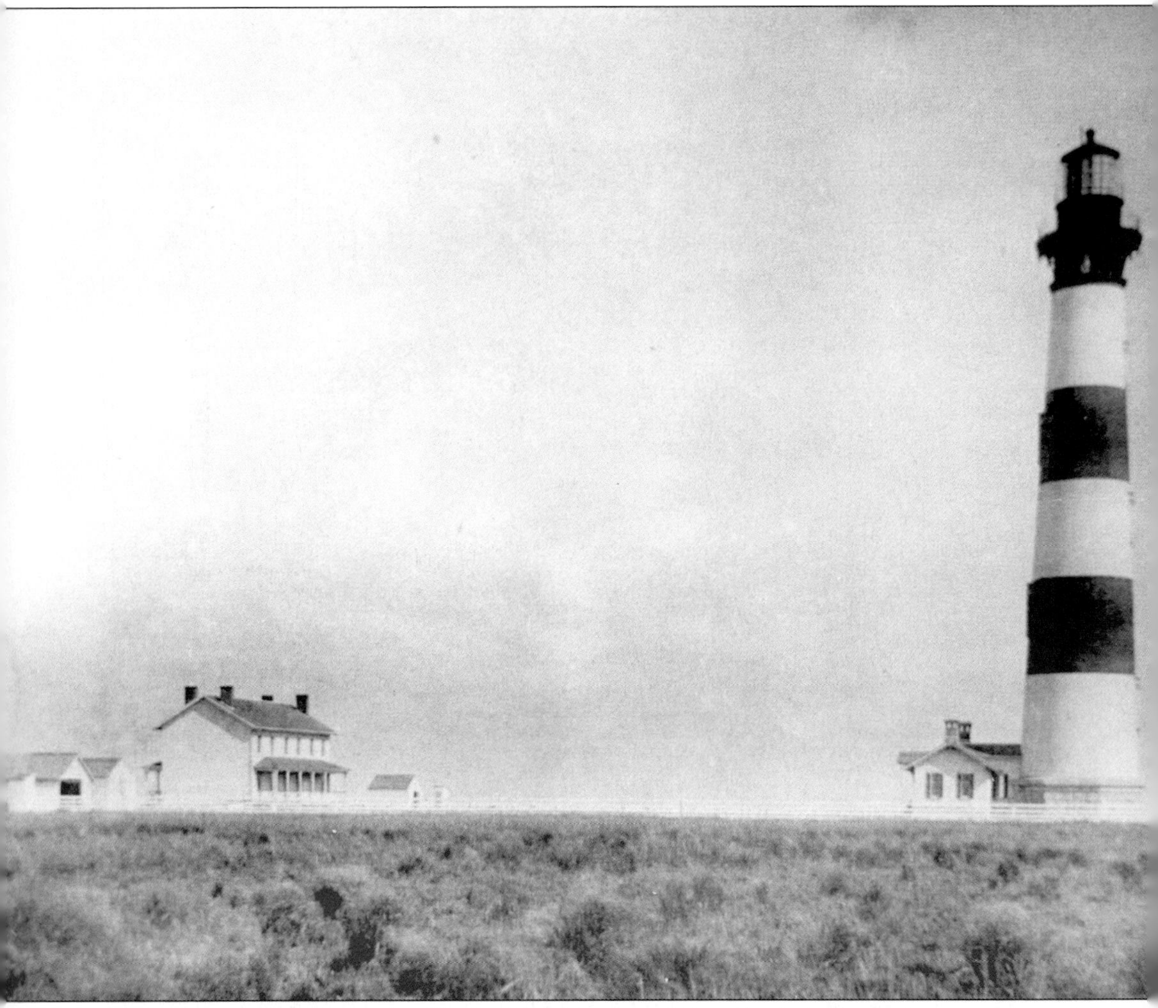

Here is another photograph of Bodie Island in the 1890s. The lighthouse is a popular tourist destination along the Outer Banks and a prominent feature of the Cape Hatteras National Seashore. (Courtesy of Outer Banks History Center.)

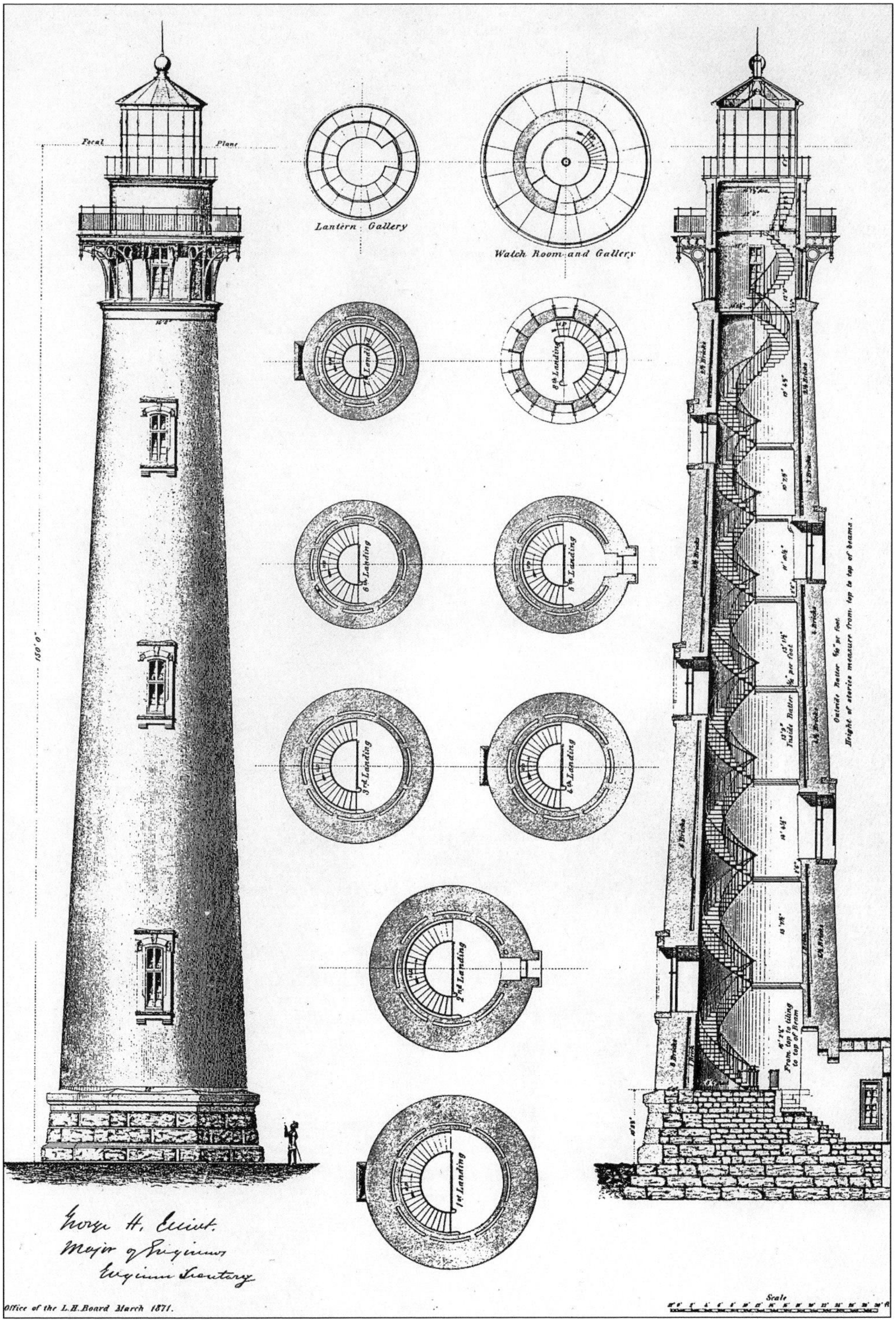

This architectural drawing of the "Body Island" Lighthouse was prepared in 1871. (Courtesy of National Archives.)

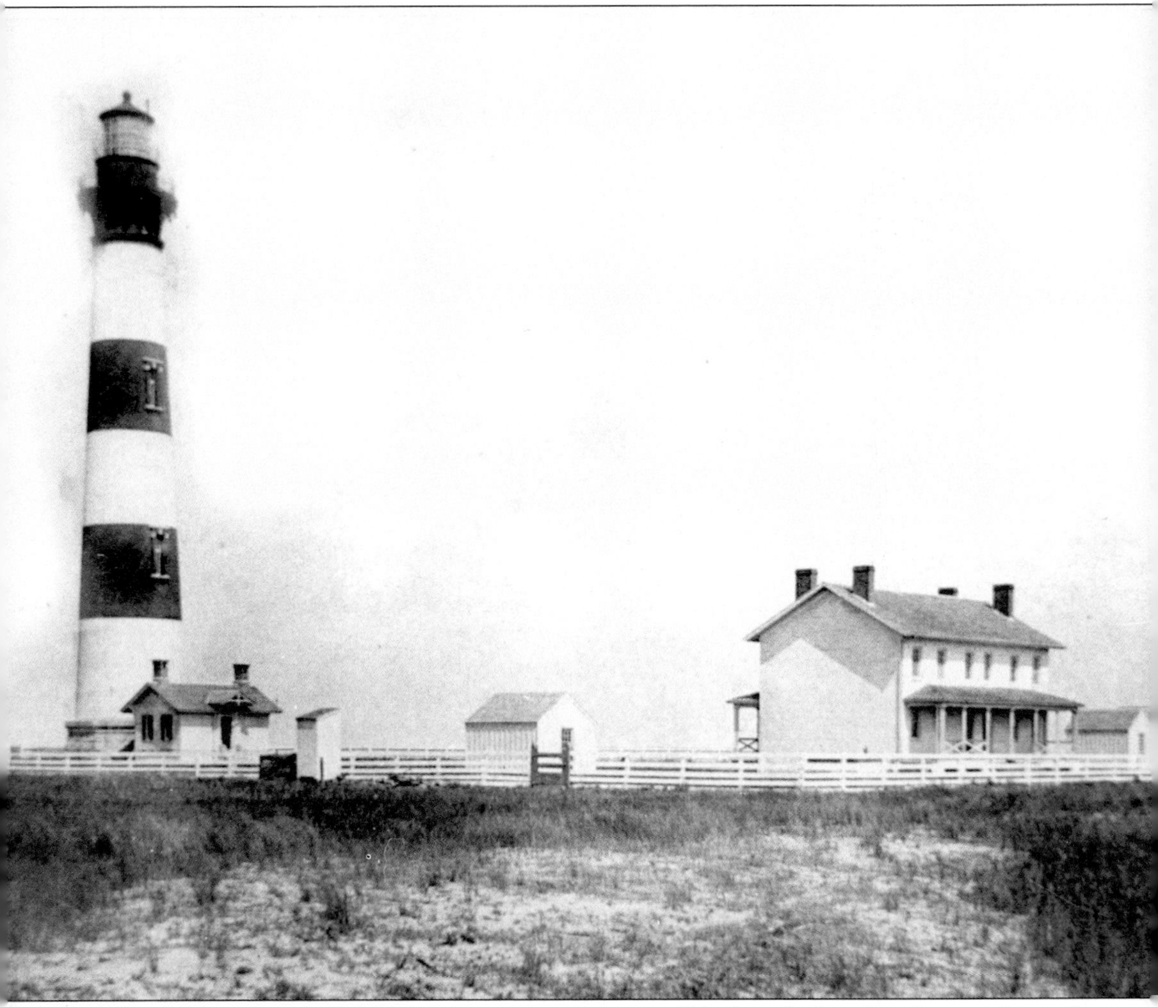

The third Bodie Island Lighthouse was given a coat of black and white bands as its daymark, distinguishing it from other lighthouses along the coast. There are 214 steps leading to the lantern room. (Courtesy of Outer Banks History Center.)

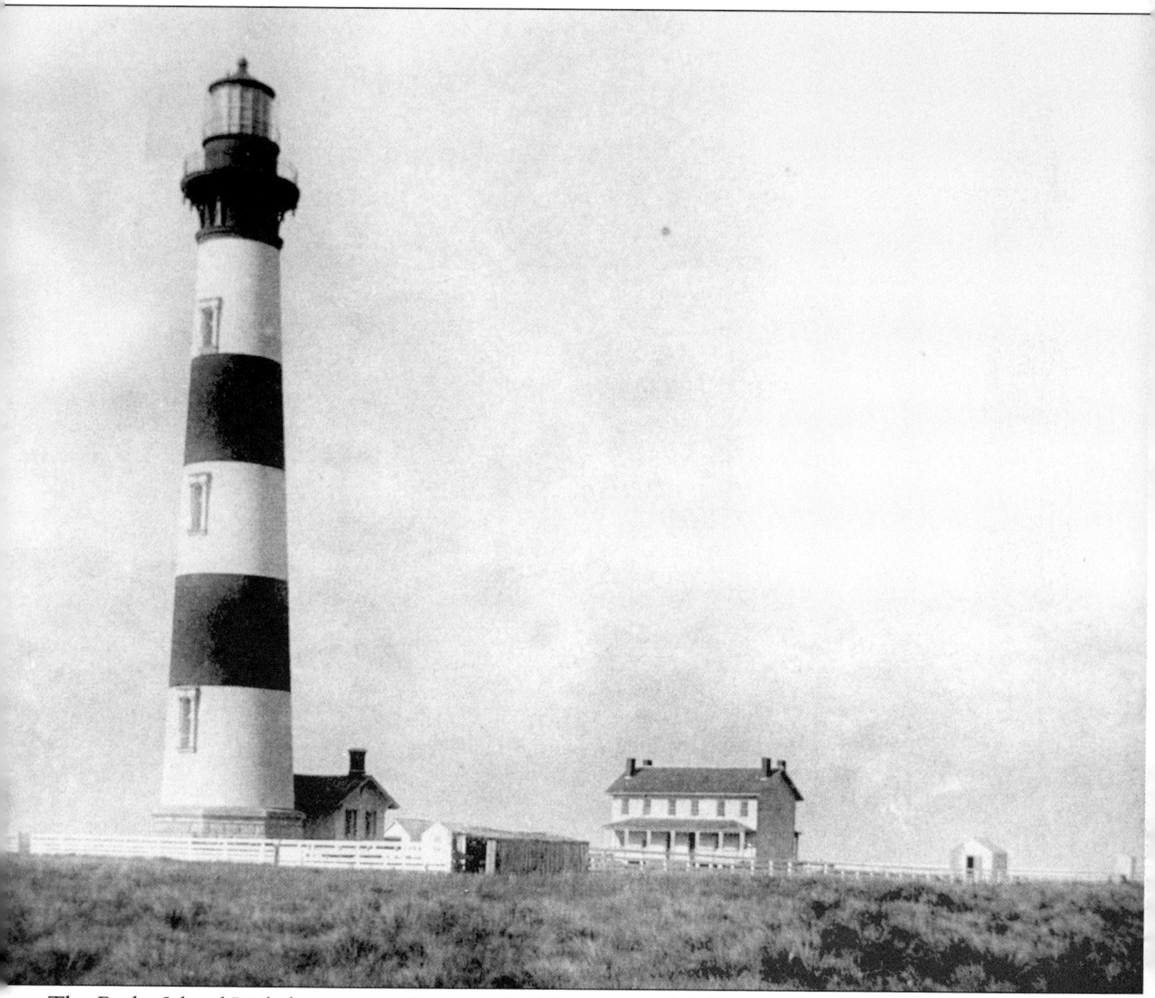

The Bodie Island Lighthouse was photographed from several different angles by an unidentified photographer in the 1890s.

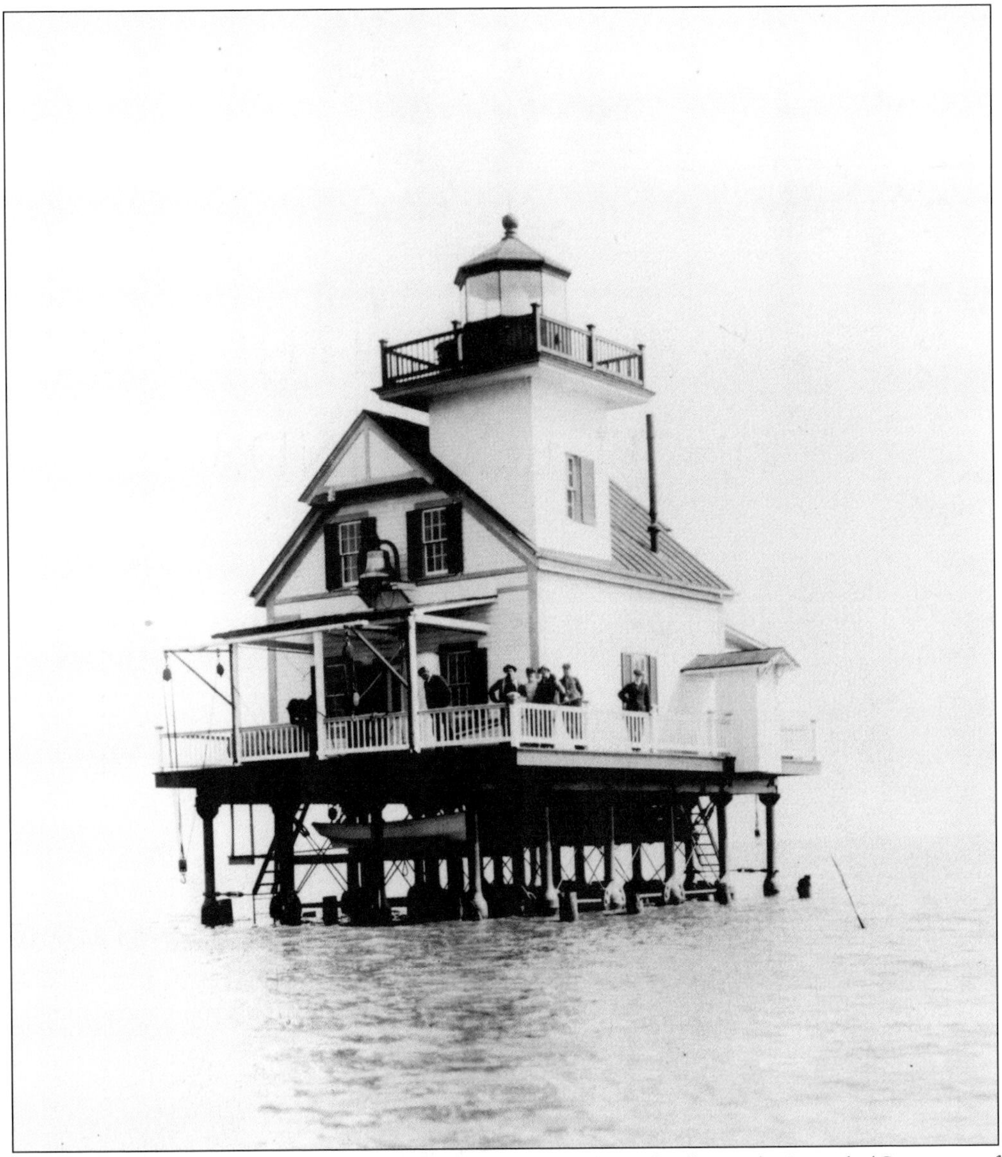

The Roanoke River Lighthouse marked the upper reaches of Albemarle Sound. (Courtesy of Outer Banks History Center.)

Ten

Screw-pile Lighthouses on the Sounds

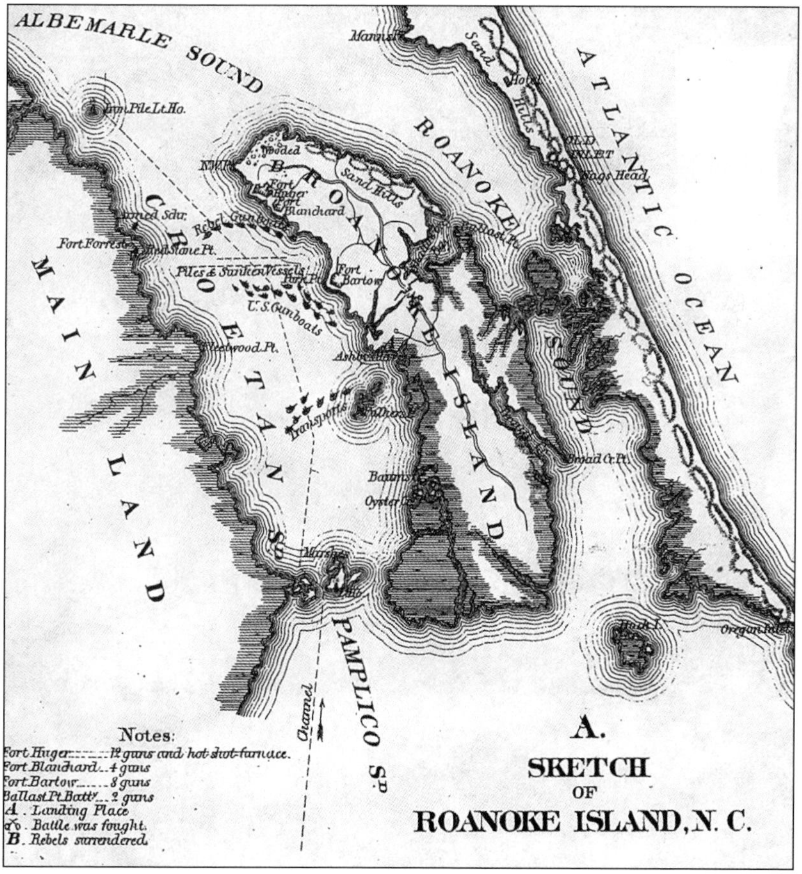

This 1862 map of the military maneuvers around Roanoke Island shows the location of the Croatan Lighthouse and the Roanoke Marshes Lighthouse.

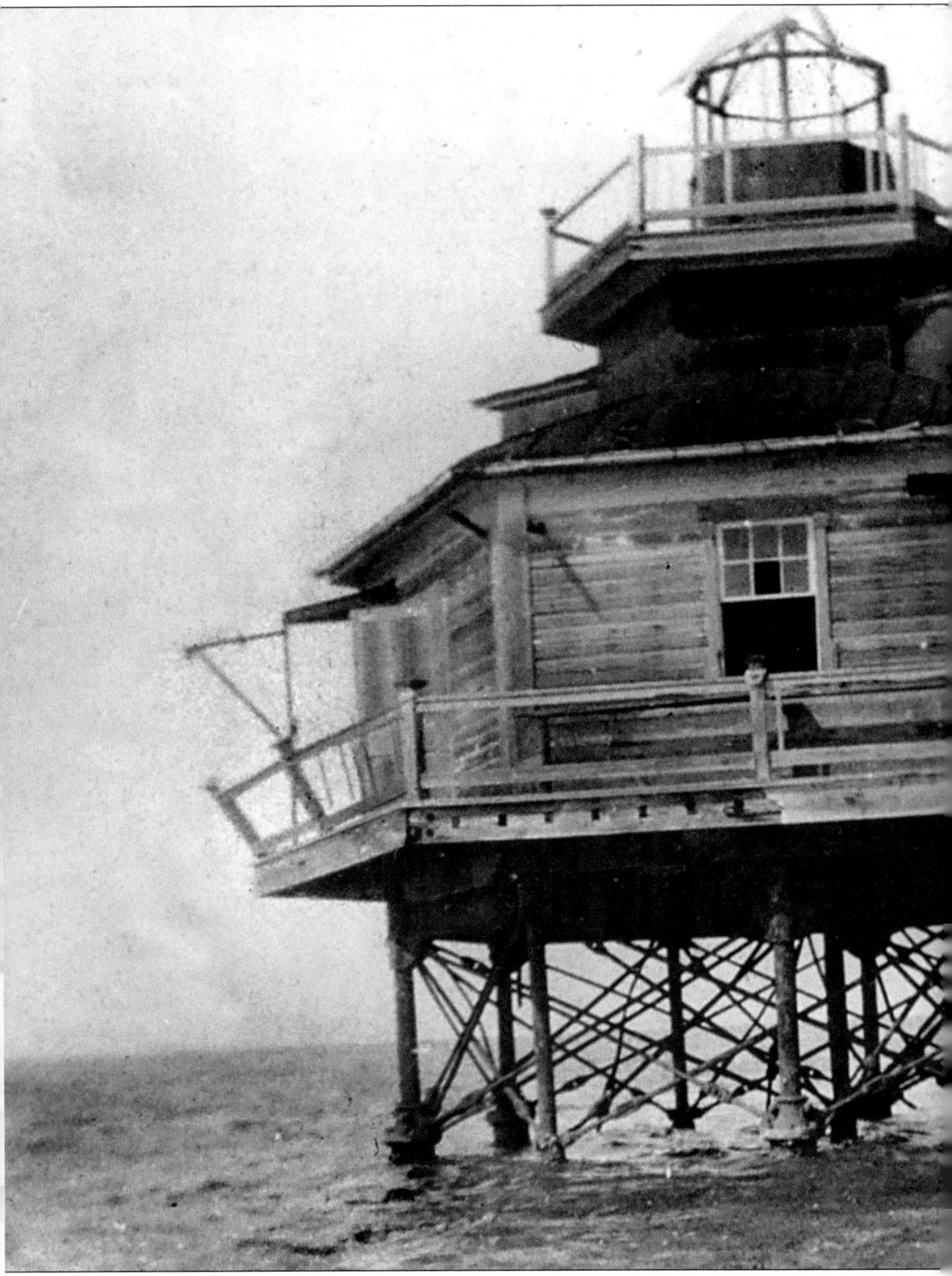

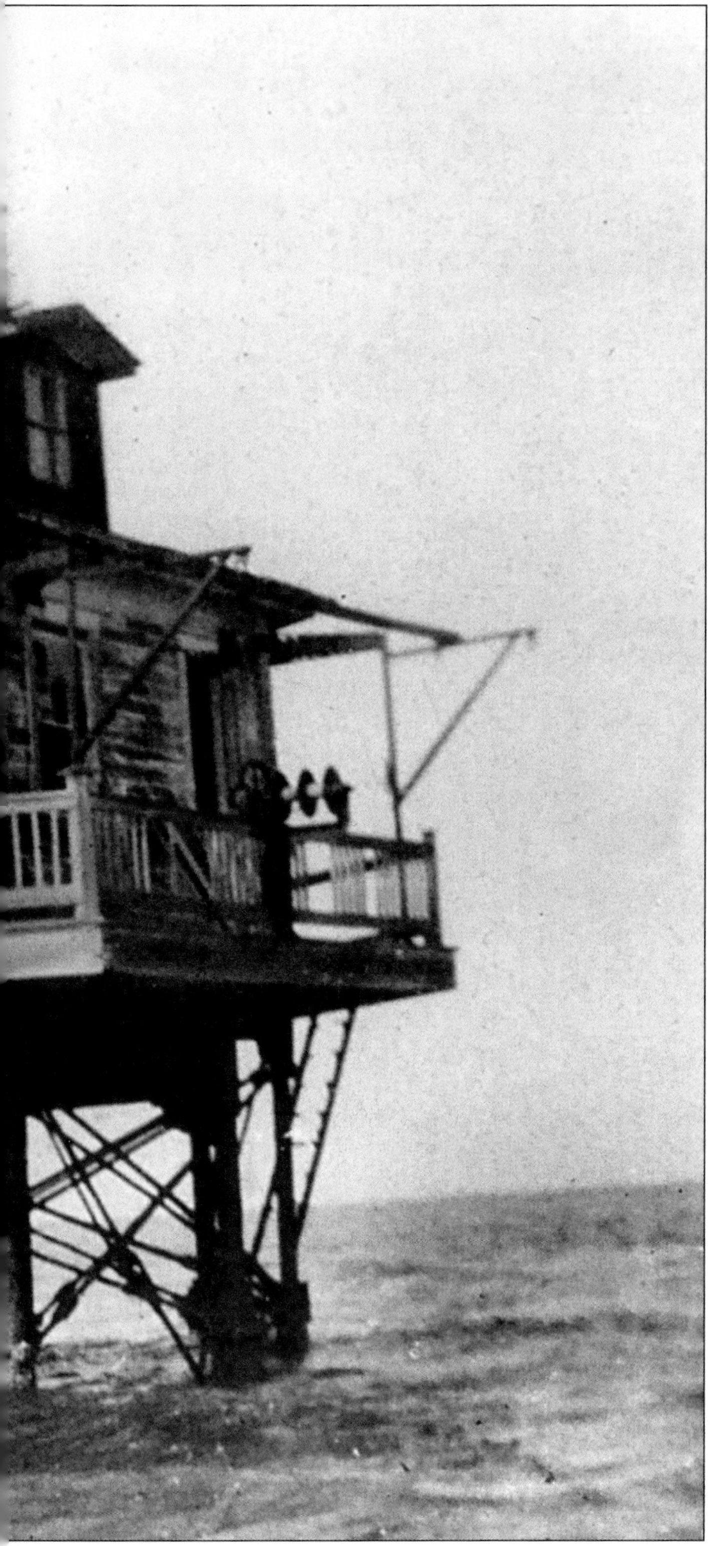

Northwest Point Light Tower, which was abandoned in 1903, is shown here in a photo taken in 1922. This was one of the lights that guided boats through Ocracoke Inlet, past Portsmouth and into Pamlico Sound. It was manned by the Lighthouse Service, but abandoned after a storm in August of 1903. (Courtesy of the National Park Service, Cape Lookout National Seashore.)

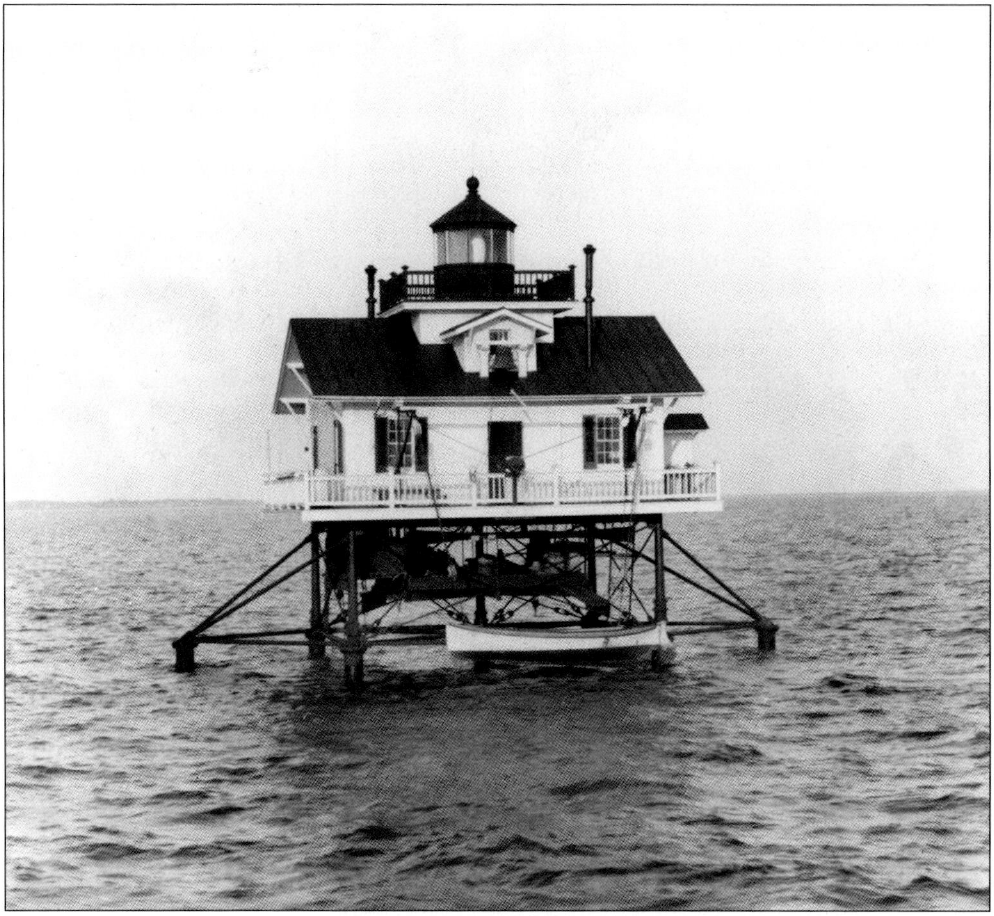

Roanoke Marshes Lighthouse marked the southern entrance to Croatan Sound, off Roanoke Island. The first lighthouse marking the entrance into the narrow channel was erected by Lucius Lyon in a marsh on nearby Roanoke Island in 1831. In 1842, the Van Pelt family claimed ownership of this site, and the United States Treasury Department was forced to remove the lighthouse. The screw-pile Roanoke Marshes Lighthouse was erected nearby in 1857, becoming the first screw-pile structure erected in North Carolina. The lighthouse served until it was decommissioned in 1955. (Courtesy of Outer Banks History Center.)

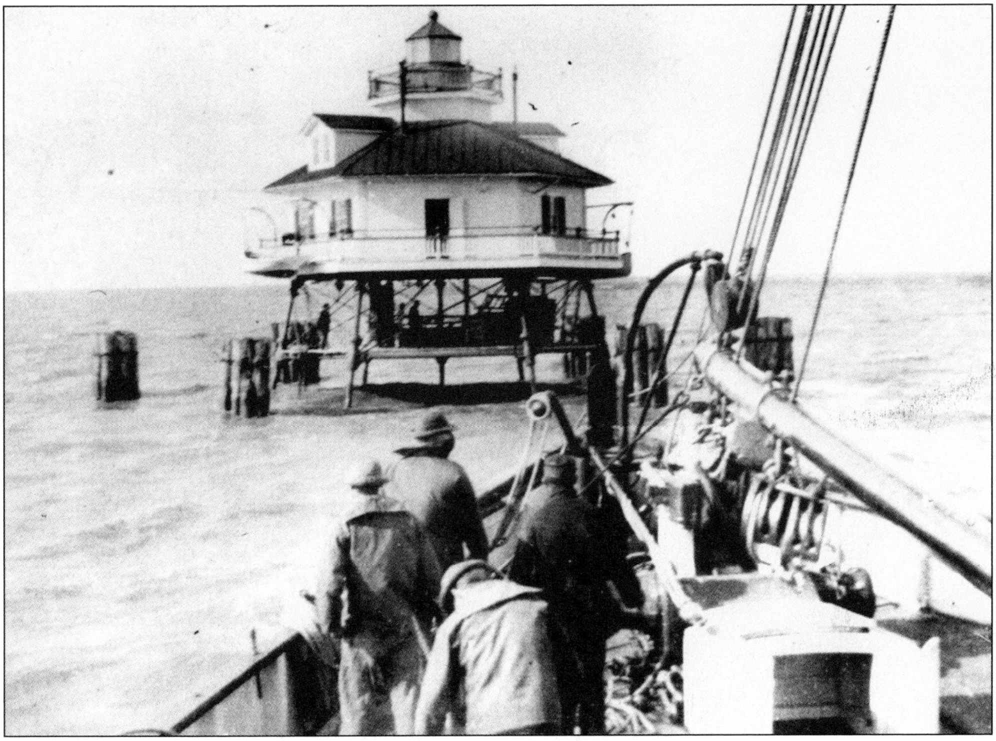

The Laurel Point Lighthouse stood over Albemarle Sound east of Edenton. (Courtesy of Outer Banks History Center.)

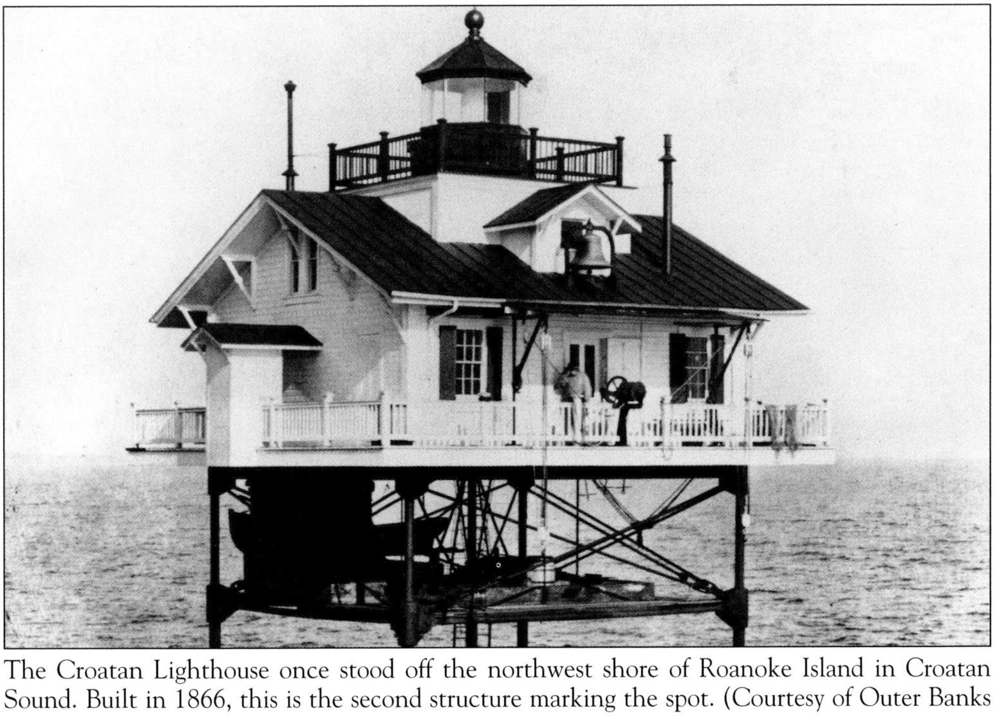

The Croatan Lighthouse once stood off the northwest shore of Roanoke Island in Croatan Sound. Built in 1866, this is the second structure marking the spot. (Courtesy of Outer Banks History Center.)

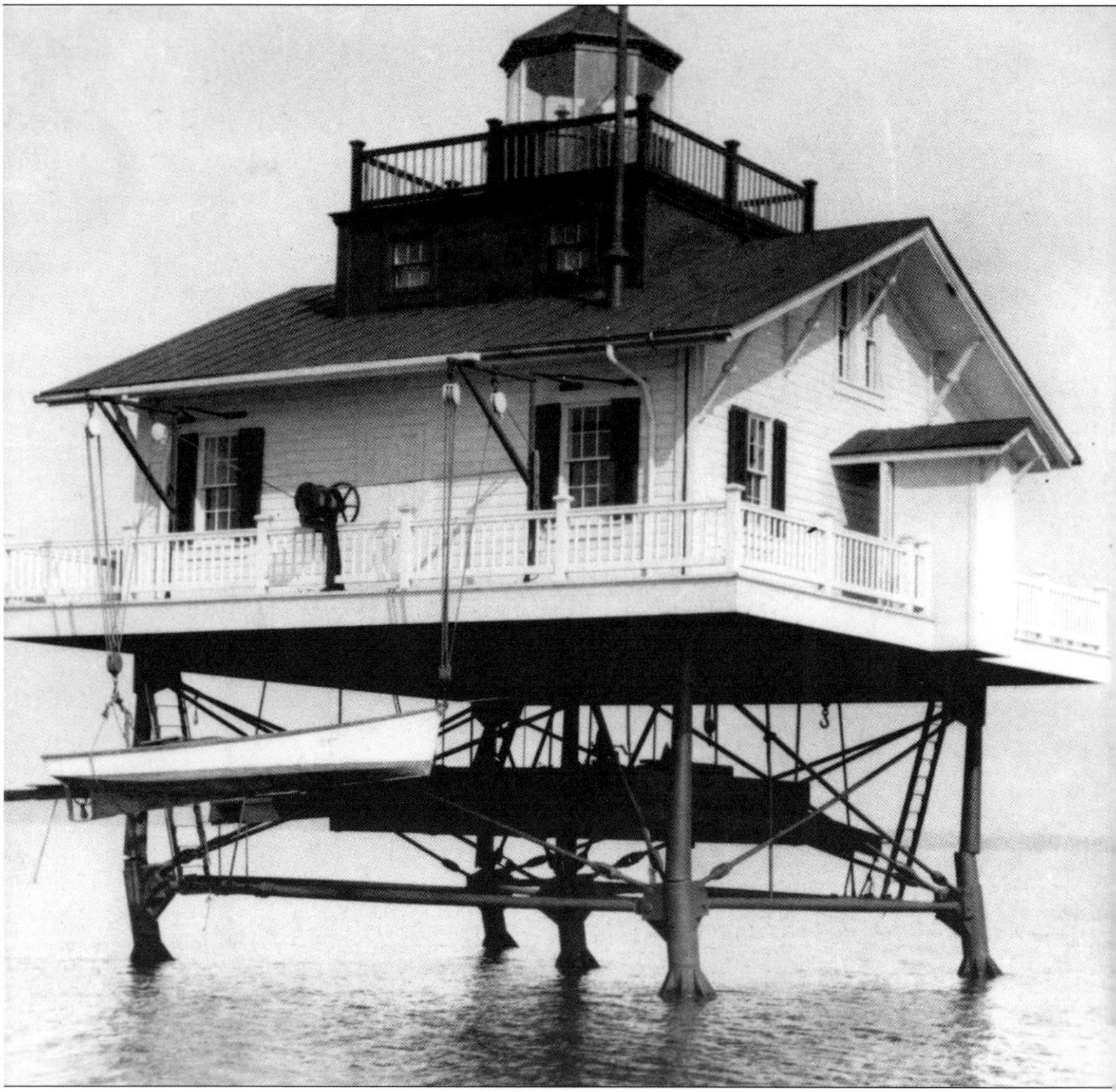

The Wade's Point Lighthouse marked the entrance to Pasquatank River, near Elizabeth City in the northeastern part of the state. A light boat marked this spot as early as 1826. The first screw-pile lighthouse was built here *c.* 1859 and was subsequently destroyed by the Confederates during the Civil War. In 1866, the lighthouse at Wade's Point was put back into service. (Courtesy of the United States Coast Guard.)

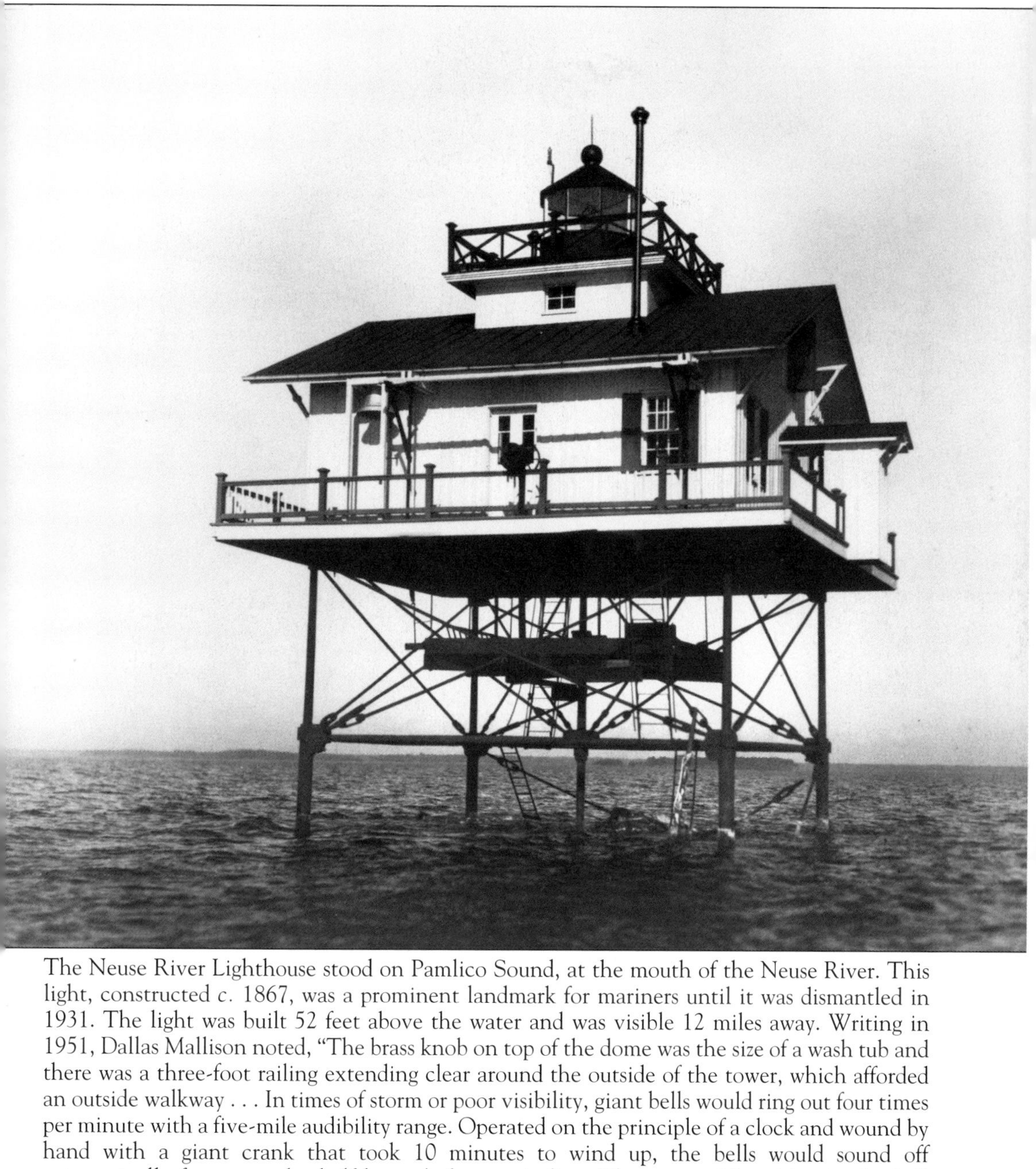

The Neuse River Lighthouse stood on Pamlico Sound, at the mouth of the Neuse River. This light, constructed *c.* 1867, was a prominent landmark for mariners until it was dismantled in 1931. The light was built 52 feet above the water and was visible 12 miles away. Writing in 1951, Dallas Mallison noted, "The brass knob on top of the dome was the size of a wash tub and there was a three-foot railing extending clear around the outside of the tower, which afforded an outside walkway . . . In times of storm or poor visibility, giant bells would ring out four times per minute with a five-mile audibility range. Operated on the principle of a clock and wound by hand with a giant crank that took 10 minutes to wind up, the bells would sound off automatically for two and a half hours before rewinding. There were 15 weights in the bell clock, each weighing 100 pounds. At least one time is recorded where the bells rung 60 hours without interruption." (Courtesy of the United States Coast Guard.)

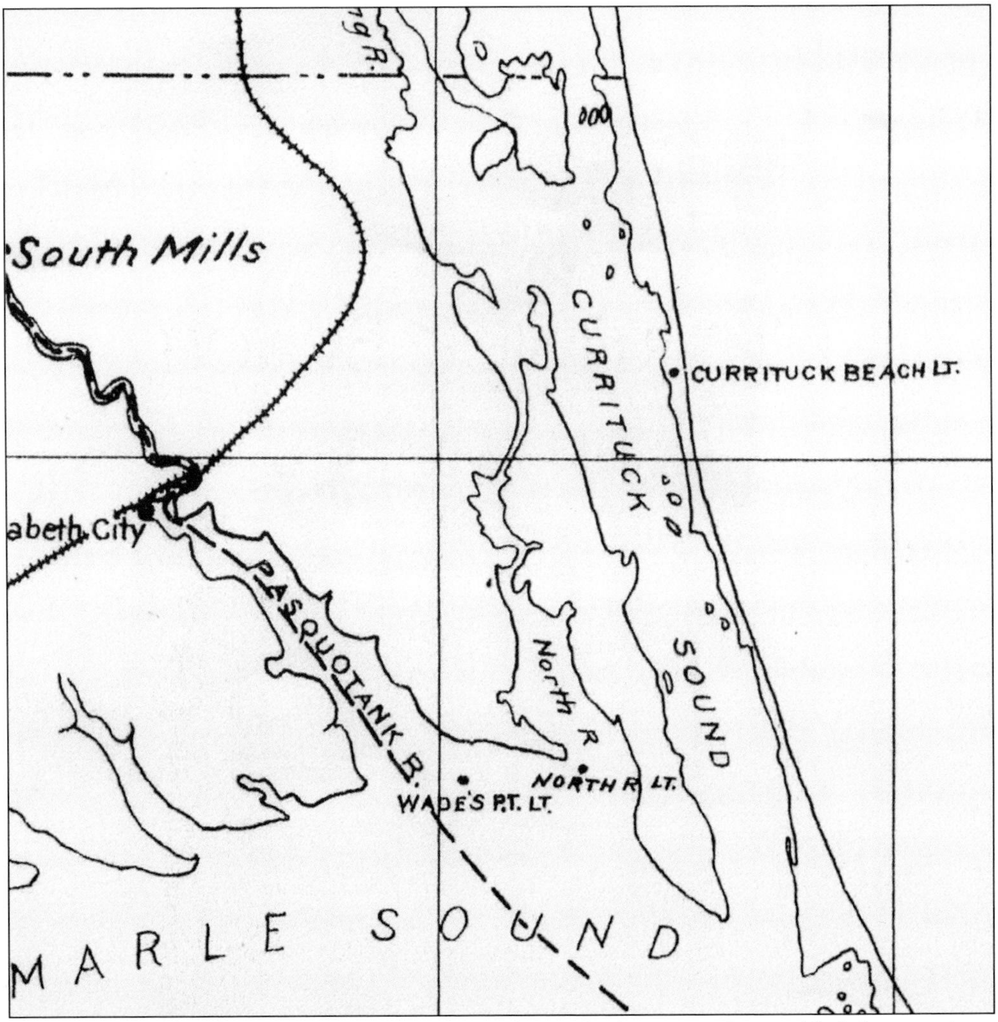

This section of a nautical chart, drawn in 1900, shows the location of several lighthouses along the northern Outer Banks and the sounds, including the Currituck Lighthouse. (Courtesy of North Carolina Archives and History.)

Eleven
Currituck Beach Lighthouse

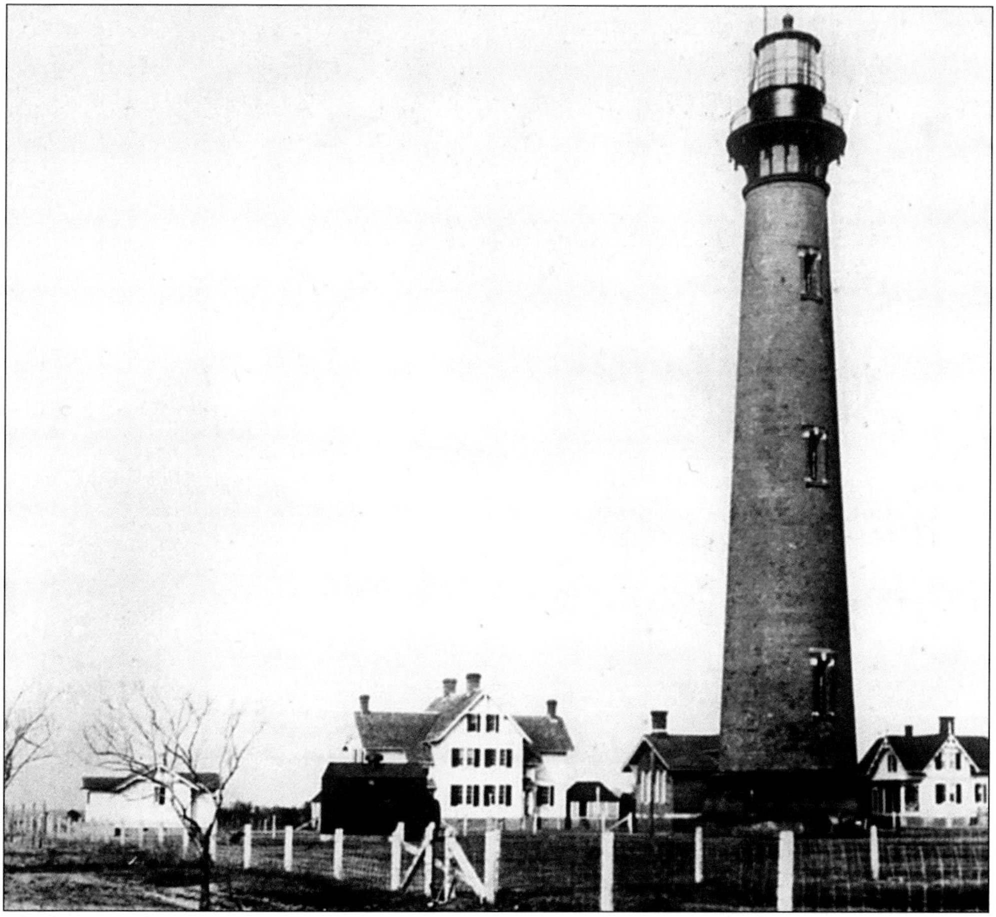

The Currituck Lighthouse is shown here, *c.* 1905. This was an important light for mariners along what was a long and dark stretch of coast between Cape Henry, Virginia, and Bodie Island, North Carolina. (Courtesy of North Carolina Archives and History.)

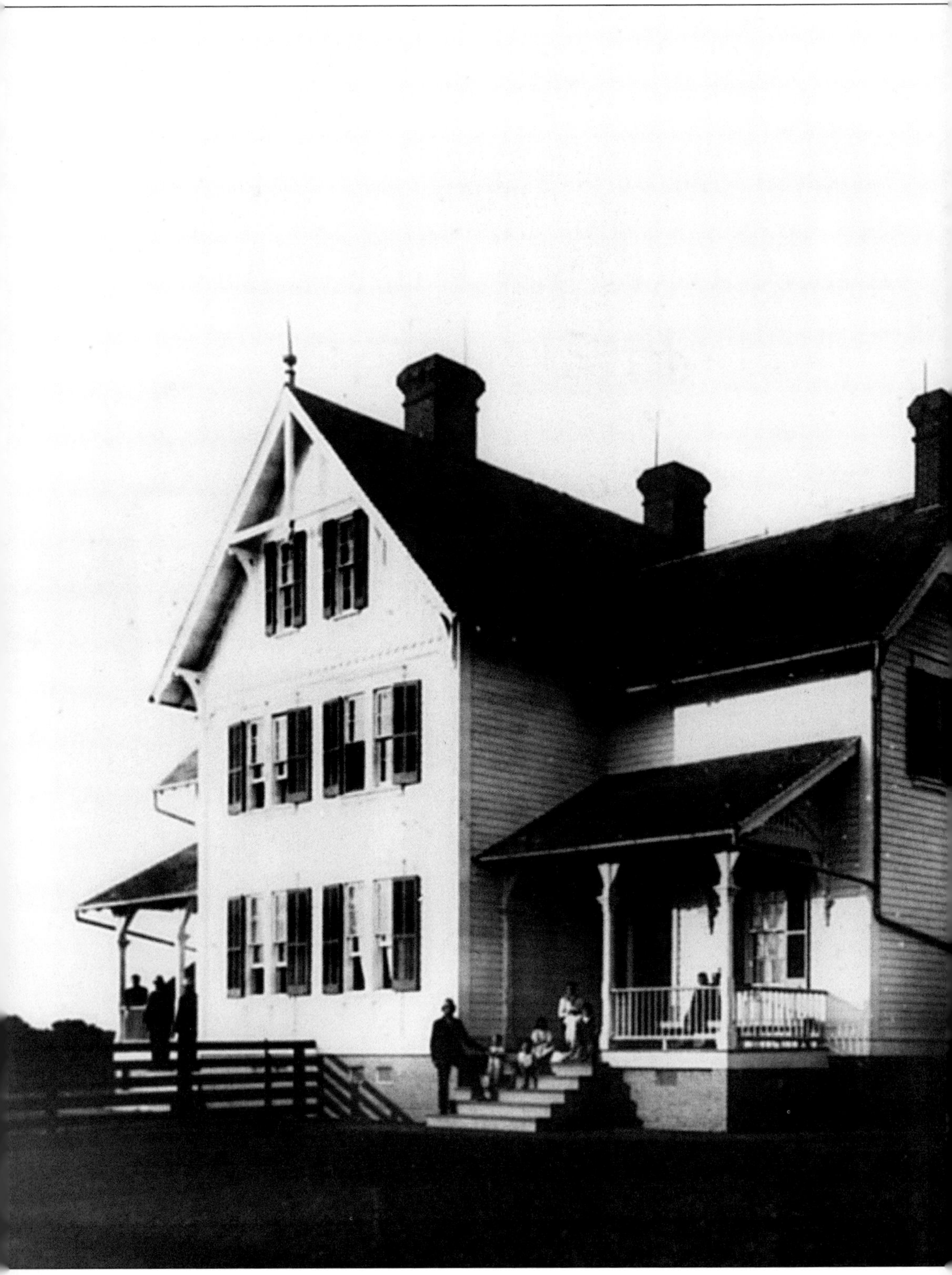

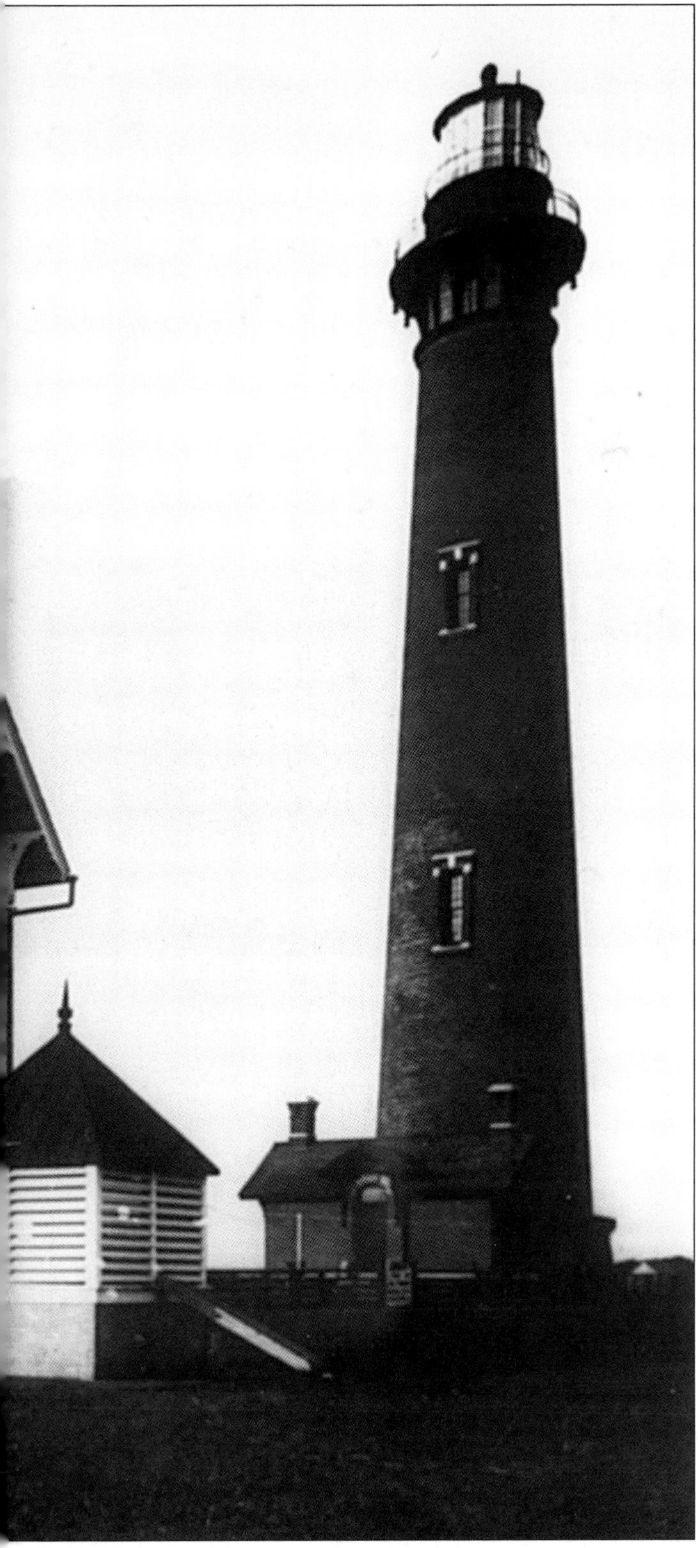

This is a picture of Currituck Lighthouse, *c*. 1880. This lighthouse began operating on December 1, 1875. It was the last tower built along the Outer Banks. Like the structures at Bodie Island and Cape Hatteras, it was patterned after the Cape Lookout Lighthouse. (Courtesy of North Carolina Archives and History.)

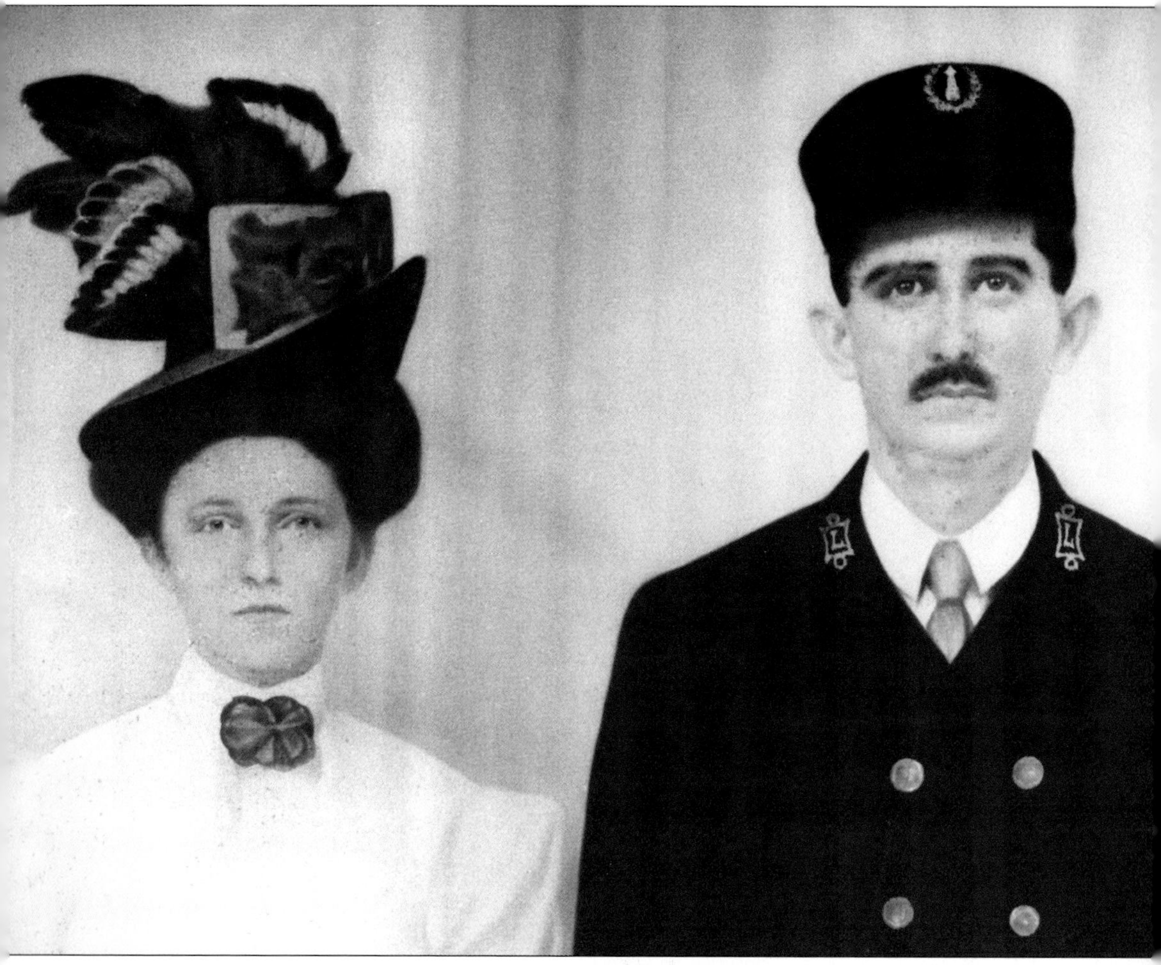

Pictured here are lighthouse keeper Homer T. Austin and Orphia, his wife. Austin was the last keeper of the Currituck Beach Lighthouse. (Courtesy of Outer Banks History Center.)

Light keeper W.J. Tate holds an important place in the annals of aviation history. Tate's wife, Addie, postmistress of the post office at Kitty Hawk, received a letter from Wilbur Wright asking for information about the area, as they were planning to conduct aviation experiments and were looking for a suitable place. She passed the letter on to her husband, who was keeper of the Currituck Beach Lighthouse. Tate wrote back to Wright, extolling the virtues of the area and providing detailed descriptions of the climate and terrain. Because of this report, the Wright Brothers chose the Outer Banks of North Carolina to conduct their test flights with their experimental aircraft. The Wright Brothers occasionally stayed with the Tate family, who sometimes helped the inventors with various tasks relating to their gliders and airplanes. (Courtesy of Outer Banks History Center.)

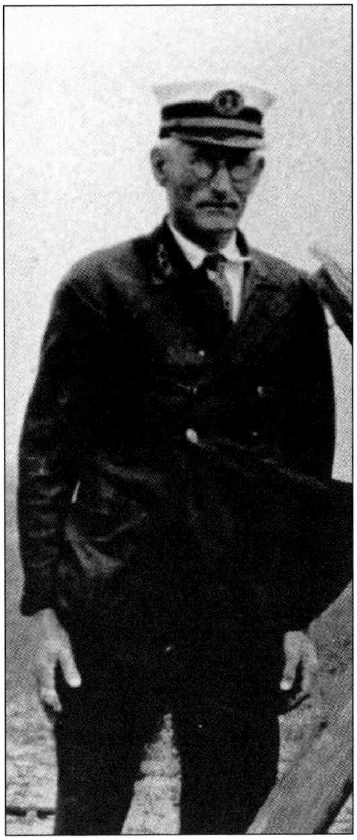

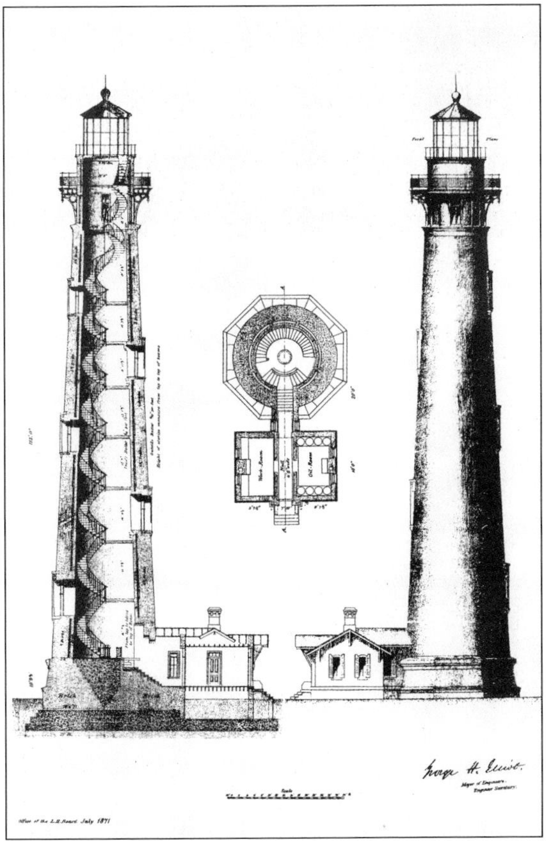

This architectural drawing of the Currituck Beach Lighthouse was prepared in 1871. (Courtesy of National Archives.)

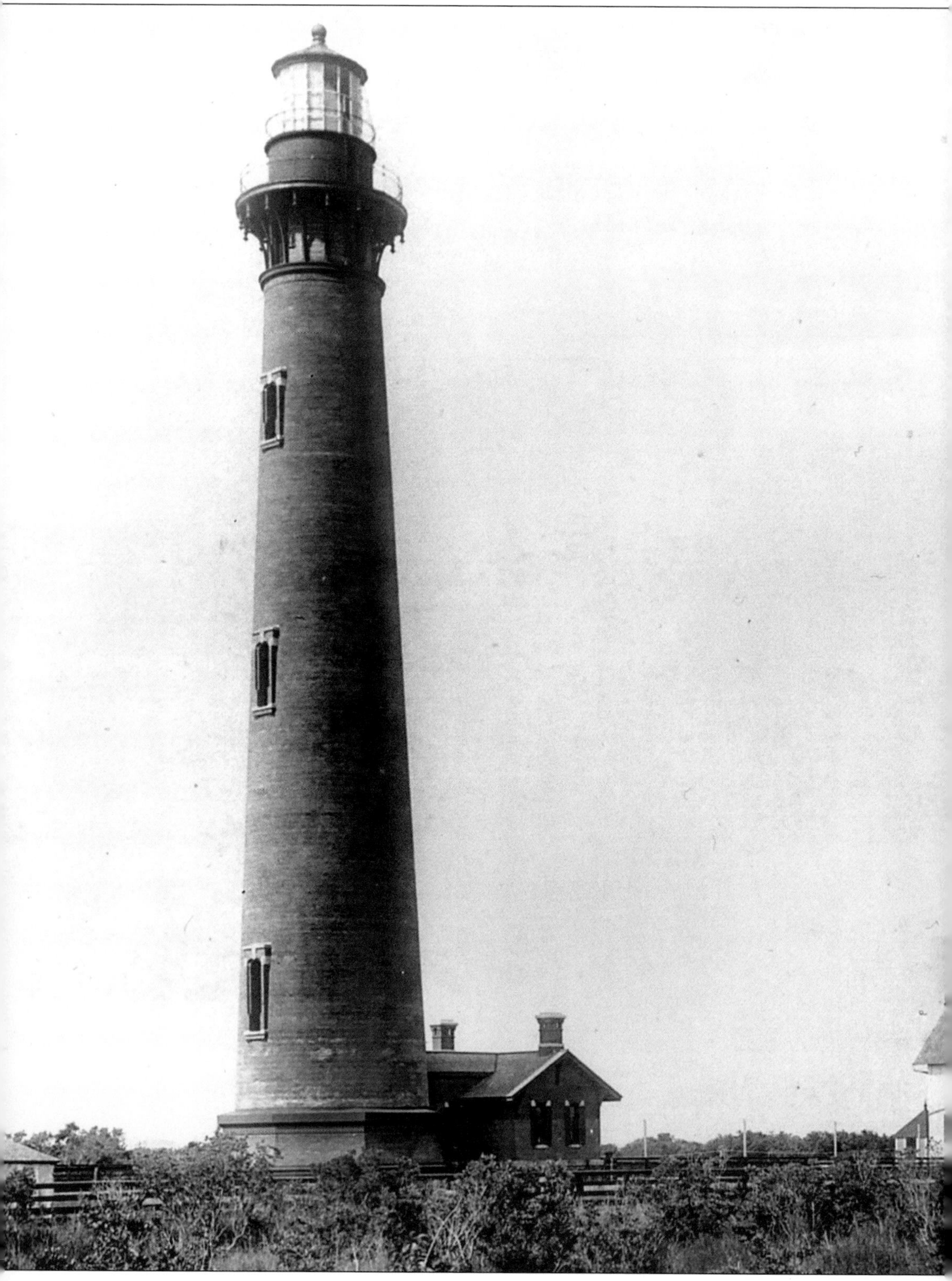

The Currituck Beach Light Station is depicted as it appeared on June 12, 1893. (Courtesy of the United States Coast Guard.)

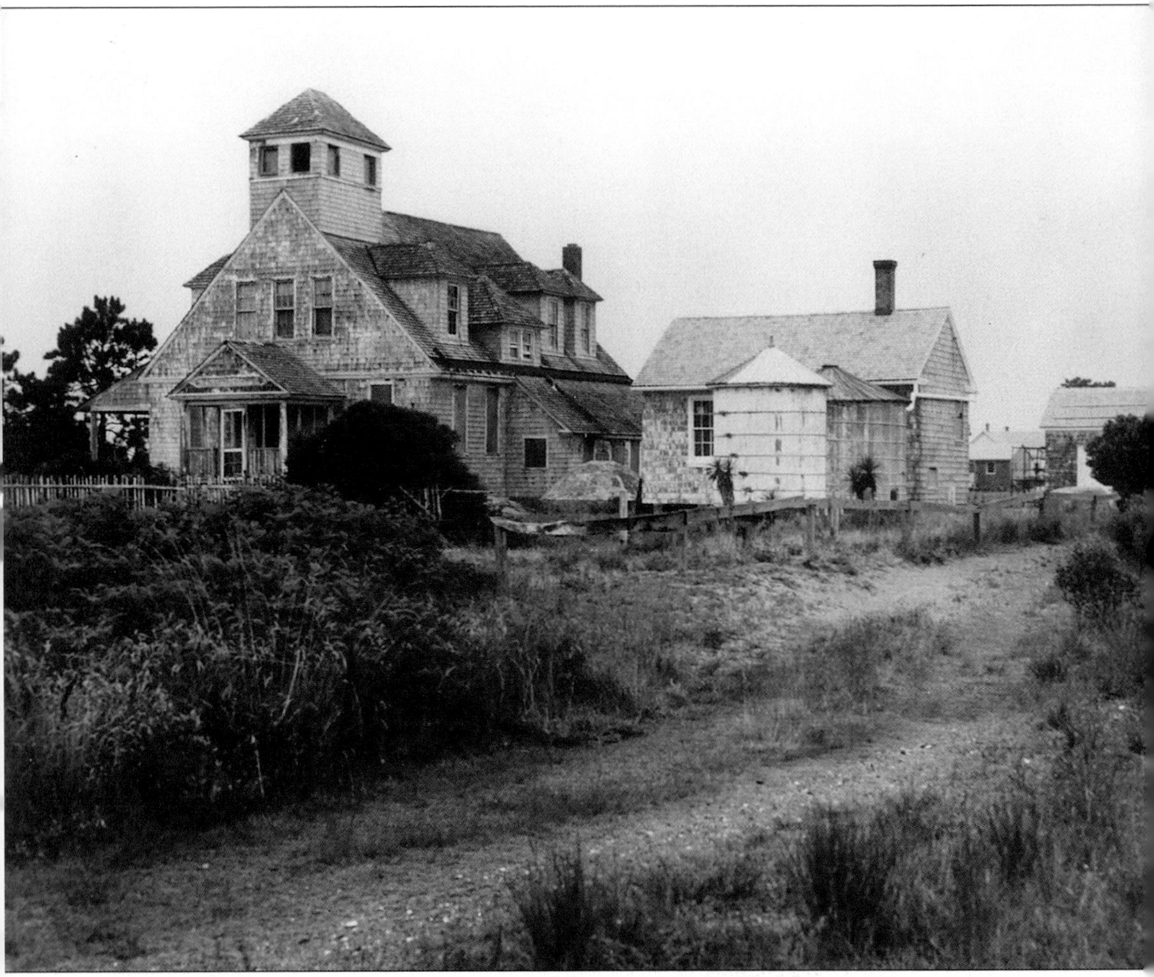

Chicamacomico Lifesaving Station was established in 1874. The structure shown here was built in 1911 and it became a model used for several other stations. In 1954, the station was abandoned by the Coast Guard and it deteriorated. A group of concerned individuals banded together to save the important landmark and formed the Chicamacomico Historical Association. Today, the structure serves as a museum and houses artifacts relating to the history of the United States Lifesaving Service and the United States Coast Guard. (Courtesy of North Carolina Archives and History.)

Twelve

LIFESAVING STATIONS

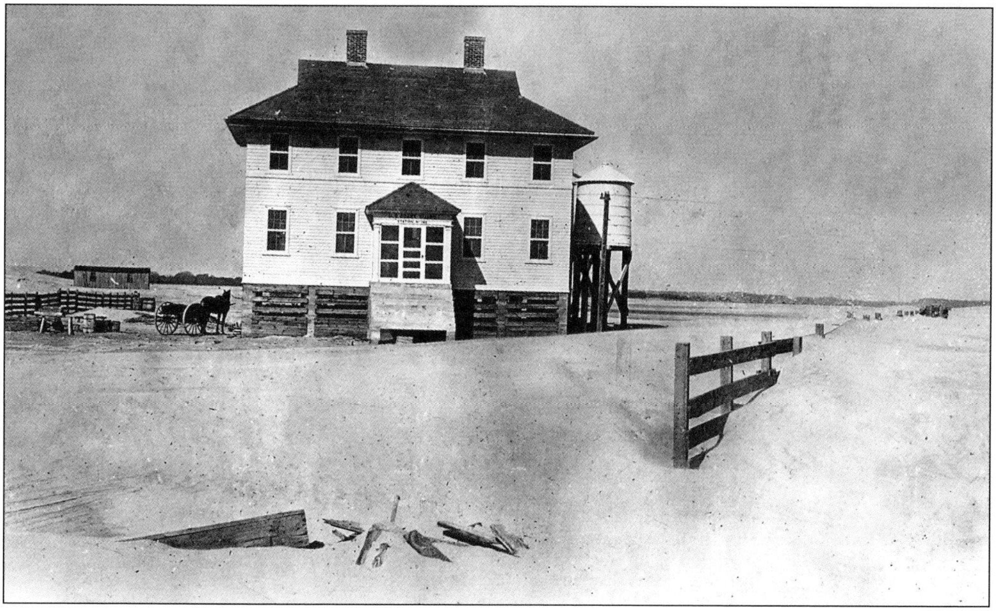

The Wash Woods Lifesaving Station, known as Deal Island in the early days of its existence, was established in 1878. It was the northernmost lifesaving station on the North Carolina coast. (Courtesy of the United States Coast Guard.)

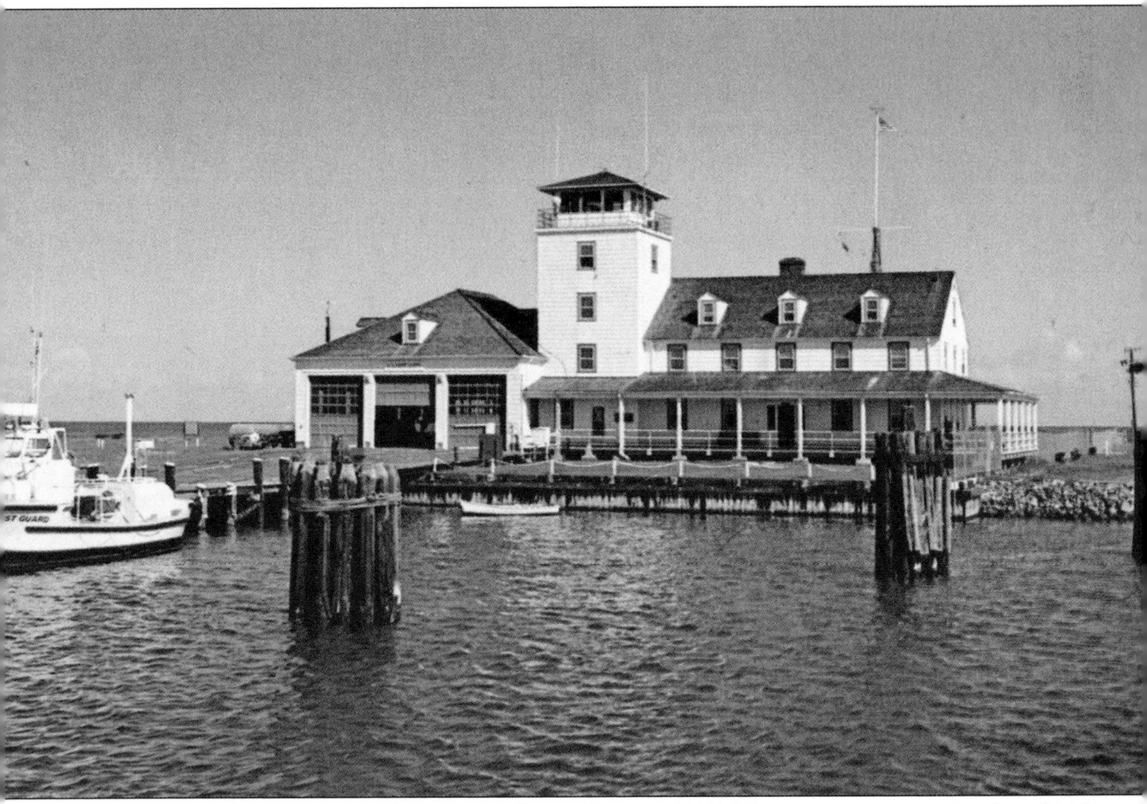

The Ocracoke Coast Guard Station is shown here, *c.* 1950. This structure, completed in 1940, replaced an earlier Ocracoke Lifesaving Station, which had been established here in 1904. (Courtesy of North Carolina Archives and History.)

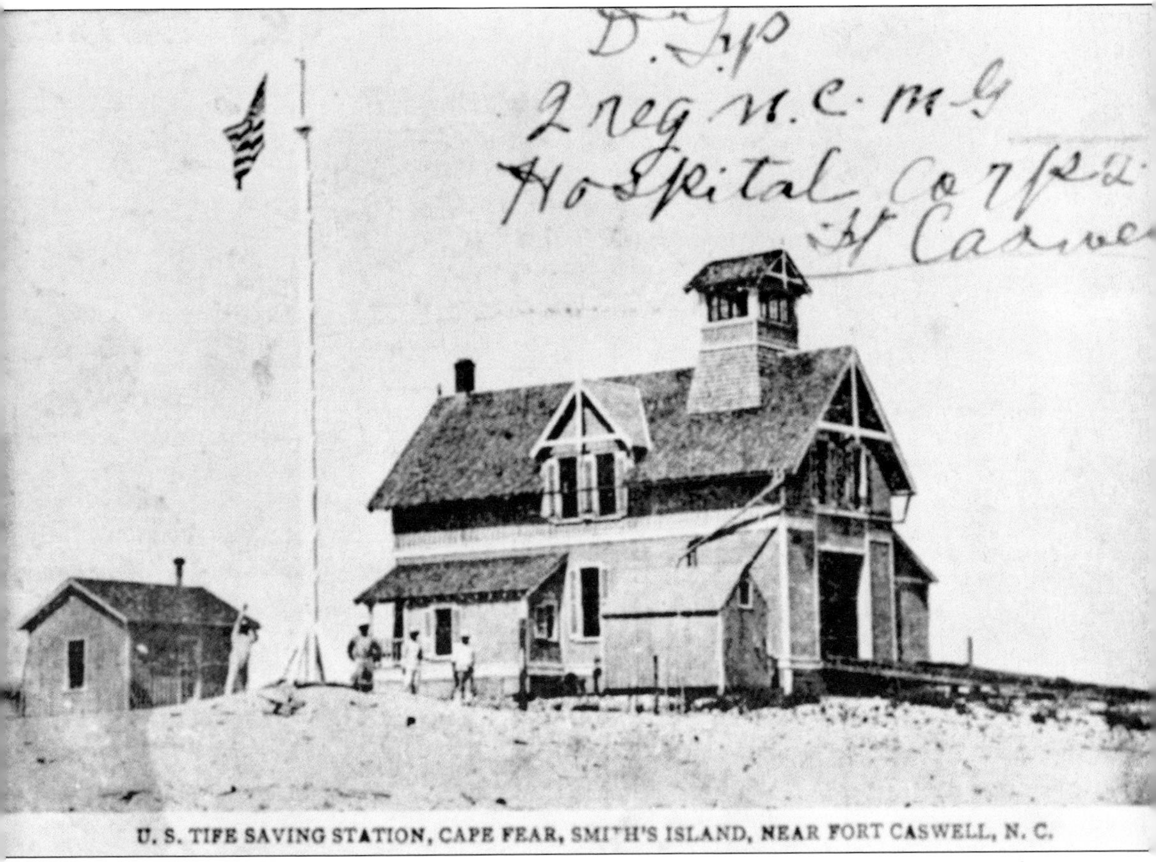

The Cape Fear Lifesaving Station, shown here in 1908, was located a short distance away from the Cape Fear Light Station on Bald Head Island. This building, built in 1882, was replaced by another structure in 1915. (Courtesy of North Carolina Archives and History.)

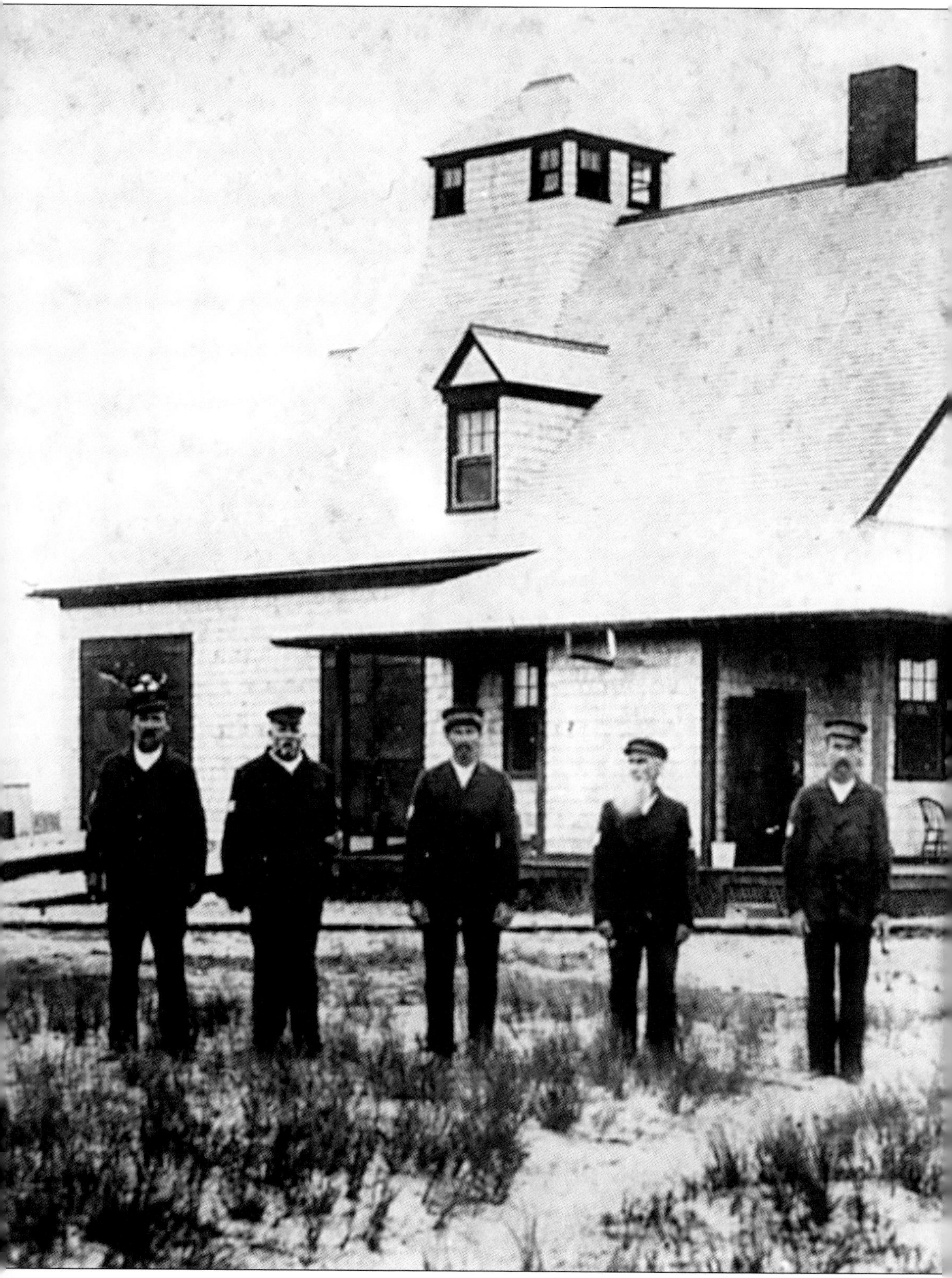

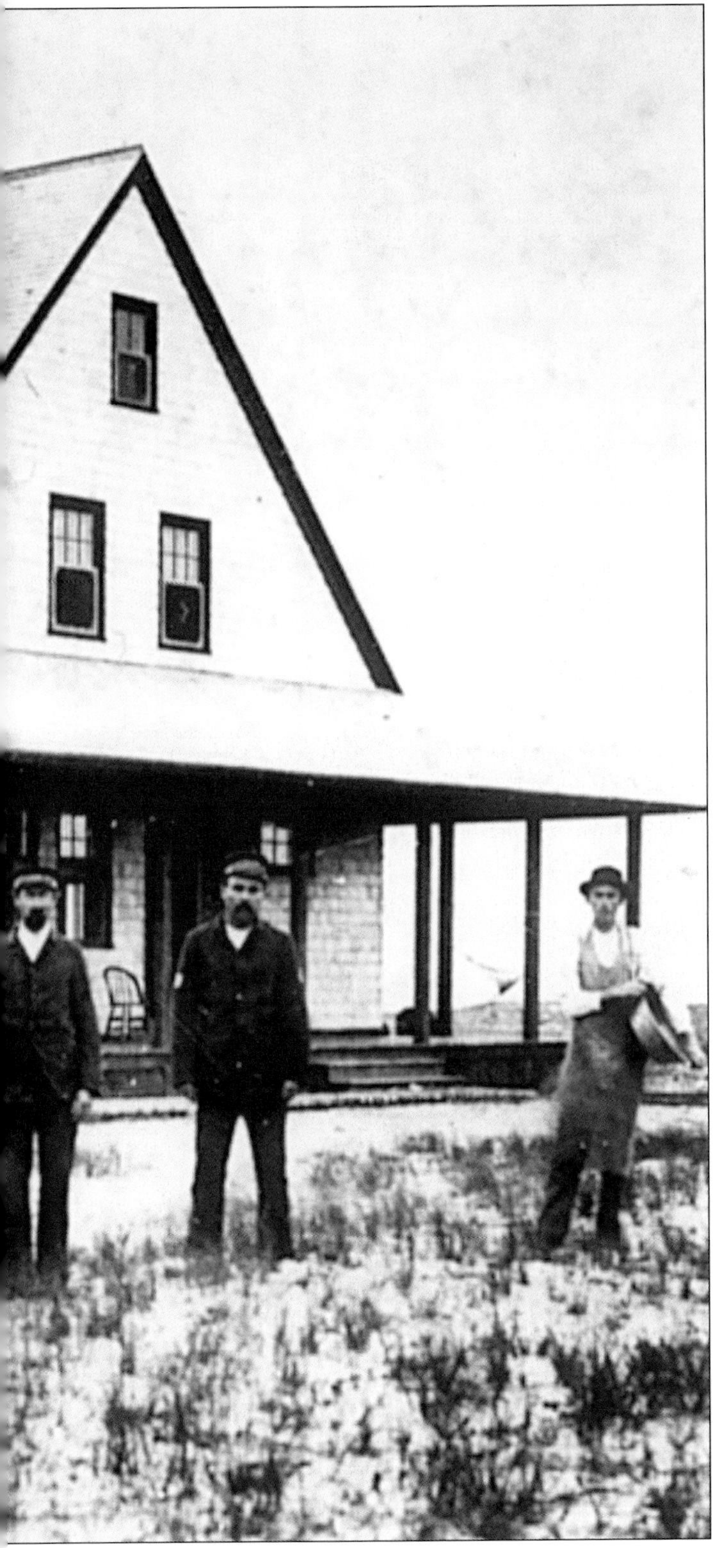

The crew of the New Inlet Lifesaving Station is shown in this turn-of-the-century photo. This station was located near Rodanthe and was operational from 1882 until 1916. (Courtesy of the United States Coast Guard.)

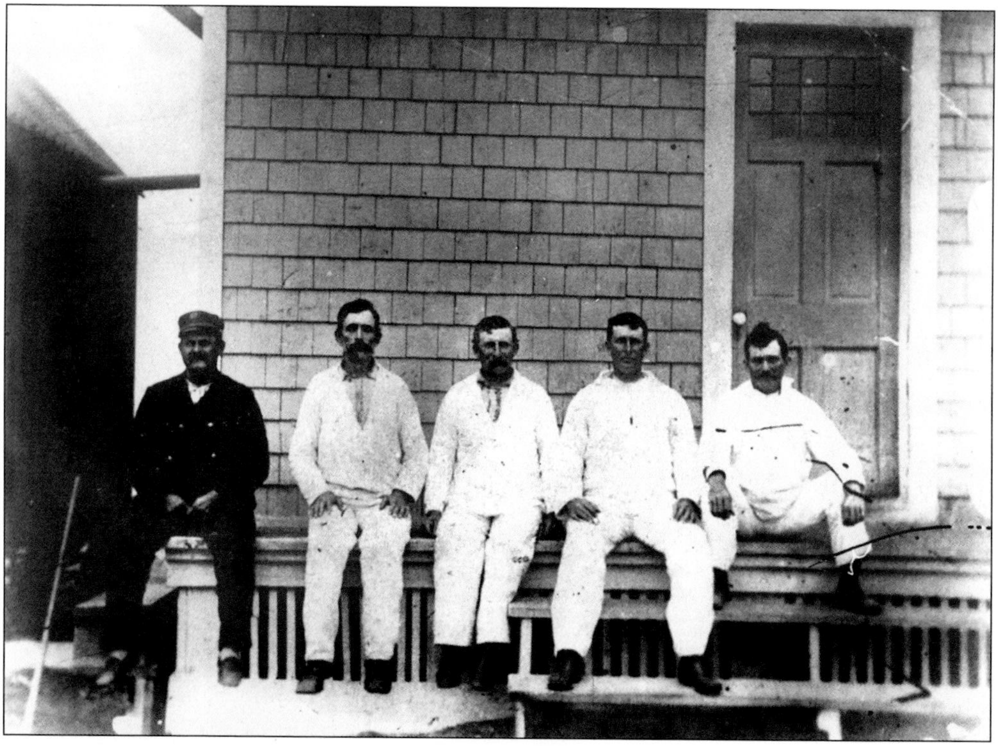

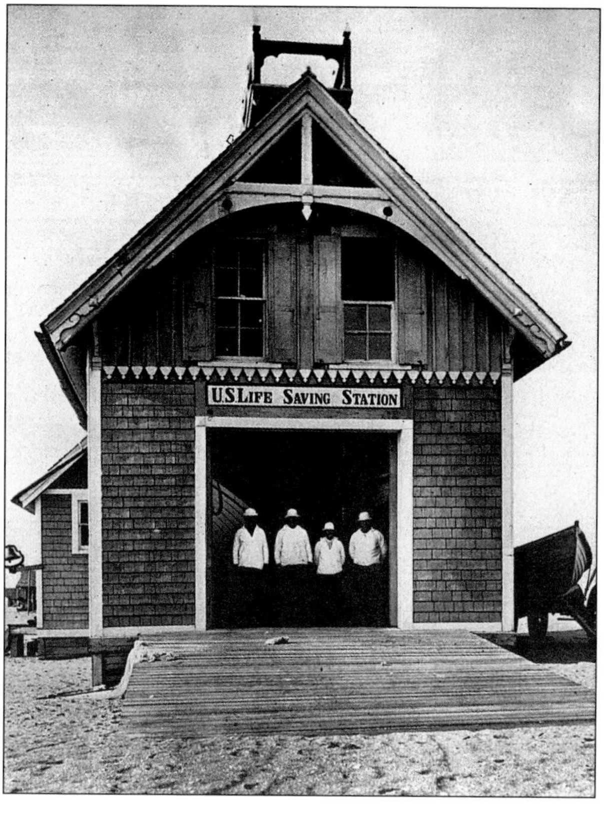

This is Kill Devil Hills Lifesaving Station in 1903. The men from this station assisted the Wright Brothers with many of their early aviation experiments. (Courtesy of the Library of Congress.)

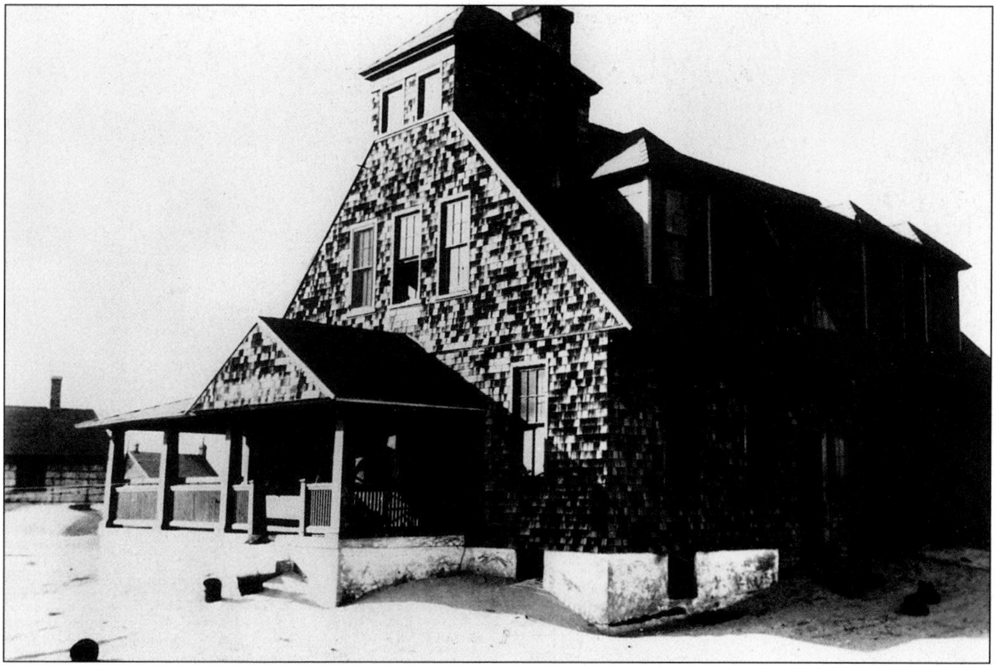

The Poyners Hill Lifesaving Station was established along the northern Outer Banks in 1878. The station was operational until 1937. (Courtesy of the United States Coast Guard.)

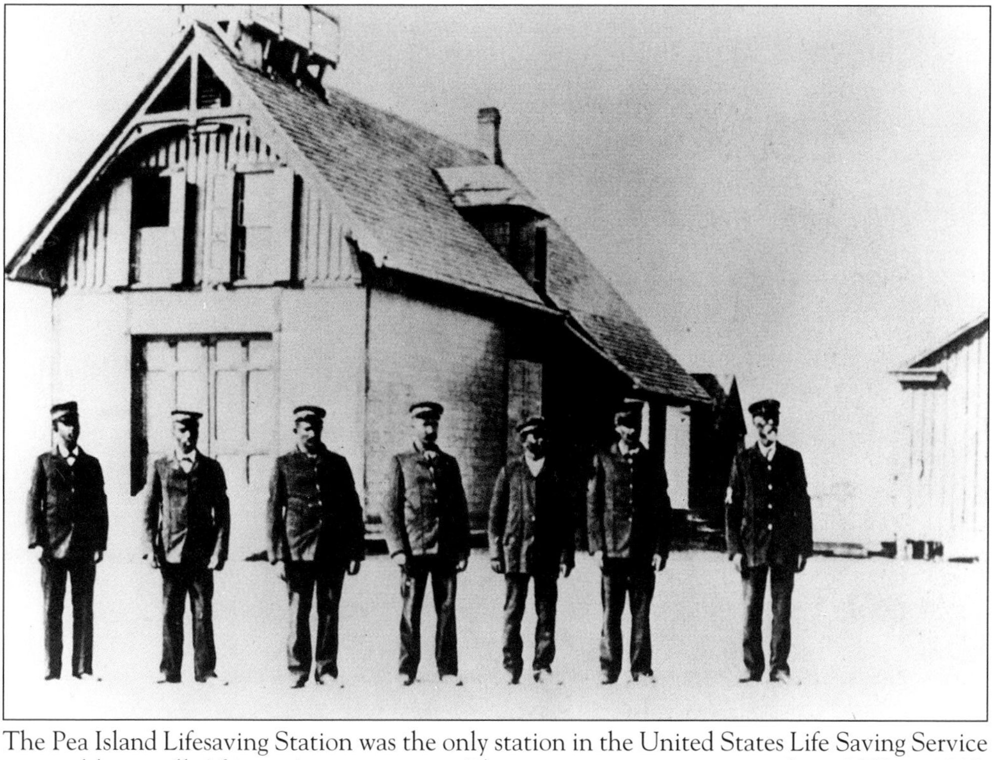

The Pea Island Lifesaving Station was the only station in the United States Life Saving Service manned by an all African-American crew. The station was in operation from 1878 to 1947. (Courtesy of North Carolina Archives and History.)

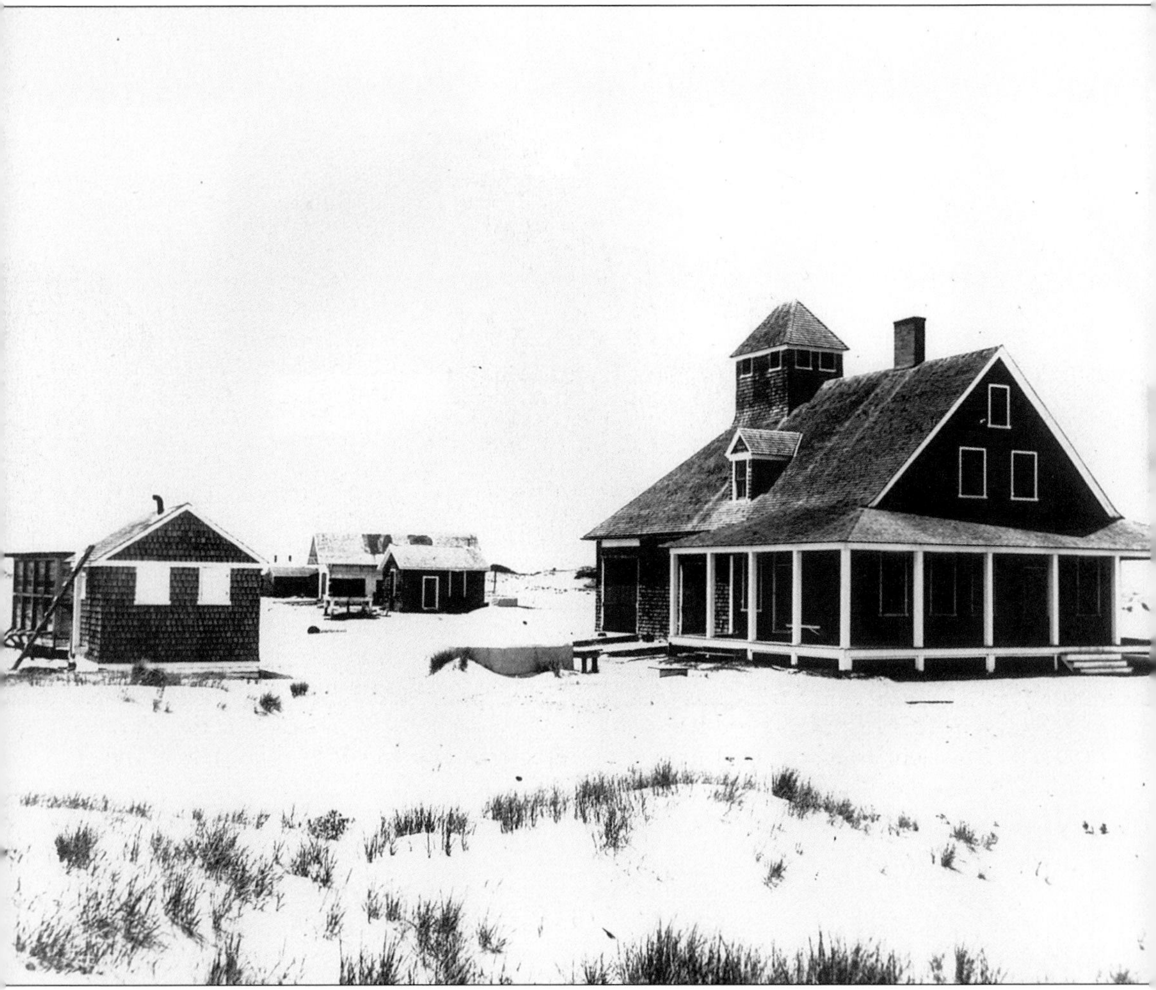

The Currituck Beach Lifesaving Station is shown here in 1927. Originally known as Jones Hill and Whale Head, this station served as an important outpost along the Outer Banks from 1874 until it was decommissioned in 1937. (Courtesy of the United States Coast Guard.)

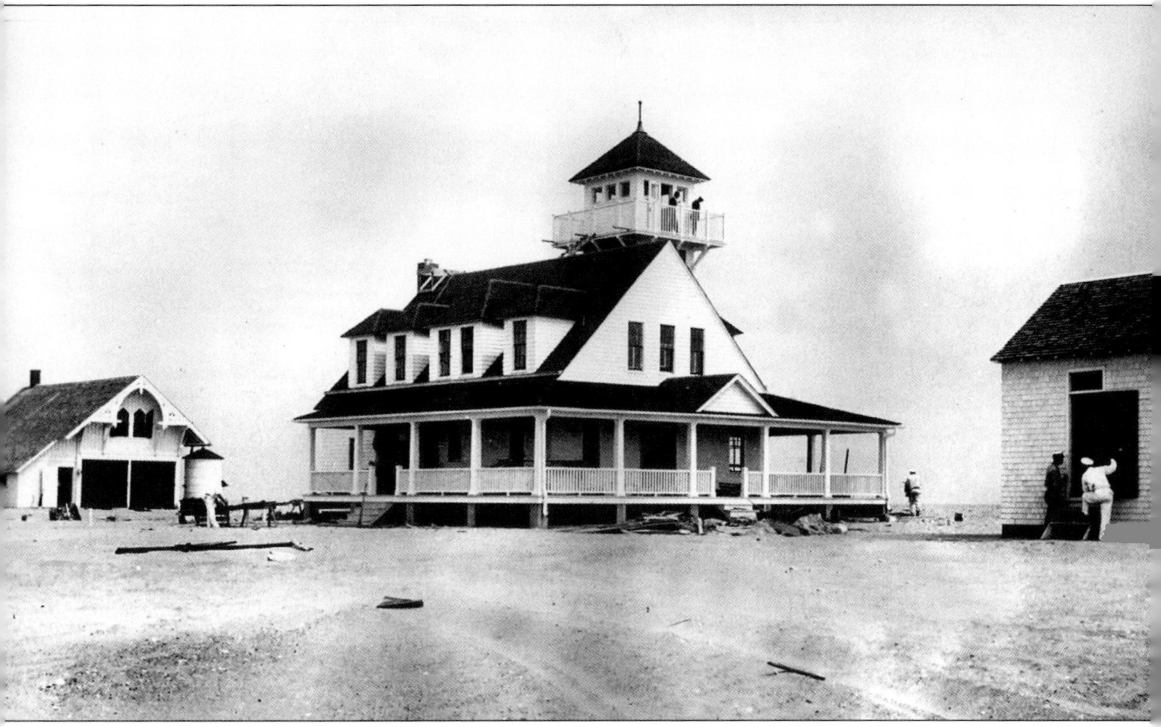

Established in 1874, the Nags Head Lifesaving Station is depicted as it appeared in the fall of 1934. This station was operational until it was decommissioned in 1957. (Courtesy of the United States Coast Guard.)

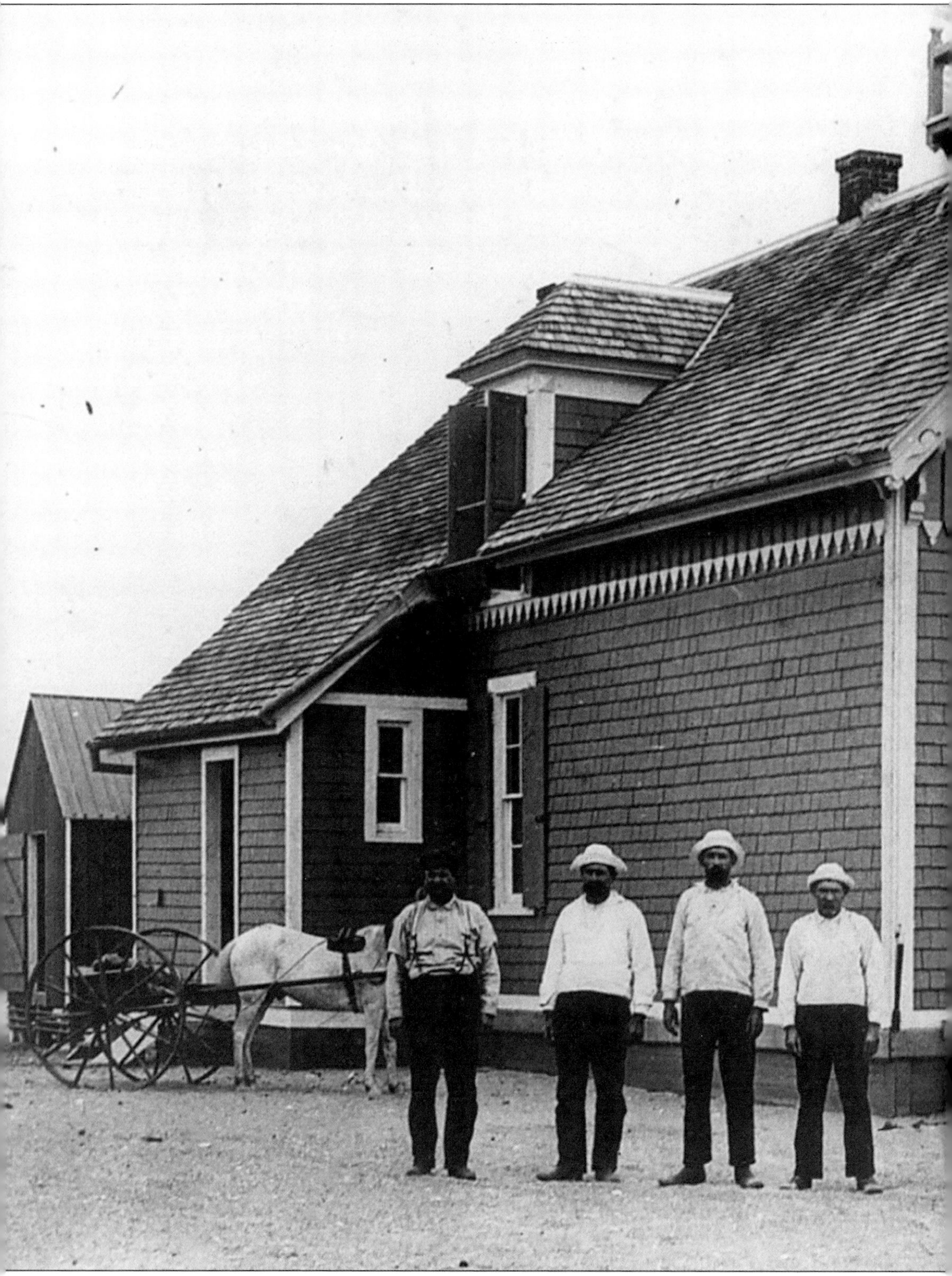

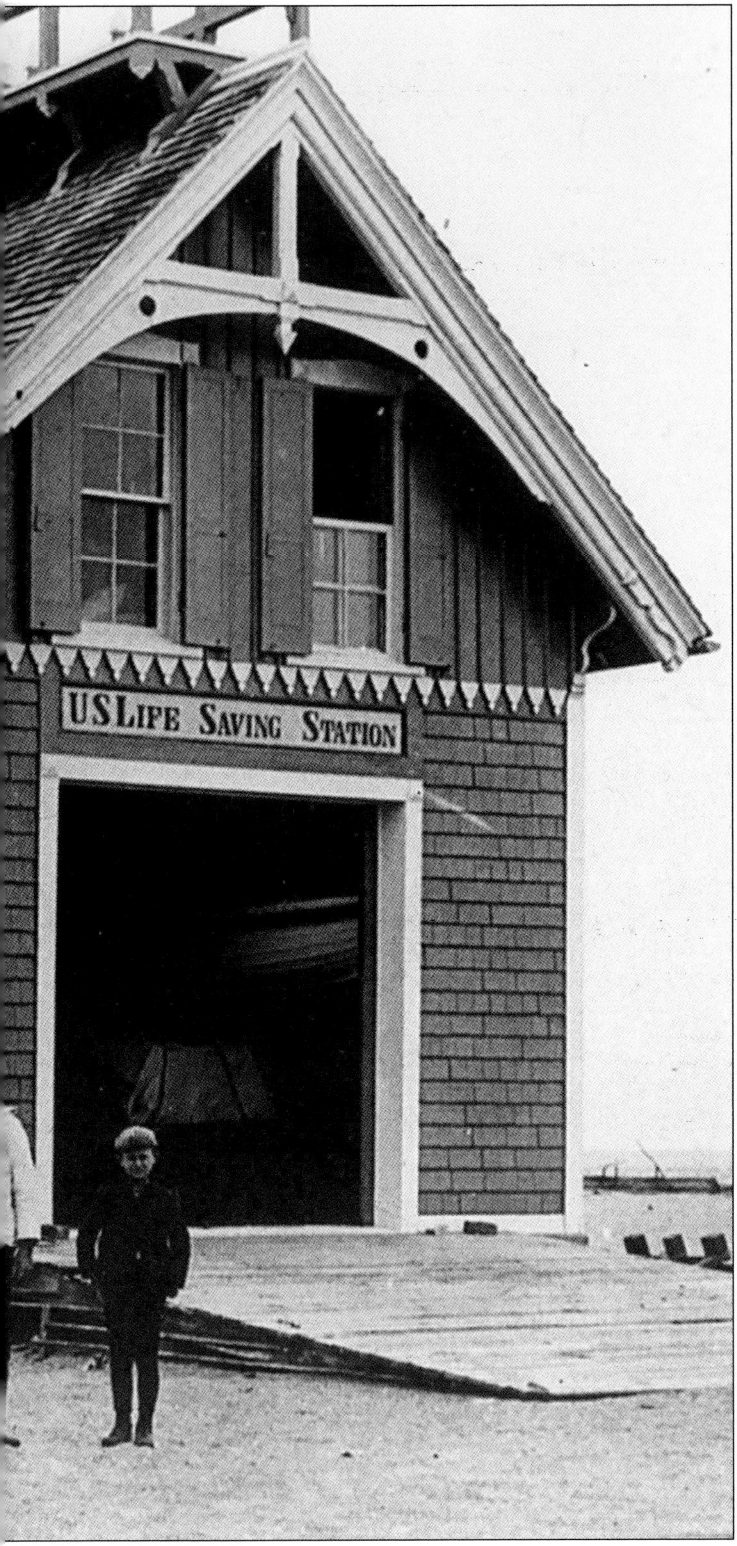

This photo shows the Little Kinnakeet Lifesaving Station, *c.* 1895. This station was located near Avon, north of Cape Hatteras, and served continuously from 1874 to 1938. (Courtesy of North Carolina Archives and History.)

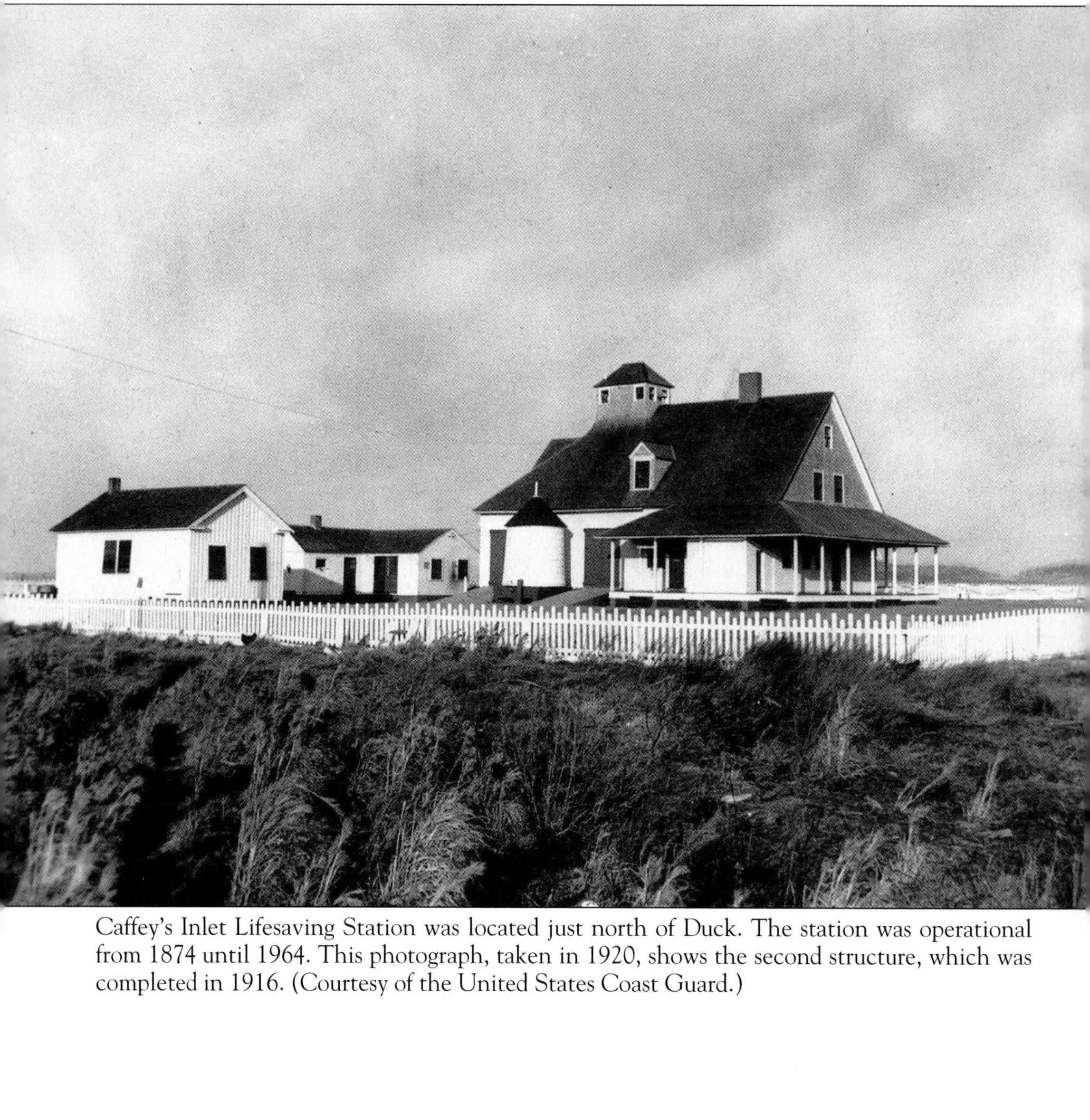

Caffey's Inlet Lifesaving Station was located just north of Duck. The station was operational from 1874 until 1964. This photograph, taken in 1920, shows the second structure, which was completed in 1916. (Courtesy of the United States Coast Guard.)

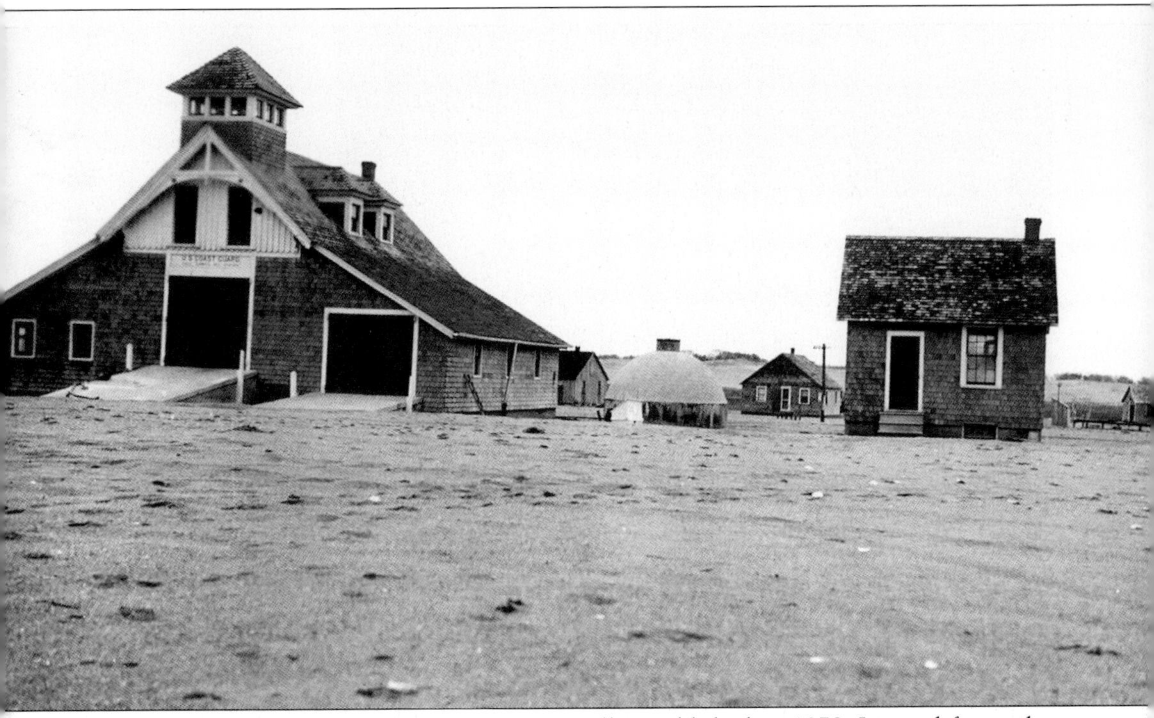

Paul Gamuel's Hill Lifesaving Station was originally established in 1878. Located five miles north of Kitty Hawk, the station was abandoned by the Coast Guard in 1949. (Courtesy of the United States Coast Guard.)

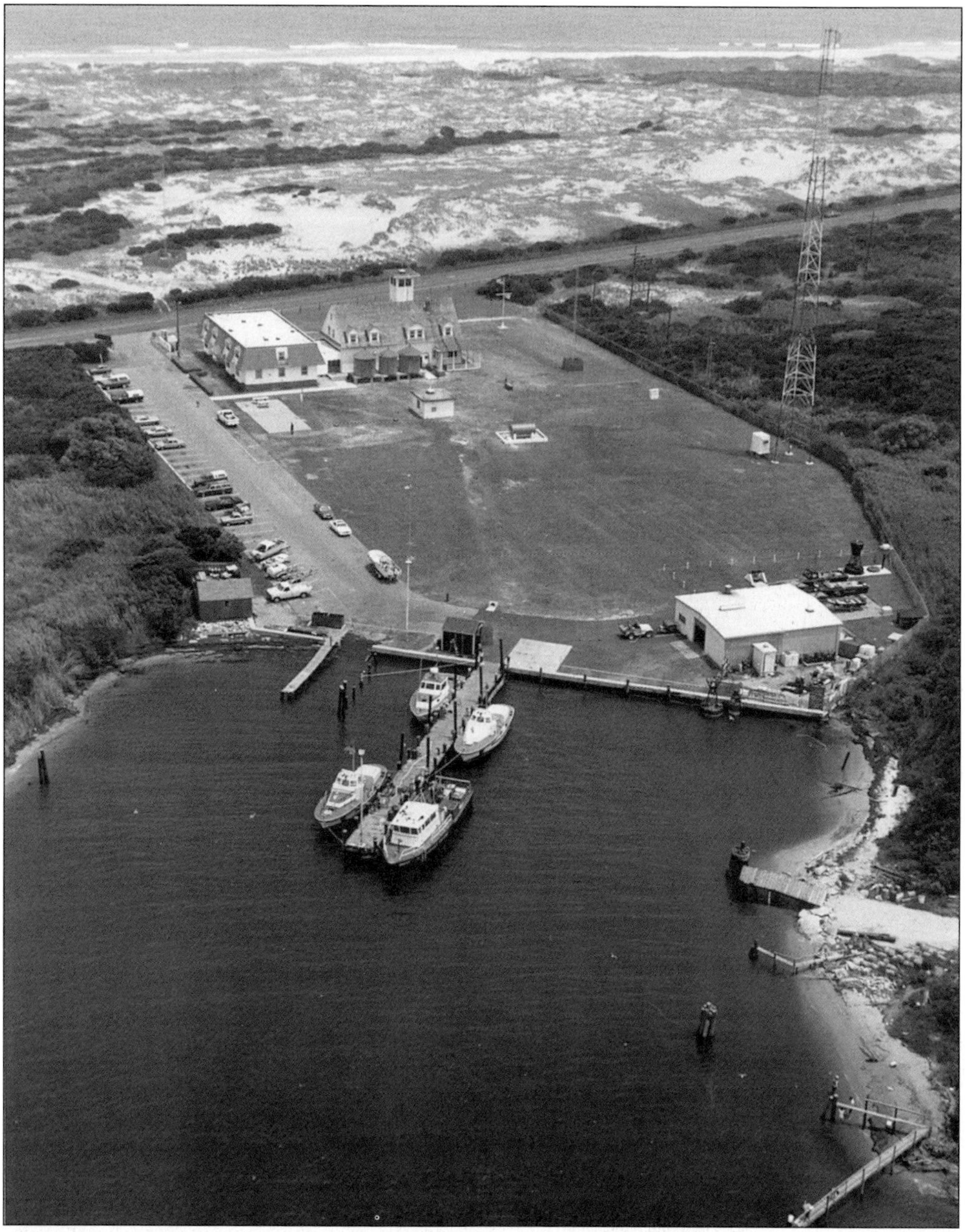

After its completion in 1898, the Oregon Inlet Lifesaving Station became a prominent landmark on Pea Island, on the south side of Oregon Inlet. The site was abandoned by the Coast Guard in November of 1988, when they moved their operation to a station near the marina along the north side of Oregon Inlet. Though no longer an active station, the buildings remain a major feature of the Cape Hatteras National Seashore. (Courtesy of the United States Coast Guard.)

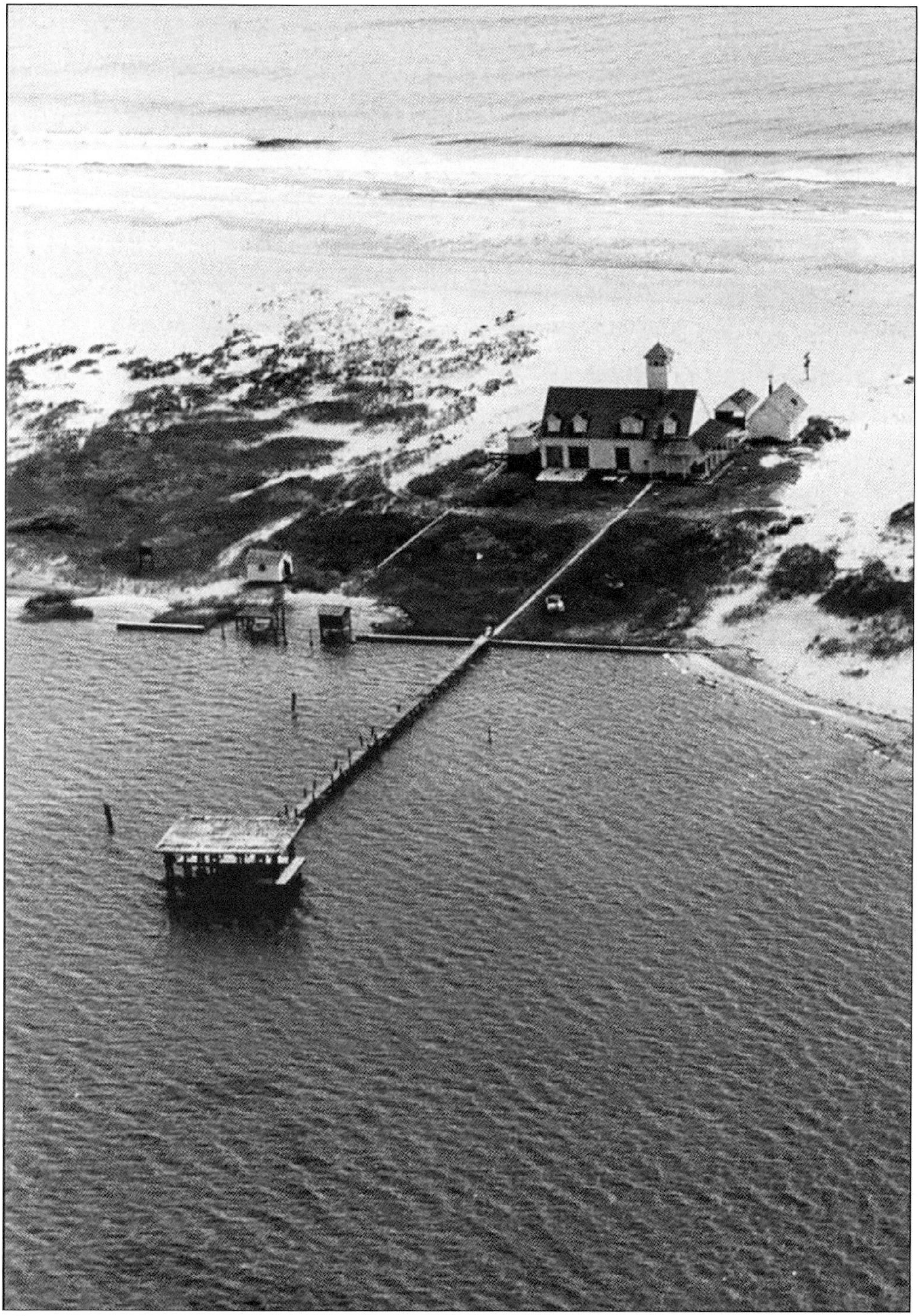

The Core Banks Lifesaving Station stood watch over the long and lonely stretch of coast between Cape Lookout and Portsmouth. This station was in operation from 1895 until 1965. (Courtesy National Park Service, Cape Lookout National Seashore)

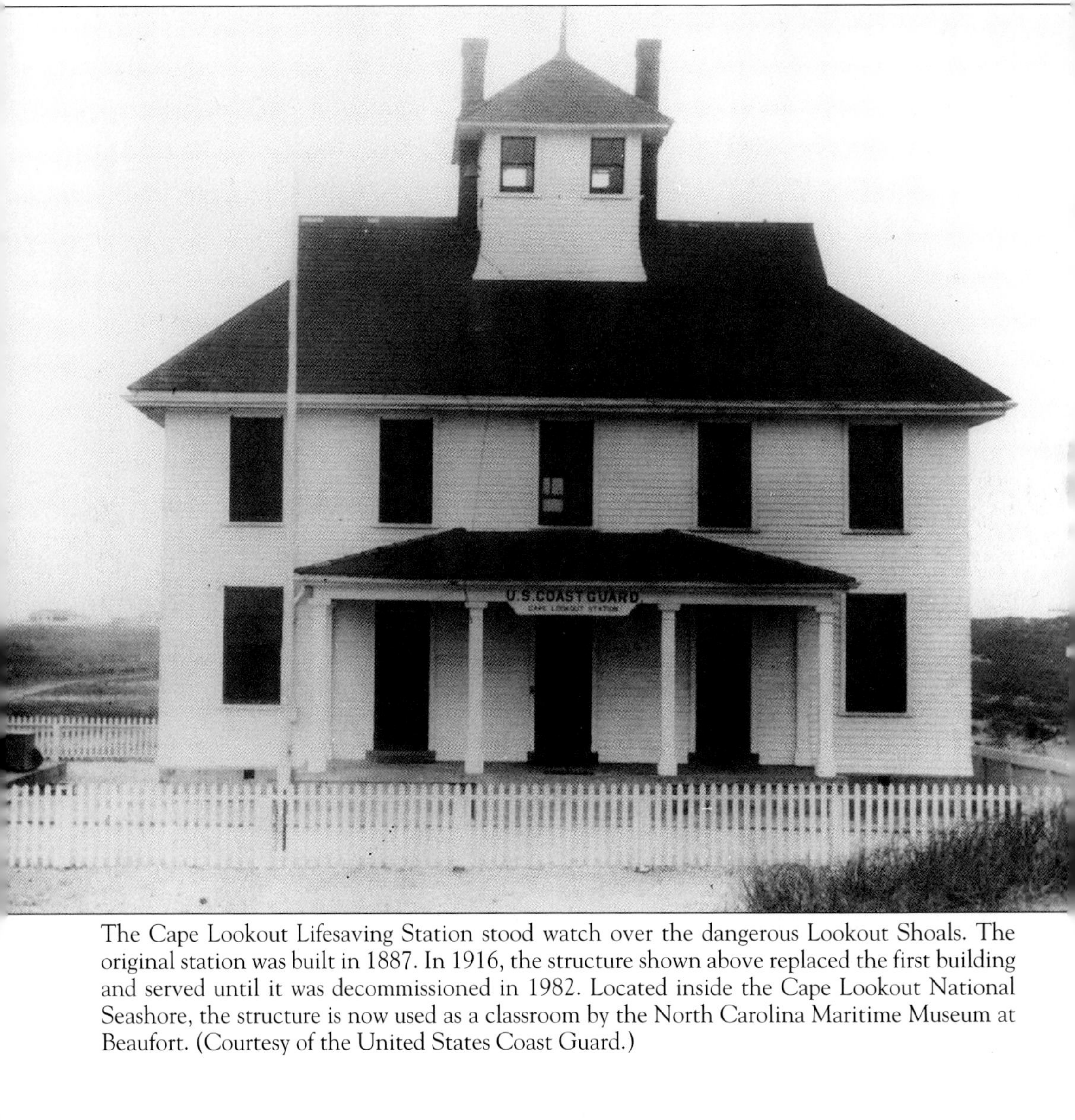

The Cape Lookout Lifesaving Station stood watch over the dangerous Lookout Shoals. The original station was built in 1887. In 1916, the structure shown above replaced the first building and served until it was decommissioned in 1982. Located inside the Cape Lookout National Seashore, the structure is now used as a classroom by the North Carolina Maritime Museum at Beaufort. (Courtesy of the United States Coast Guard.)

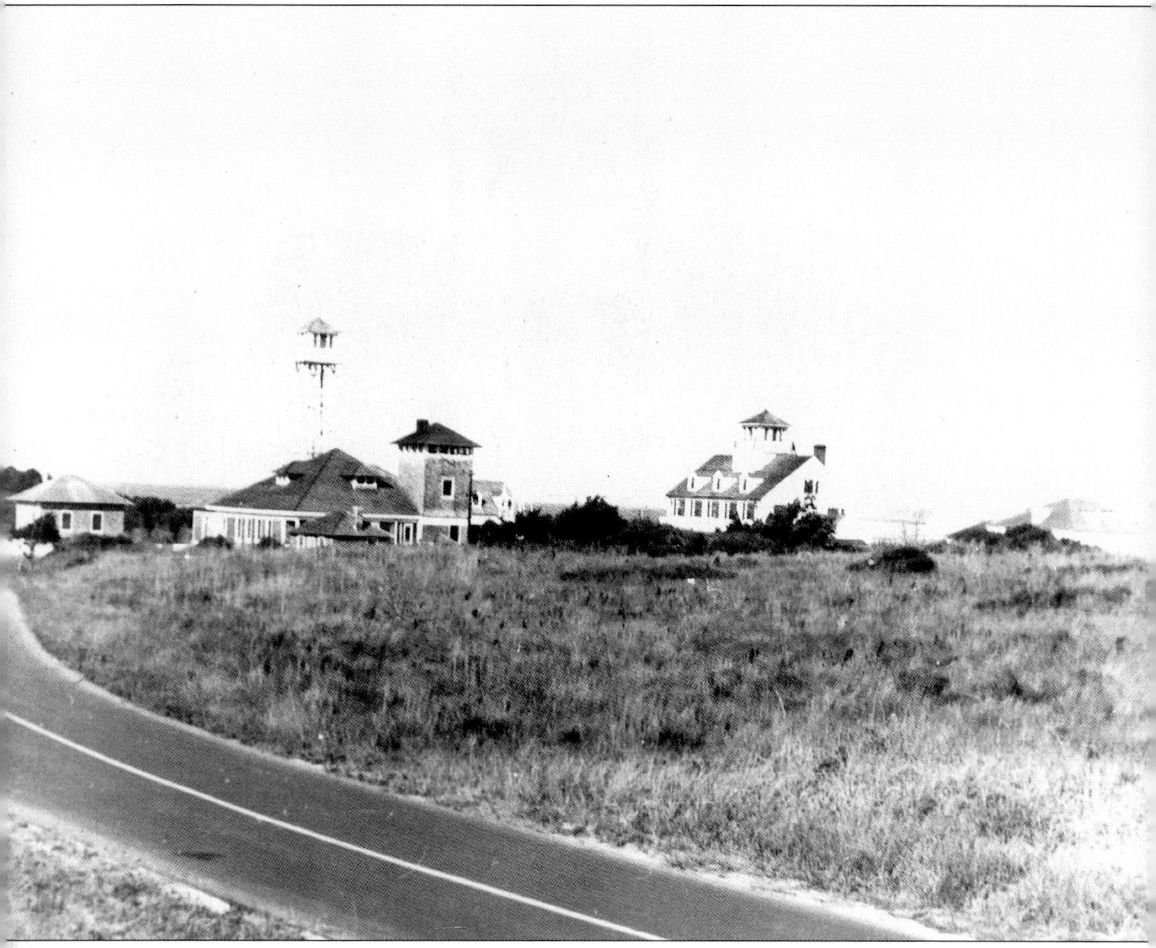

The Fort Macon Lifesaving Station was established in 1904. It stood watch over Beaufort Inlet and the vessels heading into the busy ports of Morehead City and Beaufort. (Courtesy of North Carolina Archives and History.)

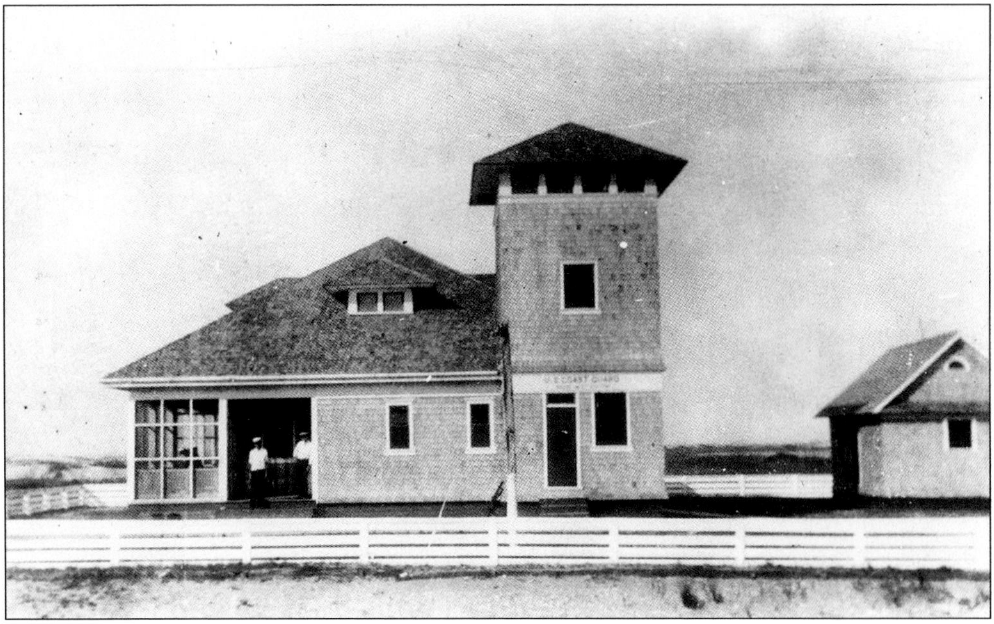

In 1905, the Bogue Inlet Lifesaving Station was established on the Bogue Banks, near Swansboro. To this day, the Coast Guard maintains a station here on the western end of the Bogue Banks at Emerald Isle. (Courtesy of North Carolina Archives and History.)

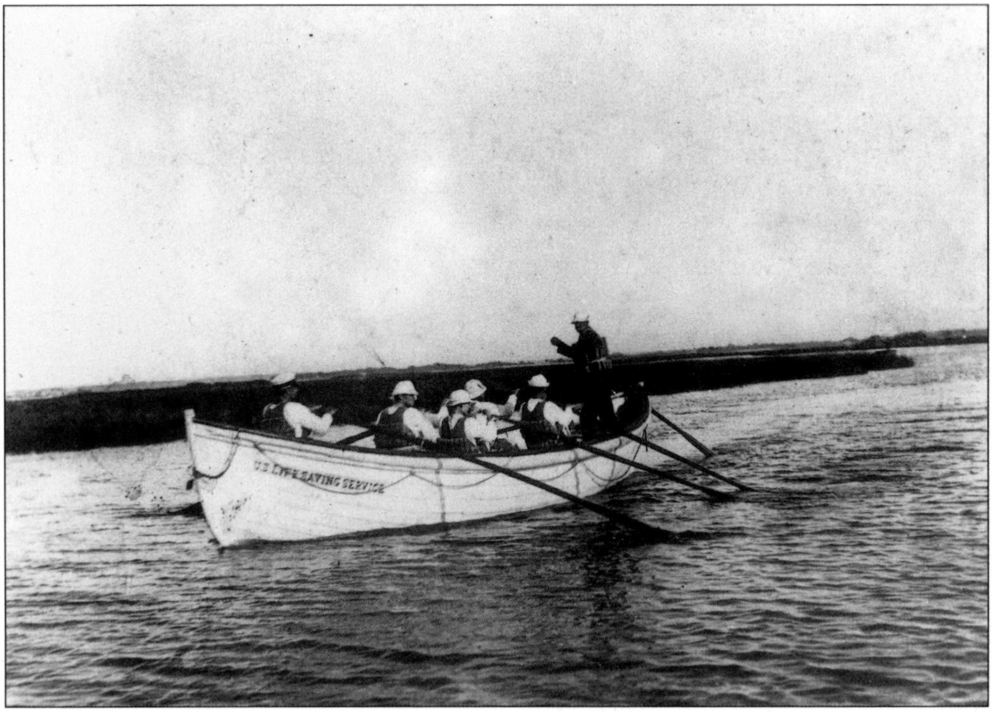

Here is the crew from the Bogue Inlet Lifesaving Station in their lifeboat on Bogue Inlet. (Courtesy of North Carolina Archives and History.)